John Thomson (1837-1921)
Photographer

1. *The Island Pagoda*. *c*. 1870–71. 100 x 209 mm.
Modern albumen stereograph from wet-collodion negative. National Library of Scotland/Wellcome Institute Library, London

JOHN THOMSON (1837–1921) PHOTOGRAPHER

Richard Ovenden

Foreword by Sir David Puttnam

Specialist photographic printing and a chapter by
Michael Gray

National Library of Scotland

The Stationery Office

Dedicated to the memory of my father, Stanley Ovenden (1922–1991)

© The Stationery Office Limited

The Stationery Office Limited
South Gyle Crescent, Edinburgh EH12 9EB

First published 1997

Designed by Derek Munn

Applications for reproduction should be made to The Stationery Office Limited

British Library Cataloguing in Publication Data
A catalogue record for this book is available from the British Library

ISBN 0 11 495833 5

Plates credited 'National Library of Scotland/Wellcome Institute Library,
London' are from modern gold-toned albumen prints in the National
Library of Scotland made by Michael and Barbara Gray from Thomson's
original negatives in the library of the Wellcome Institute. The Wellcome
Institute's permission to reproduce these images is gratefully acknowledged.

CONTENTS

FOREWORD

BY SIR DAVID PUTTNAM

Like the film-maker, the photographer looks at the world with a special eye. Both must combine a close attention to detail with the ability to step back and capture something of the essential character of a place and its people. Atmosphere is just as important to the moving picture as to the still. The greatest photographers and film-makers are able to capture these essential but often indefinable qualities with consummate ease, and to present them to the viewer in ways that are totally unexpected.

The work of John Thomson, as presented in this book, does just that. His vision acted like a zoom lens on the countries which he visited. He stood back and absorbed the nature of the landscape, the quality of the light, and photographed what he saw and felt. But as he gradually moved in closer, his photography became more specific, more focused: architecture, streets, factories, shops, right down to the essential component of any society, be it Chinese, Cypriot, Siamese, Cambodian, or British: the individual.

The range of Thomson's photography is breathtaking, but the quality which strikes the viewer most is his ability to get under the skin, so-to-speak, of whoever, or whatever, he was photographing. In the intrusive, long-lensed world of the 1990s paparazzi, our impression of early photography is often dominated by the stilted, wooden portrait work of mediocre studio-photographers which survives in much greater quantities than the work of the great photographic artists. Thomson's work, it seems to me, doesn't lend itself to this kind of oversimplification. It is marked by an immediacy and a democracy of outlook. John Thomson's photographs not only circumvented the stifling formalities of Victorian Britain, thereby allowing us to meet, face-to-face, some of the individuals whom the respectable reading-public would normally have crossed the street to avoid, but they also managed to bypass the secrets and sophistications of Imperial China's own rigid social hierarchies.

Taking a photograph today is extraordinarily easy – one click and technology does the rest – but in the first decades after its invention, the practicalities of making pictures were far from straightforward, and it is easy to forget how much more complicated and exhausting the entire process of taking a camera to the Far East was. The climate and terrain of Asia make enormous demands on those of us who are not used to the extremes of heat and humidity; and coping with the linguistic and cultural barriers must have proved even more problematic in the middle of the nineteenth century, to a man often travelling alone, and encumbered with the paraphernalia of early photography. The fact that he succeeded in travelling such immense distances is impressive enough and suggests that his skills as a traveller must rank as being almost as significant as his breathtaking talents as a photographic artist.

Photography provided – and continues to provide – a unique insight into the lives of our fellow human beings. It connected Thomson's readers in the 1870s with a different kind of living just as much as photographers today like Don McCullin or Sebastiao Salgado allow us to share all the varieties of experience of people in South America, Africa or Asia. The streets of London still provide a living of sorts to the poor, the homeless and the hungry in much the same way as they did in 1876 and 1877 when Thomson photographed the street people of his day. Thomson's photographs were intended to jolt the consciences of the comfortable Londoners who bought his books, and it's encouraging to report that even today photographers are busy documenting the lives of the successors of Thomson's London street folk in order to raise awareness of their plight among the complacent and uncaring in our 'post-modern' society.

Richard Ovenden's book tells the extraordinary story of one of photography's great pioneers and unsung heroes. The remarkable images that are reproduced in the book are testimony to the power of photography to reach into our lives and provide a direct link to a different age.

ACKNOWLEDGEMENTS

Four people in particular have aided the progress of this project through help, advice, and assistance above and beyond the call of duty. The participation of Mike and Barbara Gray has been essential. Not only have they provided the specialist albumen printing, but their massive experience and knowledge of all aspects of early photography has been as important as their kindness and comradeship. I owe a particular debt to Hilary Thomas, who not only made her private collection generously available for research and exhibition, but freely provided me with information from her own considerable researches into the Thomson and Petrie families. I hope I have done justice to her ancestor. John Hillelson also allowed me to consult material in his own collection, and gave me the benefit of a lifetime of research and interest in John Thomson.

The Library of the Wellcome Institute for the History of Medicine has provided considerable support for this project, and the work of the Curator of Iconographic Collections, William Schupbach, and that of David Brady, has been particularly important. The outstanding facilities and generous assistance which they have provided, both for this book, and the exhibition which was originally the occasion for its publication, have considerably eased curatorial burdens.

The idea for this project arose from conversations with Alex Hamilton and Julie Lawson, and to them both I owe an enormous debt of thanks. Julie Lawson, in particular, has supported and encouraged me in many ways, not least in reading drafts of the text. The work of Sara Stevenson and Julie Lawson at the National Collection of Photography in the National Galleries of Scotland has been a constant source of inspiration, and without their efforts, this project could not have been completed.

I am also indebted for help and advice to David Bruce; Mark Haworth-Booth and Janet Skidmore, Victoria and Albert Museum; John Falconer, India Office Library; Murray Simpson and Jo Currie, Edinburgh University Library; Joanna Scadden and Paula Lucas, Royal Geographical Society; Evelyn Draper, Science Museum Library; Terence Pepper, National Portrait Gallery; Jim Lawson and Halla Beloff, Edinburgh University; Stephen Lloyd, National Galleries of Scotland; Alison Morrison-Low and Allen Simpson, National Museums of Scotland; Tristram Clarke, Scottish Record Office; Roger Taylor and Philippa Wright, National Museum of Photography, Film and Television; Elizabeth Edwards, Pitt Rivers Museum; Joanna Soden, Royal Scottish Academy; Caroline Kerlin,

Birmingham Central Library; John Sanday, Preah Khan Conservation Project; Wilson Smith, Edinburgh College of Art; Ann Jones, Heriot-Watt University Archives; Michael Pollock, Royal Asiatic Society; Fraser Simm, George Heriot's Hospital; Pam Roberts and Debbie Ireland, Royal Photographic Society; David Pearson, National Art Library; and Roberta Wue, Asia Society, New York. Nick Pearce, Oriental Museum, Durham University, shared ideas and information, and kindly read a draft of the book, saving me from numerous errors.

Within the National Library of Scotland I have received an overwhelming amount of support and encouragement from many colleagues, but I would like to mention, in particular, Peter Marsden, Graham Hogg, John Scally, Barbara Hegarty, Jacqueline Cromarty, and Kenneth Gibson. The support of Ann Matheson and Alan Marchbank has been vital to all stages of this project.

Finally, I owe the biggest debt to my wife, Lyn, and daughter, Caitlin, who have both shared and endured the innumerable hours which have gone into this project. Their patience, kindness, and support are only the more obvious ways in which they keep me going.

Richard Ovenden

INTRODUCTION

Forty years ago who could have foretold that the modest sensitive plate was destined to play a part so important in the history of progress?

JOHN THOMSON*

John Thomson was born in Edinburgh just six days before Queen Victoria acceded to the throne, so it must come as little surprise that much of his life was conducted in a thoroughly Victorian manner. With enormous energy and stamina, he travelled from his native Scotland to the edges of the British Empire and beyond. He covered enormous distances with his camera, he took large numbers of photographs, and eventually wrote a voluminous quantity of text to accompany them. His subject matter covered an equally impressive sweep, ranging from architecture, archaeology, and landscapes, to individuals and groups, both in the street and in the studio. He tackled each category with equal skill and success. His books were large and impressive volumes, copiously illustrated, and he readily embraced new technology to achieve the most effective means of disseminating his photographic work.

For Thomson, the ten years he spent in the Far East – four of those travelling in China – were to be his making. Using the material he collected in the Far East as his capital, he became one of the first of that breed of modern professional photographers whose careers do not depend purely on the number of prints sold, or on the number of lucrative commissions gained, but on the *publication* of their photographic images through conventional print media. By a mixture of magazine and book publishing, and an astute appreciation of changing markets and interests in literature, he manipulated the traditional media in order to reach as wide and varied an audience as possible. Thomson not only made money, and a name for himself, he also helped to create the 'paper world' that existed in the studies, libraries, and drawing-rooms of nineteenth-century Europe. Thomson's special contribution to this phenomenon was the magisterial sweep of his photographic vision, and the 'new knowledge' that photography could impart enabled the European reading public to comprehend the world in a way that had hitherto been impossible.[1]

But the Far East was not the only sphere in which John Thomson made a significant contribution to photography. His short series of photographs taken in the streets of London in the late 1870s charted the lower orders of a city and a culture obsessed with hierarchy, and at the same time opened up a new avenue for photography. Much of the attention accorded to Thomson by photographic historians and critics in the twentieth century has focussed on this small body of work.[2]

*'Taking a Photograph', in *Science for All*, ed. Robert Brown, 2 vols (London, [1877-1882]), I, p. 262.

This book offers a balanced appreciation of John Thomson's life and work, and fills in some of the large gaps in our knowledge both of his career and his development as a photographer and a writer. Like most nineteenth-century photographers, he recorded little of his innermost thoughts in his published work, and in the absence of surviving letters, diaries and journals, we can only guess (albeit in an educated way) at the reasons which lay behind the decisions and choices that he made. The primary focus of this book is therefore on the photographs themselves. Two sources for these photographs in particular have been used. First, the images found in his own photographically-illustrated books, reproduced here in the main from examples in the collections of the National Library of Scotland. Second, the large trove of his original glass-plate negatives preserved in the Library of the Wellcome Institute for the History of Medicine. This latter collection is of particular importance, since it provides a means of returning to the moment when the images were created and offers a physical link with Thomson himself. The plates are now in various states of preservation. They bear the marks of corrosion, accidental damage, mishandling, and later manipulation, and have suffered through the sheer passage of time, and the immense distances they have travelled in their lead-lined packing cases. It is miraculous that they have survived in any state of preservation at all. But the plates also reveal intimate details of the photographer himself: his thumb and fingerprints in the emulsion, his signature scratched with a stylus, and the marks of masking and cropping to perfect the image: all tangible proof of his intimate involvement with the photographic process. The modern prints which have been made from these negatives and which are reproduced in this volume have been created using techniques – as far as we can determine – that Thomson himself used, for it has been our aim to remain as true to the photographer as possible. The marks of damage evident on these prints merely testify to the history of the man who created them. Rather than distracting from the image, they are emblematic of Thomson's experiences as a traveller.

Throughout the main sections of this book, Thomson's special skills and experiences as a traveller form a consistent and unifying theme. From the time of his first journey, made when he was still a young man, Thomson's life followed an almost Conradian path, as he travelled at first within the ever-expanding British Empire, and then outside its sphere of influence into realms dominated and influenced by even older imperial powers.[3] Like the African journeys of Marlow, the hero of Conrad's *Heart of Darkness*, Thomson's journeys in Asia were often long and arduous, sometimes tedious, and sometimes dangerous. Both men were unrelenting, forcing themselves to surmount the many obstacles which they encountered in a search for inner truths and hidden knowledge. Like Marlow, Thomson survived to tell his story to an audience living, to a great extent, at the heart of the Empire, in London. If Conrad's story, therefore, is a metaphor for self-examination, then Thomson's own life and career mirrored this, his photography on the streets of London seeking to examine the self of the great city, the soul of the British Empire. John Thomson's journeys were dominated by the quest for light, a prerequisite for photography, and he found light in the darkness both of the outer reaches of Asia (considered by some to be as dark as Africa, the 'dark continent'), and in the underbelly of Victorian London, whose streets seemed as dark and dangerous to the middle classes as the jungles of Cambodia.

In his lifetime, John Thomson's reputation rested as much on his achievements as a traveller as on his photography. For his European audience in particular, he was known as 'China' Thomson: a recognition of the role he played in bringing a wider knowledge of that great and ancient land to the west. Europe in the nineteenth century held an ambivalent attitude towards China, as the words of one European traveller to China, Louis de Carné, indicate:

> China! This word alone awakens the idea of a people that has triumphed over space by the extent of its empire, and over time by its duration. One feels in the presence of a nation, unchanging alike in its customs and maxims; and which, notwithstanding the revolutions which agitate it, and the invasions it undergoes, opposes to the current of events and ideas a sort of colossal petrifaction. Imprisoned in the meshes of an idiom which makes intelligence subordinate to memory, and in a network of institutions which regulate even the attitudes of the body, China has, nevertheless, anticipated Europe in its social life, in science, and in art; but the most fruitful inventions have remained sterile, as though Providence had willed this race should pass abruptly from a premature youth to an irremediable decrepitude.[4]

Europe's knowledge of the 'flowery land' had begun in earnest during the seventeenth century (through the missionary activities of Jesuit priests such as Verbiest, Le Comte, and Kircher[5]), and the eighteenth century witnessed a number of cultural, religious, scholarly, and commercial exchanges between Europe and China. But it was during the nineteenth century that European (indeed *western*) interest in Asia in general and China in particular became a fact of major significance. This interest was primarily commercial: Europe saw enormous commercial potential in China, and to a great extent realised this, using China both as a source of new commodities and as a market for old ones. Along with this economic interference came political, military, and eventually cultural contact on a massive scale, and with these exchanges came observations and observers of many kinds. But as these men – travellers, writers, artists, and scholars – came to know more of this enormous and ancient society, they found it impossible to comprehend fully the complexities, sophistication, and seeming contradictions that China encompassed.[6] Louis de Carné spoke, therefore, for a whole generation when he expressed his astonishment at these apparent contradictions. To some extent this was an inevitable result of looking at a country (or more appropriately, a *region*) like China from a European perspective, from a culture brimming full of revolutions: industrial, scientific, social, political, and religious. The rapid change which western civilisation underwent during the nineteenth century made it hard to observe the long progress of Chinese civilisation with anything other than impatience.[7]

Although photography was a product of several of these revolutionary developments, its novel treatment of time – its ability to render chronology irrelevant – made it uniquely appropriate to observe China with a wider compass than had hitherto been possible, and to relate these observations back to western audiences in a new and revolutionary manner. The most astute of these observations, and the most effective of the subsequent disclosures, were those of John Thomson.

John Thomson's journeys up the great rivers of Asia – the Mekong, Pearl, North, Min, and Yangzi – were not only feats of human endurance and logistical and mental organisation, but they enabled Thomson to understand from within something of a land known principally to his audience from the peripheries only. He sought to survey and document the lands in which he travelled, but unlike many nineteenth-century photographic expeditions, his was not one accompanying conquest or domination (political, economic, cultural). Thomson's approach was born of a spirit of enquiry, and a desire to gain a true understanding of what he saw. Along with those of only a handful of other photographic artists his portrayal attempted to encompass an entire society: distant, sometimes exotic. To an ambitious Victorian like Thomson the possibilities of photography made such a task, in his eyes, achievable.

But he did not operate in an artistic vacuum. His photography depended as much on influences from his own culture as on the profound impact that other cultures had upon his own aesthetic. Some of these influences are more implied than explicit, but others have left traces within Thomson's writing, such as the art theories of John Ruskin,[8] and romantic poetry.[9] Some influences are more visual than intellectual. Take the photograph 'The Fruits of China' (PLATE 2), for instance. It is a still-life, set up in Thomson's studio in Hong Kong, and its subject matter, composition, and treatment, owe as much to the influential series of fruit and flower photographs taken by Roger Fenton in the early 1860s (PLATE 3), as to the rich tradition of Dutch seventeenth-century still-life painting.[10]

2. *The Fruits of China.*
c. 1868–1871.

254 x 305 mm. Modern albumen print from wet-collodion negative. National Library of Scotland/Wellcome Institute Library, London

The technical parameters within which Thomson's photography operated were dictated by the capabilities of what is known as the 'wet-collodion' process, the most commonly used process to create a photographic negative in the second half of the nineteenth century.[11] This technology was complex in its operation, the equipment cumbersome to handle, the process time-consuming, and it depended on a large number of variables for consistency and quality; but it was nevertheless a process which enabled images of extremely high definition to be recorded. The images produced were therefore ideally suited to the great photographic endeavours of the nineteenth century, in particular the great photographic expeditions and journeys which sought to document new lands, peoples, and sites for the consumption of those either unwilling or unable to undertake the journeys for themselves.[12] John Thomson's photographs are supreme examples of wet-collodion photography, and, like a true Victorian, Thomson was aware of the importance, not only of the era in which he lived, but of photography's place within it: 'We are now making history', he wrote, 'and the sun picture supplies the means of passing down a record of what we are, and what we have achieved in this nineteenth century of our progress'.[13]

3. Roger Fenton, *Still Life*. *c.* 1862.

350 x 430 mm. Albumen print from wet-collodion negative. Royal Photographic Society, Bath

4. *Honan Soldiers*. 1871. 100 x 204 mm.
Modern albumen stereograph from wet-collodion negative. National Library of Scotland/Wellcome Institute Library, London

*This image, taken in Amoy in 1871, is one of the few images of Thomson in the Far East, and may be considered
the only self-portrait of the photographer.*

CHAPTER 1

CREATION

It has always been my ambition to see photography take its proper place as a means of illustrating exploration.

JOHN THOMSON*

FORMATION

The Edinburgh into which John Thomson was born, on 14 June 1837,[1] was a cultural, legal, religious, and scientific capital of major importance. Both in terms of size of population, and more importantly in terms of the influence the city had on the rest of Britain in general and Scotland in particular, Edinburgh was enjoying its heyday. Commerce may have underpinned this status, but it was its intellectual *milieu* which gave Edinburgh an edge over the other cities of the north. The presence of the University, and the medical establishments (the Royal Colleges of Physicians and Surgeons), together with the various scientific and intellectual organisations (the Royal Society of Edinburgh, the Royal Scottish Society of Arts, the Select Society, the Royal Institution) and legal institutions (the Faculty of Advocates, and the Society of Writers to the Signet) encouraged an exhilarating burst of scientific and intellectual activity which marked the city out from the middle of the eighteenth century until the end of the nineteenth. The Edinburgh of the eighteenth-century 'Enlightenment' might have dimmed slightly, but it was nonetheless a city where the arts and sciences flourished side by side.

As a child of parents of relatively modest means, John Thomson was not particularly well placed to take full advantage of the opportunities which could be found in Edinburgh, and it is not altogether surprising that he was eventually to decide that better prospects could be found among the cities of the Far East, which attracted merchants, traders, and others eager to make a name for themselves, and not afraid of working hard in order to get on.

John Thomson's father, William, was a tobacco spinner who later moved into the retail trade as a tobacconist.[2] He had married Isabella Newlands in 1819, and John's early years were spent in the family home, at first in Portland Place, and by 1841 in a larger flat in Brighton Street, in the Old Town of Edinburgh, an area predominantly occupied by the working and lower middle classes, and popular with tradesmen, shopkeepers, and small entrepreneurs.[3] Although his home was also close to the University, Thomson was not born into the right social background to be guaranteed an education at what was one of Britain's most important educational institutions. We cannot be sure of the cultural or intellectual atmosphere in which he was raised, nor do we know what sort of schooling he received, but we do know that by 1851 he had become apprenticed to an optician

*Thomson to A.R. Hinks, 15 February 1921, Royal Geographical Society Archives.

and scientific instrument maker in Edinburgh. It is unlikely that he would have gained such a desirable position without having attained a reasonable standard of schooling, and there were a number of elementary schools in the Old Town where he could have received such an education.[4] We also know that he held a fairly strong religious faith throughout his life, and this may well have been instilled into him in the parental home. The exact flavour of his Christianity does not come across strongly in any of his writings, but interwoven in the narrative threads of his books are comments which reveal a thorough knowledge of the Bible, and from his wife's letters to him during their years apart, we know that she regularly attended a Methodist Chapel on the Isle of Man, and he in turn wrote urging her to attend regularly.[5]

Without the financial wherewithal to send their son to university, the question of how best to equip him for life must have weighed heavily on William and Isabella Thomson. By the time of the 1851 Census, his parents had used what contacts they had in the city to find a place for John as an apprenticed optician.[6] Given the importance of the optical and scientific instrument trade in Edinburgh in the nineteenth century, and the fact that the trade itself was regarded as one which held great potential, it is likely that his parents may have had to pay a fee, or 'premium' to his Master for agreeing to take him on as an apprentice.[7] The practice of registering apprentices was breaking down in Edinburgh by the middle of the nineteenth century, and it is therefore very hard to determine which Master he was apprenticed to,[8] but a strong clue is to be found among the papers of the Royal Scottish Society of Arts. On 9 December 1861, John Thomson was proposed for election to the Society by James Mackay Bryson, a leading member in one of Edinburgh's most important families connected with the making of scientific instruments, who also ran a successful optician's business from premises on Edinburgh's most prestigious retail thoroughfare, Princes Street.[9] In the Society of Arts Roll of Members, Thomson is described as an 'Optician', indicating that he must have completed his apprenticeship, although his absence from the lists of opticians in the trade directories for this period indicates that he did not in fact have his own business.[10] The reasonable implication to be drawn from this evidence is that Thomson had been apprenticed to Bryson throughout the early 1850s (he was thirteen at the time of the 1851 Census, the normal age to begin serving as an apprentice), and by 1857 or 1858 had completed his training. By

Fig. 1. David Octavius Hill and Robert Adamson, *Mr Bryson, Horologist.* c. 1843–47.

205 x 151 mm. Salted paper print from calotype negative. National Library of Scotland

proposing Thomson for membership, Bryson was conferring recognition upon his protégé, and steering him through a kind of intellectual rite of passage.

Although direct evidence of Thomson's apprenticeship to Bryson is lacking, a further tangible link between the two is that Thomson attended the Edinburgh School of Arts, an educational institution which was the direct forerunner of Heriot Watt University. The School of Arts, a 'mechanic's institute', had been founded in 1821, and in 1852 had changed its name to the Watt Institution and School of Arts, after the scientist and engineer James Watt, who had himself made scientific instruments in Glasgow in the eighteenth century. The Bryson family was very closely connected with the School: Robert Bryson (Fig. 1), the father of James Mackay, had been instrumental in its foundation in 1821,[11] and both James Mackay and his brother had attended the School in the 1840s.[12] Robert Bryson and his fellow master mechanics had founded the School for the purpose of providing further education for the journeymen and apprentices who were in their employment. This spirit of philanthropic 'improvement' was not unique to Edinburgh, but the School of Arts had the advantage of benefitting from the flourishing scientific community which existed in Edinburgh at this time, and the School could boast the brilliant scientist Sir David Brewster (Fig. 2) as a Director. The School of Arts formed part of an important development in British education in the nineteenth century, the origins of which can be traced back to George Birkbeck's class of artisans at Anderson's Institute in Glasgow in 1800, and which took off in the first two decades of the nineteenth century in a number of industrial towns and cities, predominantly in the north of England and Scotland. By 1840 no fewer than seven hundred formal mechanic's institutes had been formed with a registered membership of at least 120,000.[13] As a nineteen-year-old, Thomson had served six years of his apprenticeship, no doubt learning a great deal, and had impressed his employer sufficiently for him to recommend that he be admitted to the School, possibly providing the 10*s* which a 'ticket' to attend the classes cost.[14]

Fig. 2.
David Octavius Hill and Robert Adamson, *Sir David Brewster.* *c.* 1843–47.

190 x 140 mm. Salted paper print from calotype negative. National Library of Scotland

Thomson attended the sessions 1856–57 and 1857–58 at the School of Arts, successfully gaining the 'Attestation of Proficiency' in Natural Philosophy in the first year, and in Junior Mathematics and Chemistry in the second. These three qualifications were required to qualify the student for the 'Life Diploma', the formal certificate to which all pupils aspired, and which he was duly awarded in 1858. Other classes were offered at the School, such as Senior Mathematics, Modelling, French, Drawing, English and Algebra, but there is no evidence of his having attended any of these other than English for which he was awarded a Watt Club Prize in 1857.[15] By no means all the students left the School with a qualification, and these achievements show that Thomson was an above-average pupil, which means that he may well have also attended lectures in Chemistry and Natural Philosophy at Edinburgh University, as this was common practice for the best pupils at the School of Arts at this time.[16] The School held most of its classes at night, so that apprentices and journeymen could attend after their working day was over. If the normal working day of an apprentice was demanding both physically and mentally, the evening classes at the School of Arts were no less taxing. The lecturers were often significant minds in their own fields, and at the time Thomson was attending, Stevenson Macadam, a senior figure in the Royal Scottish Society of Arts, took the Chemistry classes; William Lees, who had succeeded his father George, took those in Natural Philosophy; James Pryde taught

Mathematics; and Daniel Scrymgeor covered English. The natural, or mechanical philosophy syllabus included optics, magnetism, electricity and heat, as well as mechanics, dynamics, motion of machines, and less purely scientific topics like 'Mill Work', 'Clock Work' and architecture.[17] The School had a good reputation in Britain as a whole, and one contemporary wrote that 'a certificate obtained by a course of study like this, and after examinations so searching and complete, is unquestionably one of the most flattering testimonials a young man can possess; it certifies at once the correctness of his conduct, the extent of his studies, and the proficiency he has made; and go where he will, and apply for what situation he may, the certificate of membership, obtained so honourably, must ever be his best recommendation as well as the most powerful stimulus to a line of conduct which should support the character he has required'.[18] At the School, Thomson would also have had access, probably for the first time in his life, to a sizeable library of books on a wide variety of subjects, but obviously with great strengths in science, technology, and mathematics. But the library also contained books on travel and exploration, and even Nicolas-Marie-Paymal Lerebours's *Treatise on Photography* (1843): possible sources of inspiration and information for the young Thomson?[19]

There were few scientific instrument workshops in Scotland at which Thomson could have served a more exacting apprenticeship than that of James Bryson. His was a prestigious establishment, and this was no doubt the source of Thomson's knowledge of the trade. Thomson certainly knew how to operate scientific equipment and instruments, as he refers in *The Antiquities of Cambodia* to 'a set of astronomical instruments, which proved useful during the journey [through the Cambodian jungle to Angkor], and subsequently, in obtaining the bearings and measurements of the great buildings',[20] and the partnership which he and his brother later entered into in Singapore prominently featured instrument making in their advertisements placed in local newspapers.[21] His experiments with microphotography, which he refers to as having taken place in 1859,[22] were also no doubt undertaken in the spirit of scientific invention that surrounded Bryson, who was also very well connected with scientists in Edinburgh, St Andrews and elsewhere, although they were the sort of experiments that young scientifically-minded men were dabbling in all over the country in the 1840s and 1850s.[23]

After having performed well at the School of Arts, and completed his apprenticeship, Thomson would no doubt have been regarded by James Mackay Bryson as fit to join the Royal Scottish Society of Arts, the primary institution for those involved with science at a practical level in Scotland. As we have seen, he was duly elected as an Ordinary Fellow of that body, although he only paid his membership for the year 1861–62, for reasons that will become clear.[24] The Society had been established in 1821 by Sir David Brewster as the Society for the Encouragement of the Useful Arts in Scotland in an attempt to provide a forum for debate and exchange of information for the sizeable number of Scottish inventors and entrepreneurs who were increasingly finding institutions such as the universities and the Royal Society of Edinburgh unable to meet their needs. Brewster's idea was to establish an organisation that would provide a 'patronage structure' along the lines of the Society for the Encouragement of the Arts and Manufactures in London. He secured influential support for 'his' Society, and, thanks also to his own high standing within the scientific community, the Society did not take long to establish itself as a vital institution in the sphere of scientific and technical innovation.[25] Thomson would have found many familiar faces at the Society meetings: not only the Brysons, but Stevenson MacAdam (who had taught Thomson at the School of Arts), and Charles Piazzi Smyth (for whom he may well have made instruments whilst working for the Brysons) were all convenors of committees during Thomson's brief time as a member.

In common with most scientifically-minded men in mid-nineteenth-century Britain, the Brysons all held a keen interest in photography. Indeed the elder Robert Bryson had sat for the important Edinburgh photographers Hill and Adamson in the 1840s, and both James Mackay and Alexander Bryson were also interested in photography. The former had joined the Photographic Society of Scotland in 1858, and he remained fairly closely connected with it well into the 1860s.[26] It is therefore probable that it was through James Mackay Bryson that Thomson came to be interested in photography, although Scotland in general and Edinburgh in particular was a great artistic and scientific centre of photographic innovation during the period 1840–60. Much of photography's earliest developments and advances were due to the role played by Sir David Brewster and his close associates at St Andrews University, and to his network of correspondents, which embraced many Edinburgh figures associated with the scientific disciplines of chemistry and natural philosophy. These included Mungo Ponton, a scientific amateur (although he was a member of the Royal Society of Edinburgh), and Andrew Fyfe, a lecturer in Chemistry at the School of Arts until his move to Aberdeen University.[27] But Brewster also played a pivotal role in bringing together David Octavius Hill and Robert Adamson, thus uniting the equal elements of science and art in a photographic partnership that has remained central to photography's progress from the 1840s until the present.[28]

Edinburgh quickly attracted a host of players on the photographic scene. Daguerrotypists soon established themselves as portrait makers on Princes Street, and, at a more advanced level, amateurs and professionals like Charles Piazzi Smyth continued to push the potential of photography further and further.[29] Allied to these endeavours were a host of related disciplines, trades, and enterprises. The Brysons' business also traded in photographic and chemical supplies, and other chemical and pharmaceutical suppliers, such as Duncan and Flockhart on North Bridge, soon began to trade in the requisites. In such an exciting and fast-moving milieu, photography would have seemed an immensely attractive pursuit to take up, and with the encouragement of the Brysons and the wider circle of initiates active at the Royal Scottish Society of Arts, Thomson would not have found information and advice difficult to come by.

In 1833 the Charter by which the East India Company had held a monopoly of the trade in tea with China and India had expired, an event which allowed British merchants in all the ports of the nation to engage in this lucrative trade. Accordingly, that April, the *Isabella* arrived at Leith from Canton with the first cargo of tea (all 7,000 chests of it) to be shipped to any British port outside London. The docking of the *Isabella* therefore gave the populace of Edinburgh its first direct and exciting encounter with goods from China, a country of which the general public had hitherto been only vaguely aware. The *Isabella*, and the many other ships that followed her, carried more than just cargoes of tea. Silk, cotton, bamboo canes, and other new commodities came into the public domain, and small boys remembered the event for years to come.[30] John Thomson, who was born just three years after the arrival of the *Isabella*, would still have been an impressionable young boy during the early years of this cultural and commercial exchange, and the sights, smells, flavours, and textures of China would have been accessible to him through the Edinburgh shops of Andrew Melrose, the tea importer and entrepreneur responsible for the *Isabella*'s trading venture. Other contacts were to be made over the next two decades between Scots and the Far East, as merchants and financiers began to exploit the commercial opportunities that were opening up, and were soon followed by diplomats, missionaries, doctors and a variety of other 'enterprising Scots'. During the 1840s and 1850s a number of these men and women returned to Scotland to tell of their experiences in lectures, meetings, and publications, giving further evidence of the wonders of the East to young Scots.[31] At the School of Arts, Thomson also had access to a library of books, which included travel literature, in particular H. Murray's *Historical Account of China* (Edinburgh, 1834), which may have given him a taste for the Orient.[32]

The promise of financial prosperity was no doubt a major factor in Thomson's mind when, in the early 1860s, he decided to travel east to join his brother William, who had moved to Singapore to set up as a watchmaker, having left Edinburgh on 30 August 1859.[33] The possibilities for advancement in the East were significant, thanks largely to the East India Company, which handled the administration of British interests and colonial government throughout India and large tracts of South-East Asia, making trade and commerce in these areas relatively easy for British traders and merchants.[34] The East India Company had no jurisdiction in China, but even here improvements in diplomatic relations had recently taken place, allowing a greater freedom of movement in the interior. The Convention of Peking, signed in 1860, granted access for westerners to Treaty Ports and to the interior of China (with some exceptions), and this enabled the sort of travelling which became the central factor in Thomson's photographic operations.

FIRST JOURNEYS

It was the journey to join his brother in Singapore that gave John Thomson his first opportunity to experience life in the Far East. He left Edinburgh on 29 April according to an entry in the Thomson family Bible,[35] although throughout his time in the Far East it is almost impossible to be certain of his exact whereabouts, as the dates of his various journeys are hard to determine with any degree of accuracy. His own travel accounts often contradict each other in terms of dates, and the suggestion that he condensed the accounts of several short trips into one for the sake of a coherent narrative must be taken seriously.[36] An advertisement taken out by Thomson in *The Straits Times*, a Singapore-based newspaper, lets us be certain that he arrived in Singapore no later than 12 June 1862. In the newspaper he advertised his services as a photographer, from his 'photographic room' at Captain Leisks, 3 Beach Road, while another advertisement in the *Straits Calendar and Directory* for 1863 indicates that he and his brother also jointly operated a business making chronometers, and optical and nautical instruments.

Singapore had been founded as a trading post by Sir Stamford Raffles (acting as an agent for the East India Company) on 30 January 1819. By 1826 it had become important enough for the East India Company to unite the island with Malacca and Penang, forming the Presidency of the Straits Settlements. The merger placed Singapore under the control of Penang, although a series of events (the dissolution of the East India Company in 1858, and the abandonment of Singapore by the India Office in 1867) were to lead to Singapore becoming a Crown Colony. By the early 1860s the island had a population of 81,000, a massive growth from the few thousand native inhabitants living on it in 1819.[37] With a typical eye for a good trading base, a large number of Chinese had settled in Singapore. They came largely from the provinces of Fujian and Guangdong, and lived hard and frugally on the island, hoping to make enough money to return home with a profit. The Malay community, the indigenous people of the island, continued to grow, but relinquished their dominant position to the British and Chinese. Indians, who came mainly as traders and labourers, could also be found on the island, where they formed its second largest community by 1860.

In the 1860s, just as today, Singapore was an entrepôt of tremendous importance to the economic life of South-East Asia, and the great potential for personal advancement which has always been a feature of such cities was no doubt the magnet which drew the Thomson brothers there. Indonesian, Siamese, Chinese, and Malayan commerce focussed on Singapore; and British, Arab, German, and American merchants fed off this more local trading network. Despite such economic growth, photography was slow to take off as a feature in the city's commercial life, probably a result both of the difficulty in obtaining supplies of materials, and of the unpredictable nature of the market for images among the western residents. John Thomson, therefore, had few rivals in the early 1860s, Sachtler & Co. being the only other firm documented at the time. But unfortunately the early 1860s were not a particularly buoyant period for the European trading community in Singapore that would have provided most of Thomson's customers.[38] The slump hit the island around 1861, largely the result of the expansion of Dutch trade in Sulawesi, and in 1864, the slump's lowest point, many firms both Asian and European went to the wall. This was only a short-lived depression, however. By 1867 Singapore was a flourishing port once more, and this trend towards prosperity was to continue, particularly after the opening of the Suez Canal in 1869, which heralded Singapore's major period of growth.[39] The period of the slump encompassed John Thomson's use of Singapore as a base, and may have influenced his decision to travel to other areas within South-East Asia, and eventually to leave and return to Britain.

Thomson travelled extensively from Singapore among the islands and some of the mainland territories of Malaya and Sumatra during the early 1860s. This period, spent journeying through the Straits of Malacca, was an important one for Thomson, who was grappling with, and eventually getting used to, life in a very different climate and culture from that of mid-nineteenth-century Edinburgh. Penang, an island some 360 miles from Singapore, was evidently his base for a short time. The island had been ceded to the East India Company in 1786, and the neighbouring mainland territory, Province Wellesley, followed in 1800. Penang's principal settlement, George Town, became the focus for British economic activity, as well as the centre of another economically active group of the overseas-Chinese. Thomson thought Penang 'strikingly picturesque', and found the climate, scenery, and natural history of the island very much to his liking, as he makes clear in his eloquent description of the island in *The Straits of Malacca*.[40] He comments: 'During the ten months I spent in Penang and Province Wellesley, I was chiefly engaged in photography – enabling me to gratify my taste for travel and to fill my portfolio, as I wandered over Penang Settlement and the mainland hard by, with an attractive series of characteristic scenes and types, which were in constant demand among the resident European population'. He also records that he hired two Madras men to act as photographic printers and assistants.

During his time in the Straits Settlements he also viewed sugar plantations, and spent six weeks in the company of planters and engineers, many of whom were 'big brawny men from the lowlands of Scotland', who showed him warm hospitality. He also made a brief visit to Malacca which he found neither interesting nor profitable. The suggestion that he visited India, probably based on the fact that he was a member of the Bengal Photographic Society, is otherwise unsubstantiated. He no doubt joined as a corresponding member from Singapore, and he depended to some extent on Indian sources for supplies of chemicals and other photographic requisites. The photograph of a destructive Indian cyclone in 1864, which has been attributed to Thomson by Stephen White, was no doubt taken by one of a number of other photographers known to have taken similar images.[41]

By 1865 Thomson had established both a settled base in Singapore and an active portrait studio providing photographic services to the growing western community in the colony. He was also operating a scientific instrument making business in partnership with his brother.[42] From his comments in *The Antiquities of Cambodia* we learn that he had access to numerous publications on Asia, possibly at the Raffles Library, or the Straits Branch of the Royal Asiatic Society, although Singapore did have an English-language bookseller who imported titles from Britain.[43] It was through reading, according to his own account, that he was inspired to travel to the 'ruined cities which the author found in the heart of the Cambodian forests'.[44]

Siam, the King, and the Cambodian Ruins

Singapore was but a five-day passage by steam-boat from Siam, and the great city of Bangkok (PLATE 5), opened up to British visitors for only ten years, would no doubt have been high on the list of places to visit for any adventurous traveller in the Far East in the middle of the nineteenth century. Given that, as we have seen, Thomson's interest in travel had been excited by reading the accounts of other travellers whilst in Singapore, it is not surprising that he should have decided to pay a visit to Siam. He travelled in the Siamese steamer *Chow Phya*, first going ashore at Paknam (on the river Menam) before arriving in Bangkok on 28 September 1865, where he vividly describes travelling 'through the floating city in the dimness of the early morning light' and gazing 'upon the towers and roofs of more than half a hundred temples'.[45] The British Consulate in Bangkok had been established in June 1856, a natural development following the Treaty of Friendship and Commerce between Britain and Siam, which was signed on 5 April 1856. Evidently the city soon after became home to a small community of expatriate Scots, as the *Chronicle and Directory for China, Japan, and the Philippines for 1866* refers to the Clyde Dock Yard and Steam Saw Mills in the city. Thomson's first task was probably to contact the British Consulate, and there he became acquainted with H. G. Kennedy. At the time, Kennedy was merely a Student Interpreter, but by 1868 he had become 2nd Assistant, a position he was to hold until at least 1871.[46] The two were to become close friends.

Thomson was keen to gain an audience with the Siamese Royal Family, and the Consulate was able to arrange this. Much of his time in Bangkok was spent taking a number of stunning formal portraits of the King, his relatives, and chief ministers, and documenting royal ceremonies, and visits to temples *(PLATES 6–7)*. The royal barge was the subject of one particularly magnificent photograph *(PLATE 8)*, and he regarded the royal progress in boats as 'one of the most imposing spectacles [he had] ever beheld'.[47] The King of Siam, Mongkut (1804-68), reigned from 1851 to 1868, and had lived as a Buddhist monk in the *sangha* of Bangkok until he became King. As a monk he had been free to develop his own interests, and had studied many foreign languages.[48] Throughout his life he had been closely concerned with the status of Siam as a nation, and accordingly followed a conciliatory policy towards the western powers, accepting their pleas for free trade and diplomatic relations. Whilst living in Bangkok, and working closely with the royal court, Thomson would probably have come into contact with another British resident, Anna Leonowens, the tutor to the sons of King Mongkut, and author of *The English Governess at the Siamese Court*, a celebrated nineteenth-century book later immortalised in the musical and motion picture, *The King and I*.[49] If he did meet her, Thomson chose not to record the exchange in his books, but he does refer to her work, pointing out several serious inaccuracies in her account of Angkor, and accusing her, in no uncertain terms, of plagiarism from the works of Henri Mouhot.[50] For her part, Anna Leonowens reproduced in her books a number of Thomson photographs, heavily doctored as wood-engravings, and rather disparagingly referred to 'James Thomson' as 'the able English photographer'.[51] Thomson's Siamese and Cambodian photographs were to find their way into several other publications during the latter half of the nineteenth century, often through the agency of his publishers Sampson Low. They appeared, for instance, in Frank Vincent's *The Land of the White Elephant: Sights and Scenes in South-Eastern Asia* (New York, 1874).

Thomson travelled on several short journeys from Bangkok, including one to Petchiburee in the company of Dr Daniel Beach Bradley, an American Missionary and editor of the *Bangkok Recorder*. Bradley clearly got on well with Thomson, who supplied him with a collection of albumen prints which is still in the possession of his descendants.[52] Thomson appears to have been printing a number of his Siamese images in Bangkok, and selling them on a commercial basis, as, in addition to the Bradley collection, Thomson images appear in an album (now in the Gilman Collection in New York) compiled by Franklin Blake, a young American from Massachusetts who was working in Bangkok for the Boston trading company Augustine Heard & Co. at the time of Thomson's stay in the city.[53]

On 27 January 1866, John Thomson and his friend H. G. Kennedy set out on a journey he later described as 'having characteristics that might fairly claim kindred with those of the deadly regions of Central Africa, that have given to the world as many books as might clothe its savage population decently in paper, and containing as many narratives of adventures and hair breadth escapes from fever and famine, wild beasts and hungry cannibals, as might keep the hair of the reading public standing on end for at least one month out of the twelve'.[54] Clearly, his life in Singapore had been quiet enough for him to read a number of accounts of the Cambodian jungle and the amazing ruins at Ongcor, or Angkor, that lay deep in its midst, and he and his companion were fired up for adventure: 'a journey holding out such prospects, could scarcely be looked forward to but with that degree of pleasure and interest which the soldier must feel going into battle, when reminded by his friends that the odds are ten to one of his ever coming out of it'.[55]

The two men procured a letter from King Mongkut to ease their passage. They set out with the express intention of reaching Cambodia, 'for the purpose of exploring and photographing its wonderful ruins'.[56] The four months from January 1866 which they spent travelling through the rough country of Siam and the jungle of Cambodia were certainly arduous, and they had to employ ten porters to transport not only the usual supplies, but all the chemicals and equipment necessary for the wet-collodion process: the travelling required considerable strength of character from the two men.[57] Their journey took them down the Gulf of Siam to Chantabroon, then on a long and difficult route to Battabung, during which the Europeans were plagued by leeches, and Thomson contracted 'jungle fever' (probably malaria), and had to be nursed back to health by Kennedy. Eventually, Mongkut's letter enabled them to get elephants to make the latter stages of their journey easier, and they finally reached the heart of the ancient Cambodian kingdom: Angkor *(PLATE 9)*. Here Thomson was the first photographer to visit what is now one of the most important sites of ancient architecture in the world. His short time in Angkor coincided with the arrival of a French archaeological expedition, the first of hundreds of visits by European scholars, and he preceded the French photographer Henri Gsell (active in the 1860s and 1870s) by a matter of weeks.[58]

The two travellers decided not to return directly to Bangkok, but headed instead for the Cambodian capital Phnom Penh, which they reached on 27 March 1866. Cambodia had become semi-independent from Siam by the Franco-Siamese Treaty of 1863, which in theory created an independent kingdom under the protection of France, but in fact the influence of Siam had remained powerful. Thomson's typically European disregard for native cultures and sensibilities recurs in his writing about Cambodia, which in 1867 he regarded as a 'miserable remnant of "Khamain"',[59] and he repeats his imperialist accusations concerning the 'listlessness and apathy' of the native peoples.[60] Thomson thoroughly approved of the French influence on Cambodia, regarding it as harnessing the 'latent energy' of the native peoples, and he thought the European buildings constructed by the French in Phnom Penh a great improvement on the 'primitive' bamboo huts in which local people lived. As in Bangkok, Thomson saw the opportunities for photography in the city and in particular recognised the commercial potential of images of the political leaders: of his surviving images, formal portraits of Norodom, the King of Cambodia (1834–1904; he reigned from 1860 to 1904), and members of the royal household predominate *(PLATE 10)*.

After a return visit to Bangkok, where Thomson presented King Mongkut with a set of photographs of Angkor (possibly those which Mongkut later gave to Anna

Leonowens, and which formed the source for the woodcuts in her book), he returned to Singapore, where he began the process of

Fig. 3. *The King of Siam's State Barge.* 1866.

Wood-engraving (from *The Illustrated London News*, 25 May 1867). National Library of Scotland

marketing his work to a wider public, and succeeded in getting *The Illustrated London News* to reproduce two of his photographs (one of which is illustrated as Fig. 3) as wood-engravings.[61] As far as can be determined, these were the first of his images to be published and this must have encouraged him to think that the images and experiences he had gathered could find commercial outlets back in Britain.

THE RETURN OF THE NATIVE

At some time in May or June of 1866, Thomson returned to Britain from Singapore.[62] Using his experiences in Siam and Cambodia (in particular the visit to Angkor), and his photographs from that trip, as his 'capital', he then adopted a number of strategies to establish his reputation as a serious traveller, photographer, and writer. There were various societies in Britain devoted to subjects which related closely to his own interests, and he used these organisations to meet other people with similar concerns, and to make contacts and look for new opportunities. Thus, at some point after the Anniversary Meeting of the Ethnological Society of London in May 1866, he successfully petitioned to be elected a Fellow. His first attempt to establish his reputation as a serious traveller came with a paper, 'Notes on a Journey to the Ruins of Cambodia', which he sent to the Royal Geographical Society on 17 August.[63] This paper also marks his debut as a writer, although his lack of experience as an author ultimately led to the paper being turned down for publication by the Society's referee, the eminent anthropologist and architectural historian James Fergusson. This setback made little impact on his determination to make his name, and for the remainder of the year Thomson set about a busy schedule of lecturing and writing that ultimately brought the recognition he had hoped for. In August 1866 he attended the thirty-sixth meeting of the British Association for the Advancement of Science in Nottingham, giving a paper to the Section on Geography and Ethnology, and showing his photographs, copies of inscriptions, and ground plans of the site, to the assembled audience of high-profile figures in the fields of geography, ethnology, anthropology, and related disciplines.[64] This may have helped his election as Fellow of the Royal Geographical Society on 26 November 1866.[65]

Another strategy which might also provide a source of income was to seek to publish his images and written thoughts as widely as possible. He approached the photographic journals in the first instance, from August to October 1866 publishing a series of articles in the *British Journal of Photography*, and on 19 November he exhibited his Cambodian images in a large and important exhibition in Edinburgh organised by the Edinburgh Photographic Society.[66] His work was in good company at this important event, as the other photographers who exhibited included Francis Bedford, William Donaldson Clark, and Charles Piazzi Smyth, and the event attracted large crowds at the Museum of Science and Art. Thomson was evidently quite a success with the Edinburgh Photographic Society, for on 17 December in the same year he lectured to the Society on Siam and Cambodia, illustrating his talk with lantern slides.[67] His lecturing continued well into 1867, his northern base proving convenient for establishing contacts in both Edinburgh and Glasgow. He gave a very well-received paper on Siam and Cambodia (again accompanied by photographs 'projected on a screen by the oxyhydrogen light') to the Glasgow Photographic Association on 21 February 1867,[68] and the Angkor photographs were exhibited at a meeting of the Architectural Institute of Scotland on 11 April, when the architecture of Angkor Wat was discussed (Fig. 4).[69] He was also keen to build on his initial good fortune with *The Illustrated London News*, and offered them more images from Cambodia, which were published on 1 February 1868.[70]

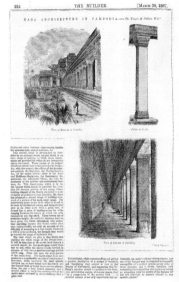

Fig. 4.
Naga Architecture in Cambodia.
1866.

Wood-engraving (from *The Builder*, 30 March 1867).
National Library of Scotland

Early in 1867, under the title *The Antiquities of Cambodia: A Series of Photographs Taken on the Spot*, the Edinburgh publishers Edmonston and Douglas issued Thomson's account of his visit to Angkor, which he had been working up since returning to Britain.[71] This was his first book, and he had been fortunate in managing to persuade one of the foremost publishers of illustrated books in Scotland to take on the project. No doubt the series of lectures that he had given had helped to establish his reputation, and certainly his acquisition of prestigious Fellowships of the Royal Geographical Society and of the Ethnological Society of London would have made a difference. The book would have been costly to produce, as it was issued with albumen prints (real photographs) pasted in as the means of illustration, and with two panoramas adding to the complexity of production. Edmonston and Douglas must have been convinced that it would find a ready audience. The involvement of one of Britain's leading scholars on Asian antiquities, James Fergusson (1808–86), may well have provided the publishers with the necessary authority behind the work.[72] Fergusson's involvement is only hinted at in the text, where an earlier work of his is referred to, but elsewhere Fergusson is fulsome in his praise of the photographs, and explicit about his role in *The Antiquities of Cambodia*:

> The greatest amount of information can be obtained from the photographs of Mr J. Thomson, and his personal communications. From these sources a tolerably connected account is condensed in my *History of Architecture* (II, p. 713, et seq), to which the reader is referred. Since that time, Messrs Edmiston [sic] and Douglas, of Edinburgh, have published a selection of Mr Thomson's photographs, with explanatory text taken, principally, with my consent and collaboration, from my work above referred to.[73]

This note, buried in Fergusson's magisterial work, may well have been intended to set the record straight, as his contribution to *The Antiquities of Cambodia* gets no recognition in that volume.

James Fergusson was a high-profile scholar and writer, and praise for Thomson in his *magnum opus* would have been taken seriously in the circles in which the photographer wanted to move. Fergusson's *A History of Architecture in all Countries, from the Earliest Times to the Present Day* was the first great comprehensive history of world architecture published in English, the first edition appearing in three volumes from 1862 to 67. The second volume was still being worked on when Fergusson became aware of Thomson's photographs and 'discoveries'. Fergusson, already familiar with the accounts of Angkor by Mouhot and Bastian, was clearly excited by Thomson's account, but it was the evidence contained in his photographs which revolutionised the way in which the historian could assess the significance both of the structures themselves and of the detail of their ornaments.

> It would have been impossible to write anything that would convey a correct idea of these ruins had it not been for the zeal and enterprise of Mr. J. Thomson, who was following his profession as a photographer in the East. At considerable risk and expense he carried his apparatus to the spot, and brought away a plan and some thirty photographs of the great temple, and views of one or two others. These he has placed at my disposal, and it is principally from them, with the information he has afforded me verbally, that the following account is compiled.[74]

With *The Antiquities of Cambodia* recently published, Thomson continued to be in demand as a lecturer, and he made the inevitable move to London, speaking to the Ethnological Society of London on 9 July 1867.[75] During this period Thomson became involved socially with the Petrie family from the Isle of Man (Fig. 5), who came to Edinburgh regularly to visit a relative who had married Sir James Young Simpson, the important surgeon who had discovered chloroform, and whose younger brother John became a close friend of John Thomson.[76] Isabel Petrie attended one of Thomson's lectures in Edinburgh, at the Industrial Museum,[77] where they met and embarked on what was to become a long and happy relationship.

Fig. 5.
Petrie Family,
Ronaldsway,
Isle of Man.
c. 1867.

Albumen print
from wet-collodion
negative.
John Hillelson
Collection

FIRST CHINA JOURNEYS

With a successful round of lectures, a series of articles, and one major publication (not to mention two Fellowships) under his belt, John Thomson returned to the Far East late in 1867.

From the confused chronology that can be derived from his own accounts, it seems that he spent part of the latter half of 1867 and the early part of 1868 in Vietnam, which, like Bangkok, was only a short journey by steamer from

Singapore. Here the European visitor was naturally drawn to Saigon, the European town built up by through French colonial interests, with large stone and brick constructions which contrasted markedly with the traditional native buildings of nearby Cholon. In Vietnam, as in Siam and Cambodia, and to a lesser extent in Penang and Province Wellesley, Thomson travelled around the country (although he did not make any long journeys), and, keeping his eyes and ears open, he began to work his observations and photographs into short articles which he eventually published in *The China Magazine*. These articles again betray Thomson's keen interest in the affairs of the ordinary people, although this close interest in the poor was offset by contact with prosperous merchants. What this writing also reveals is that Thomson found it impossible to enter into a deep understanding of the culture in which he lived for several months, since, despite his efforts to gain as much knowledge of the Cochin-Chinese as he could, prejudices and mis-assumptions litter his writing. Like most nineteenth-century European writers on Asia he was unable to shake off his cultural cloak and appreciate the past and present experiences of the people he encountered without comparing them to western cultural paradigms.

Early in 1868 Thomson moved his base of operations, which at this time meant his commercial portrait business, from Singapore to Hong Kong (PLATES 11–12). The colony had been captured from the Chinese by the British earlier in the century, and had established itself as a powerful entrepôt, a crucial trading station for British colonial and commercial interests in East Asia. This period in the nineteenth century was one which saw Hong Kong grow considerably, its population alone increasing in size from 117,471 in 1866 to 124,198 in 1871.[78] Given that Singapore was still in the grip of a depression, the decision to move east was not a difficult one for Thomson to make. Also, his appetite for new places and experiences had not dimmed, and he must have felt that his prospects of marriage to Isobel Petrie would look decidedly better if his business were able to expand. Hong Kong was the natural choice. As in other growing Asian cities (in particular, those in India), Scots had been quick to realise the commercial and social opportunities to be had, and John Thomson therefore discovered in Hong Kong a vibrant community of expatriates with which to socialise and do business. The issue of *The China Punch* which came out on 9 December 1867 described a typical social gathering of Scots in the city:

> About a hundred Scotchmen and their friends sat down to dinner at the Club on Saturday … 'Hotchpotch' and 'Haggis', 'Cockie Leekie' and 'Collops', 'Finnon Haddocks' and 'Shortbread', 'Cauld Kail', and 'Custocks' were included in the Bill of Fare, and after good justice being done to them 'Willie brewed a peck o'maut' and the company settled themselves firmly in their seats preparatory to 'making a night of it' after the approved Scotch fashion.[79]

With such a convivial group of his own countrymen evidently making a good living in the colony, Hong Kong would have seemed a natural place to make a more permanent base, and Thomson duly announced the opening of his studio in the Commercial Bank's Building in Queen's Road, in the *China Mail* of 11 March 1868.[80] By late September he had enough saleable prints to be able to advertise forty of them in the *Daily Press*.[81]

Hong Kong, unlike Singapore, had a well-established group of commercial photographic studios operating when Thomson arrived. In addition to several native Chinese photographers, a number of Europeans had established businesses there, the most important of which was that operated by W. P. Floyd.[82] Thomson and Floyd, as the two most prominent western photographers in the colony, inevitably developed a commercial rivalry that manifested itself as a price war. Floyd advertised his photographs as 'unsurpassed for quality by any photographer in China' and reduced his prices in July 1868, while in September Thomson advertised his own series of 'instantaneous views' of Hong Kong, with a special emphasis on current events, prompting further price cuts by Floyd, a move which almost bankrupted Floyd's business until it was saved by patronage from the Governor of the island.[83]

Thomson was keen to diversify his business, and, in addition to running his commercial studio, he became involved, as we have seen, in the production of the illustrated weekly publication, *The China Magazine*. The use of real photographs to illustrate a magazine was unusual, and it was probably this which encouraged the *China Punch*, under the title 'Ready in Three Weeks', to make satirical capital at Thomson's expense:

> No. 4 of the CHINA MAGAZINE – The Conductor begs to inform subscribers that Mr J. Thompson A.B.C.D.E.F.G.H.I.J. and sometime W. and Y. has undertaken the photographs published in number 1. 2. & 3., and they will be sent to the undertakers as soon as possible. The Conductor has now much pleasure in stating that every thing is in train, and feels convinced that the *China Magazine* will take a prominent status in a paying line. Photographs of scenes in Hong Kong, the Swiss Cantons, Cochin-China Fowls, the Siamese Twins, Malacca Canes and Penang Lawyers, chiefly from negatives by Mr Thompson, will appear during the present quarter. The Conductor is in a position to announce the above, having already received two negatives, thus making it a positive fact ... Illustrations. 1. Street Gambler – by a Share Broker. 2. Chinese Sempstress – by a Thimble-Rigger. 3. River Seen in a Coach in China.[84]

With Thomson just having returned from Britain, and proudly placing the letters F.R.G.S. and F.E.S.L. after his name, the editors of the *China Punch* no doubt thought him fair game. In fact, the fault probably lay with the editor of *The China Magazine*, who announced in the April 1868 issue 'that Mr J. Thomson, FRGS and FESL, has undertaken the photographs with which the Magazine will, in future, be illustrated. From the high character of Mr Thomson's productions and from the approbation awarded to them in Europe, as well as in the East, the conductor believes that subscribers will have reason to be well satisfied with this change'.[85] Unfortunately, Thomson and *The China Magazine* soon parted company, for reasons which remain obscure, although it has been suggested that he did not approve of the editorial decisions regarding his article on the art of photography.[86] What seems more likely is that the magazine could not sustain the expensive practice of pasting in albumen prints, a labour-intensive task that few journals were able to sustain for long periods in the nineteenth century.[87]

Despite this setback, Thomson's commercial work continued to expand and diversify in Hong Kong. Edinburgh contacts, no doubt made during his period promoting his Cambodian experiences, proved valuable in securing the contract to produce an album of photographs to accompany Andrew Wilson's book *The Ever Victorious Army*, which had been published in Edinburgh by William Blackwood. The book is an account of General Gordon's period controlling the allied forces in China during the Taiping Rebellion, where the military prowess of the troops led to the force being dubbed 'The Ever Victorious Army'. The British edition of the book had no illustrations except a map, and, anticipating that '300 will be easily disposed of in China',[88] Wilson organised the production of this companion volume, Thomson acting solely as the Hong Kong 'end' of the enterprise, and probably printing the images in his own studio, although he was not responsible for taking them. In the end, Blackwoods printed just over a thousand copies of the text, and the accompanying album was no doubt intended to be issued with the few hundred that were sold by the firm's agents in Hong Kong and Shanghai.[89]

The year 1868 continued to be a significant one in Thomson's life. Not only were his professional activities coming together, with his studio established in a new base and commercial ventures opening up, but his private life was also the scene of significant developments. Isabel Petrie, by now engaged to Thomson, followed her fiancé to Hong Kong, where they were married on 19 November. Shortly afterwards the couple travelled to Canton, Thomson using the trip to make some pictures.

The following year, 1869, showed further promise for the photographer, whose business was evidently expanding. His experience in dealing with authors and publishers was also beginning to pay off, as he was commissioned to provide the photographs for a memento volume compiled by the Anglican Colonial Chaplain to Hong Kong (1867–70), William Roberts Beach, to commemorate the visit of the Duke of Edinburgh who had been travelling around the Far East aboard HMS *Galatea* (PLATE 13). The cruise had begun in February 1867, and was to last, on and off, until 1871, although the ship only stayed in Hong Kong during the first two weeks of November 1869. Beach rushed the volume out, hoping to cash in on the massive excitement which the visit aroused in Hong Kong, and the book, *Visit of His Royal Highness the Duke of Edinburgh ... to Hong Kong in 1869*,[90] was marketed in Hong Kong by Noronha and Sons (the Government Printers), and in Britain by Smith, Elder and Co., the profits being promised to the Building Fund for St John's Cathedral in Hong Kong. Thomson already had a reputation in the colony, as Beard knew his photographs would 'form one of the chief attractions of the work',[91] although he realised that the expense of tipping-in the seven images would considerably increase the production costs. The project was also an opportunity for Thomson to develop his portrait work among the political and social élite, and the frontispiece to the book is a three-quarter-length portrait of Alfred, Duke of Edinburgh himself. This publication, the first photographically-illustrated book published in China, was quickly followed by the second book for which Thomson was responsible, *Views on the North River*. This was published in Hong Kong, again by Noronha, and this time the photographs (pasted-in albumen prints) were emphasised over the textual element of the book. No doubt expensive to produce, it probably had a small print-run, and copies of it are now very scarce indeed.

Soon after the birth of Willie, their first son, John and Isabel Thomson decided that the Far East was not the right place for a European mother and her child, and so on 23 June 1870 Isabel and the baby son left Hong Kong on a boat bound for Britain. Two other factors influenced this decision. In one letter to her husband Isabel refers to his brother William's debts in Singapore, which John was forced to take over.[92] Isabel also suspected that she had become pregnant again, and with her health suffering in Hong Kong they no doubt decided to err on the side of caution. Her first letter to John from the boat confirmed that her suspicions were right. [93] So, with one son, and another child on the way, John decided that he was best focussing his attentions on his writing and photography, to gather enough material to ensure the financial security of his family once reunited. In the meantime he knew that his wife and child would be cared for by Isabel's family. The boat called at Singapore, where Isabel had to collect her brother-in-law William, who had stayed on in Singapore, and, without his brother's guiding hand, had drifted into a spiral of debt, illness, and alcoholism. He had clearly acquired a reputation in Singapore for his unruly behaviour whilst under the influence of alcohol, and Isabel was forced to write to her husband that 'no ship's Captain would undertake the responsibility of giving William a passage home'.[94] Isabel went to stay with her family on the Isle of Man when she finally reached Britain, and it was there that their second child, John, was born. William was dispatched with family money to America, where he continued to be a drain on his brother, although the latter did all he could to support him and his daughters.[95]

THE GREAT TRAVELLER

Between 1870 and 1872, a time spent on his own, but with a network of western contacts ready to be exploited, John Thomson built up both the experience and desire to undertake a series of major journeys in China. Without his family, he had the freedom to spend long periods away from his base in Hong Kong. It was at this point that he undertook four distinct large-scale journeys which were to produce the most important photographs made by him in China, and which fuelled his aesthetic and emotional response to the country. These momentous journeys took him up the North Branch of the Pearl River, up the River Min to the area around Fuzhau (with a related excursion to Formosa), to Peking and the surrounding country, and finally up the great river Yangzi.

But, during this period, he also made a series of shorter visits to other coastal cities and ports in China. These included a lengthy stay in Canton (*PLATE 14*), which resulted in a large number of important photographs, and trips to Macau (*PLATE 15*), Swatow (now Shantou in the province of Guangdong), the port city of Zhaozhou, and Amoy (Xiamen), all easily accessible and connected to Hong Kong by the daily steamer service. Some of these cities, especially the Portuguese colony of Macau, were popular resorts for the foreign residents of Hong Kong, and would have been natural places for any westerner to visit, but Thomson also made frequent trips to Shanghai, much further away from Hong Kong, where he made photographs and established contacts among the large population of westerners. He would later return there, using it as a base for travelling up the river Yangzi.[96]

Initially, much of this period was spent in and around the city of Fuzhau, some thirty-five miles up the River Min from the coast. Fuzhau (now known as Minhow) was one of the great tea cities of China, and in the early nineteenth century it was the major Chinese port for the famous tea clippers sailing to Europe and north America. The city flourished in this way because of the deep-water anchorage a few miles to its south. Known as 'Pagoda Anchorage', this centered around a small island, home to both a dockyard and the sizeable Fuzhau Arsenal, and was a site which Thomson likened to the Clyde docks. Fuzhau was home to a flourishing community of western merchants, financiers, tea-planters and an assortment of hangers-on trying to make something of themselves in the Foreign Settlement on the south bank of the River Min. The more respectable westerners lived in large, cool, spacious stone-built houses, very different from the wooden structures which housed the sizeable Chinese population. Thomson observed that the foreign residents formed 'a very agreeable community',[97] a comment which may refer to the relatively large number of Scots resident in Fuzhau at the time.[98] 'Petty feuds, of course, occur among them, as they have an abundance of leisure on their hands when the tea season is over; but, as a rule, they employ their spare time more wisely than in local squabbles, and seek healthful recreation among the mountains and glens of the province.'[99] The magnificent scenery was also a major reason for Thomson's prolonged visit to Fuzhau, and he made several shorter expeditions from the city, amassing a collection of negatives which form what is his strongest series of landscapes (and which is discussed below, pp. 142–46). However, the landscape did not monopolise his artistic sensibilities while he was in Fuzhau, for a portion of *Foochow and the River Min*, and parts of the Fuzhau section of *Illustrations of China*, examine the types and conditions of the poor, a subject that was becoming increasingly important to Thomson as his journeys progressed. The monastery at Gushan, evidently on many western travellers' list of places to visit, was also the subject of some particularly evocative Thomson photography. 'This Temple seems to be the Jerusalem of this part of China', wrote Robert Fortune twenty years before,[100] and like Thomson he was particularly taken with the 'majestic grandeur' of the Gushan peak itself.[101] From Fuzhau Thomson made other journeys. While on a sailing trip to Shanghai, he stayed for almost a month on a yacht owned by an English merchant. Rather more prosaically, he also visited a leper village near Fuzhau with a local missionary, the Reverend Mr Mahood. A further excursion up the Min River was to Yenping City with Justus Doolittle, an important American missionary. Doolittle had been sent to China by the American Board of Commissioners for Foreign Missions, first arriving in Fuzhau in 1850, and with his immense experience of China he was an important contact for Thomson. He was a prolific writer and publisher, and his output included religious tracts in Chinese and *The Social Life of the Chinese* (first published in New York in 1865). From Fuzhau Doolittle also edited the *Chinese Recorder and Missionary Journal*, an organ which supported Thomson's work in many ways, advertising his photography, publishing his writing, and giving favourable reviews of his publications. Thomson also collaborated with Doolittle on a Chinese-English Dictionary, providing a section on photographic terminology.[102]

In April 1871 Thomson made a separate and distinct journey to the island of Formosa (Taiwan), only eighty miles by steamer from the important coastal city of

Amoy (Xiamen), where he had been staying and photographing the city and inhabitants. 'My purpose was to go into the heart of the island to see the aborigines', he later wrote,[103] but there may have been a personal reason for visiting the island. James Laidlaw Maxwell was a brilliant young medical doctor, who had studied at Edinburgh, Würzburg, and Berlin, before taking the degree of MD at Edinburgh University in 1858. The following year, Maxwell took up the post of Medical Missionary in Formosa, based at Taiwan-fu, and connected to the Foreign Mission Board of the Presbyterian Church in England. Thomson and Maxwell may well have encountered each other in Edinburgh, possibly in the late 1850s, and Thomson may well have visited the island as much to renew an old acquaintance, as to encounter the island and its 'aborigines'. The two men made an expedition into the interior of the island, about which relatively little was known in the west, as the jungle was dense and the island was dominated by a high and jagged mountain range. Maxwell's medical mission in Taiwan-fu was clearly very advanced by contemporary standards, and the fame of the 'good foreign medicine-man' encouraged many on the island to undertake long journeys to the hospital. In *The Straits of Malacca* Thomson observed that Maxwell 'enjoys many opportunities for spreading a knowledge of Christianity, for gaining converts ... in a place like this the life of such a man is no enviable one ... his is a lifetime devoted to self-sacrifice and systematic toil'.[104] By 1872, Maxwell had returned to Edinburgh, and was using some of Thomson's photographs of Formosa during his lectures to medical audiences. Maxwell later moved to the Henry Lester Institute for Medical Research, Shanghai, and became Medical Advisor to the International Mission to Lepers, and to the Chinese Mission to Lepers, before returning to Britain where he became Secretary of the London Missionary Association.[105]

After the excitement of the interior of Formosa and his encounter with the hill-tribes, Thomson returned briefly to Hong Kong. In the previous year he had already been involved in negotiating the sale of his studio, and it would take almost another year for the transactions to be completed.[106] But once these negotiations had started, Thomson felt free to embark on the final stages of his journeying around mainland China, beginning with a visit to Peking, China's greatest city.

Peking, Princes, and the Yangzi

Thomson's stay in Peking was longer than his visits to most other Chinese cities, no doubt because the opportunities for taking interesting and potentially important photographs were far greater in the capital than anywhere else in China *(PLATE 16)*. 'I have not space to relate a tenth of what I beheld or experienced in this great capital', he was to write later,[107] and his Peking photographs are among the most interesting of all his Chinese images, showing an experienced photographer using all his skills and relishing the rich and varied material which was to be found there. He was able to make important contacts with other Britons living in Peking, some associated with the British Legation, others with medical and missionary activity. The British Legation supplied important assistance for all British visitors to the city, and behind its high walls provided a little genial civilisation of a distinctly European kind. It was very much a home-from-home. A Fives Court, a Billiards Room, and a Bowling Alley were provided for recreation and relaxation, and more serious pursuits could be had in its reading room for newspapers and journals and in its library. In every sense, the Legation provided 'a little nation by itself' for the weary traveller.[108] Thomson certainly made contact at a high level. Although Thomson was working for *The Illustrated London News* as a correspondent, the British Minister in Peking, Sir Thomas Wade, gave him the job of photographing Li Hongzhang, a senior Chinese official, whom Thomson visited in the company of E. H. Parker, a consular official. Li Hongzhang had been presented with an album of Thomson's photographs by Wade, in the hope that he would consent to have his own taken; eventually permission was granted, although the encounter was not an easy one.[109] As in Bangkok, Thomson no doubt used his British diplomatic contacts to engineer portrait sessions with a number of the most senior Chinese politicians and Government officials.

It may have been his religious contacts that brought him to call on the Rev Dr John Dudgeon in Peking.[110] Dudgeon had been sent to China by the London Missionary Society in 1863, moving to Peking the following year where he oversaw a hospital connected with the Society. He accompanied Thomson on a number of visits around the city, as well as travelling with him to the Wanshoushan.[111] Another Briton in Peking at this time was Stephen Bushell, the talented Sinologist, and already an authority on Chinese art and antiquities. He acquired a number of Thomson's photographs whilst in Peking, and these were used to illustrate his book on Chinese art.[112] Thomson's religious connections also brought him together with Alexander Wylie of the London Bible Society and sometime Shanghai representative of the British and Foreign Bible Society. He had been in China since 1847, and travelled with Thomson and a Mr Welmer (a Russian) from Peking to the Great Wall in October 1871.[113]

The confused nature of the dates in Thomson's own travel accounts makes it impossible to say exactly when he left Peking. The dates on the negatives, although written in his hand, were added some time after the plates were exposed and processed, and cannot be relied upon either. What *is* certain, is that after leaving Peking he returned to Shanghai for some time, establishing rooms for himself in the Chamber of Commerce Building, where he set about printing as many of his negatives as he could, and organising what was already being referred to as 'The Thomson Collection'.[114] From Shanghai he also took the opportunity to make his last – and most extensive – photographic journey in Asia, up the great river Yangzi.

'Shanghai has always been able to hold its own as the great Chinese emporium of foreign trade', noted Thomson, and the foreign settlement in the city, which he regarded as a 'model settlement', had become a busy European-style seaport, with modern western buildings: a place of great commercial activity. It was therefore an ideal location for Thomson to make useful contacts, the 'splendour and sumptuousness' which he found no doubt encouraging his hopes of finding subscribers for a book project.[115] But the geographical location of Shanghai also meant that it was the natural base for a journey up China's greatest and most important waterway, the Yangzi.

Thomson travelled up the great river at first by steamer as far as Hangzhou, some six hundred miles above Shanghai, and the highest point on the river that was navigable by steam ship. Hangzhou was one of the ports supported by a British Trade Concession since 1861, and, although well positioned at the confluence of the rivers Han and Yangzi, it did not attract the sort of trade which many British merchants had hoped for. After a brief stay, Thomson began the final leg of this long journey with two American companions. The boat was intensely cold at night, and the travellers had to exist in close proximity to the skipper and his wife for the entire journey, enduring their pungent tobacco fumes – an aspect of the journey which was not to Thomson's liking. This is how he describes part of the voyage:

> Let the reader imagine himself afloat in such a vessel as I have described, with such a crew, on a river red like the soil through which it flows, and from half a mile to a league in breadth; let him conceive himself ascending the stream between low level monotonous clay walls; he will then have a picture of our craft and our surroundings for many days as we pursued our voyage upwards to the Gorges.[116]

On 18 February 1872 the party eventually got as far as Wushan in Sichuan Province, no less than 1,200 miles west of Shanghai. The magnificence of the scenery made the endurance all the more worthwhile, and one of Thomson's final bursts of photographic activity on China secured some of his most enduringly beautiful images. He then returned to Hangzhou, and finally to Shanghai, via Nanjing *(PLATE 17)*. After completing his business in the city he visited Ningbo, from there travelling to the beautiful Snowy Valley, nearby.

Cypriot Excursions

Between his return to Britain during in the autumn of 1872 and his death in 1921, John Thomson travelled very little. Perhaps his ten years in the Far East had flushed the need and desire to travel out of his system; more likely the pleasures and pressures of a growing family encouraged him to devote his energies to securing a steady income and establishing a career with a long-term future. This phase of his life, one divided between disseminating his images and knowledge of China as widely as possible and building up his career as a studio-based photographer, was punctuated, however, by one final overseas journey – to Cyprus in 1878. On 4 June of that year, a treaty (or 'defensive alliance') known as the Cyprus Convention was signed between Britain and Turkey. It was the result of political, historical, and military developments among the great powers active in the Levant at the time. Under the Treaty, Great Britain gained control of Cyprus, and Sir Garnet Wolseley was appointed Lord High Commissioner. As a consequence, the British Navy arrived off Larnaca on 2 July 1878, and on the 22nd Wolseley landed with British and Indian troops, and a proclamation was issued announcing him as Her Majesty's High Commissioner for the island.[117]

At a time when western interest in the Middle East was very high, and given the significance of Cyprus's biblical, classical, and medieval associations, it was a golden opportunity for Thomson to be the first British photographer and writer to survey the present state of the Empire's newest acquisition. He travelled overland from London, through Paris to Marseilles, and sailed from there to Alexandria.[118] Thomson's ship arrived off Larnaca *(PLATE 18)* on the morning of 7 September, and during the next day he soon became familiar once more with the problems of tremendous heat and intense sunlight that he had come up against on many of his Far Eastern photographic journeys. His journey around Cyprus was largely undertaken by mule, and often involved staying with the natives of small, simple villages in the hills, something which allowed him to gain an understanding of the ordinary people.[119] Nicosia evidently impressed him greatly, and his travels included the other principal settlements on the island: Kerynia, Morfu, Paphos, Limmasol, and Famagusta. At Kerynia he hired a Dragoman as an Arabic guide[120] in order to visit the monastery of St Pantalemoni,[121] and journeyed extensively through the hilly region of the island. In addition to the photographs that he took, Thomson took the trouble to note the state of the island in general, its principal topographic features, its main sites of antiquity, and its industrial and agricultural infrastructure. These observations were aired the following year, in a paper which he gave on Cyprus to the Royal Geographical Society.[122]

What is unclear is the motivation which lay behind this visit. The opportunity for a photographer and writer to publish a survey account of the island must certainly have been seen by Thomson, and commercial considerations would no doubt have been important. He stressed in the introduction to *Through Cyprus with the Camera* that he desired to record the island soon after Britain took control so that a record of its dilapidated state could be made as 'a source of comparison in after years'.[123]

It is probable that, being the first writer and photographer to visit Cyprus after the start of British control, he may have required official permission to travel there. Perhaps Thomson and his publishers, Sampson Low, Marston, Searle and Rivington, approached the Foreign Office for a commission to provide an 'official' survey account, as a sort of 'cultural' propaganda mission. What is interesting is that Thomson's paper to the Royal Geographical Society refers to the strategic potential of the harbour at Famagusta, while the comments raised in response to his paper by other members of the Society similarly dwell on the opportunities the island offered. 'If the time ever came when Famagousta should be called upon to play a part similar to that which it did in the middle ages, as a great fortress of the Mediterranean, all the conditions were present for adapting it to the circumstances of modern warfare.'[124] The political climate no doubt encouraged patriotic remarks like this to be made in gatherings of this kind, but it may also be significant in determining Thomson's reason for the Cyprus journey that the volume was dedicated to Sir Garnet Wolseley, the chief British official on the island.[125]

At the end of the day the commercial product of this journey, a two-volume book, reveals the work of a seasoned photographic traveller well used to the problems of photography in difficult, unfamiliar climates, and familiar with the hardships of travelling alone with only the support of locals who could not always be relied upon, no matter how hospitable they might be. In his November lecture to the Photographic Society of Great Britain he described his motivation as being simply to 'obtain a series of photographs which would convey some idea of the place and the people; and, secondly, to procure such information as would be valuable toward the same end, as to present to the public a faithful reproduction of what I saw and heard during my travels'.[126] Thomson lectured (with the aid of lantern slides) to both the Photographic Society of Great Britain and the Royal Geographical Society, and in February 1879 published his expensive two-volume survey of the island. The work, a 'royal quarto', retailed at five guineas (£5 5s), making it very expensive indeed. The publishers boasted in their adverts that 'a copy of this work has been ordered for the Royal Library, Windsor', probably in order to encourage sales among the aspirant middle classes.[127]

5.

6.

5. *Bangkok, Capital of Siam. c.* 1865. 122 x 158 mm.
Woodburytype. National Library of Scotland

6. *Interior of Temple. c.* 1865. 203 x 253 mm.
Modern albumen print from wet-collodion negative. National Library of Scotland/Wellcome Institute Library, London

7.

8.

7. *Crown Prince of Siam. c.* 1865. 252 x 203 mm.
Modern albumen print from wet-collodion negative. National Library of Scotland/Wellcome Institute Library, London

8. *1st King's State Barge. c.* 1865. 200 x 504 mm.
Modern albumen prints from two wet-collodion negatives. National Library of Scotland/Wellcome Institute Library, London

9.

9. Nakhon Wat, North End of West Front. 1865. 186 x 234 mm.
Modern albumen print from wet-collodion negative. National Library of Scotland/Wellcome Institute Library, London

10.

11.

10. *Norodom, King of Cambodia.* 1865. 240 x 183 mm.
Modern albumen print from carbon transfer. National Library of Scotland/Wellcome Institute Library, London

11. *Hong Kong Facing the Harbour. c.* 1868–69. 180 x 224 mm.
Albumen print from wet-collodion negative. National Library of Scotland

12.

13.

12. *Chinese Artist, Hong Kong. c.* 1868–71. 102 x 200 mm.
Modern albumen stereograph from wet-collodion negative. National Library of Scotland/Wellcome Institute Library, London

13. *The Galatea carrying H.R.H. The Duke of Edinburgh.* 1869. 253 x 305 mm.
Modern albumen print from wet-collodion negative. National Library of Scotland/Wellcome Institute Library, London

27

14.

15.

16.

14. *Chinese Lady holding Parasol, Canton. c.* 1868–71. 101 x 202 mm.
Modern albumen stereograph from wet-collodion negative. National Library of Scotland/Wellcome Institute Library, London

15. *Macao: Façade of Church.* 1872. 307 x 254 mm.
Modern albumen print from wet-collodion negative. National Library of Scotland/Wellcome Institute Library, London

16. *The Kwo-Tsze-Keen, or National University, Peking. c.* 1871–72. 302 x 245 mm.
Collotype. National Library of Scotland

CHAPTER 2

PUBLICATION

*The Camera should be a power in this age of instruction for the instruction
of age ... Photography is alike a science of light and a light of science ...*

JOHN THOMSON*

STARTING OVER

When Thomson returned to Britain from Hong Kong sometime in the middle of 1872, having made the decision to leave what had been a successful base for his photographic journeys for four years, the principal motivation behind his decision was almost certainly the desire to establish a normal family life with his wife and children. Isabel Thomson, like many wives of British merchants and businessmen, had found the heat and humidity of Hong Kong very difficult, and during two years of life without her husband, had had to raise a family with the help of friends and relatives, living a somewhat lonely life on the Isle of Man. What must have made the decision to leave the Far East easier for John was the knowledge that he was returning to Britain with the opportunity to use both his photographs and his skills as a writer to communicate with a wider public. With his Chinese journeys just completed, and a body of work which, he must have guessed, would prove to be of great interest to the armchair travellers of Victorian Britain, his prospects were good. The challenge he now faced was to promote and disseminate his work.

In November 1872, Thomson, living in south London, approached The Chiswick Press, perhaps Britain's leading firm of quality printers, to obtain an estimate for what was to be his third photographically-illustrated book and arguably his most exquisite: *Foochow and the River Min*.[1] The idea of publishing a work on China had been conceived well in advance of his return to Britain, although to begin with Thomson had envisaged a serial publication along the lines of *The Art Journal*. With photographs reproduced by the collotype process, his original idea was to publish it in eight quarterly parts over two years, each part containing six large photographs and eighteen small. The publication was to include letterpress text by leading writers on Chinese affairs, and would be entitled 'Illustrations of China and the Chinese', the subscription costing twenty-four dollars a year.[2] By the beginning of 1872 he already had a number of subscribers, some no doubt in Shanghai, where local press reports were effusive in praise of the proposed publication, others in Britain where his wife had been pressing loyal friends to subscribe.[3] But by the time he returned to Britain a change of mind had taken place, and Thomson was thinking in terms of a single volume devoted to Fuzhau and its scenery, with a larger production on China as a whole to come later. The homeward

*John Thomson, 'Proverbial Photographic Philosophy', *British Journal Photographic Almanac* (1875), p. 128.

Fig. 6.
*Life in China
Part I: The Feast
of Lanterns.*
1872.

Wood-engraving
(from *The Graphic*,
7 December 1872).
National Library of
Scotland

Fig. 7.
*Life in China
Part II.*
1872.

Wood-engraving
(from *The Graphic*,
7 December 1872).
National Library of
Scotland

voyage would have given him ample time to ponder the options and he must at that time have begun work on selecting the images and writing the accompanying text. His visit to The Chiswick Press in November 1872 also implies that he had sufficient capital to consider investing it in a book project.

But before tackling the production of *Foochow* itself, Thomson approached *The Graphic*, an important weekly illustrated magazine with a large circulation among the middle classes. It had an established reputation for high-quality wood-engraved illustrations (often derived from original, commissioned art-work) and a strong interest in social concerns. Thomson's street images of China, presented as a series entitled 'Life in China', fitted in well with the magazine's profile, the combination of unusual oriental figures and practices, together with strong visual effects, proving good for a series of sixteen parts. (Figs. 6–7). The first, consisting of seven illustrations, together with text, appeared on 30 November 1872, and the last came out on 18 October 1873. The first issue introduced the artist as having been travelling in China for five years, and having 'returned to this country to publish a work entirely illustrated with his photographs, printed by a permanent process': a good advertisement, as well as regular money.[4]

Having started the process of disseminating his work, albeit via the interpretations of a commercial wood-engraver, Thomson began to concentrate on the means of reproducing his photographs to higher standards, and under his own control. His first duty was to the subscribers of *Foochow and the River Min*, and it was with this work in mind that he visited The Chiswick Press. He obtained an estimate for a volume of double crown folio size, with ten pages of letterpress, the remainder of the book being taken up with mounted photographs, the printing of which would be handled elsewhere. Although the Press archives do not indicate it, the title-page of the book informs us that the photographs were reproduced by the carbon process, and printed by the Autotype Fine Art Company, also of London. At this time Thomson also obtained an estimate for the printing of 600 'letterpress photographs of China' (that is to say photomechanical reproductions of his photographs), which must have been for the first volume of *Illustrations of China*, indicating that large-scale publishing was high on his agenda.

Foochow was published privately, for subscribers only, the eventual owners being British merchants and tea-planters whom Thomson had met during his time in Fuzhau. Indeed, the preliminary narrative highlights the intended audience: 'The views, however, of greatest interest to the residents of Foochow [Fuzhau] are those taken on the Yuen-foo branch',[5] and he later refers, somewhat tongue-in-cheek, to his 'subscribers' who 'have every opportunity of making themselves masters of the subject of tea'.[6] In fact, Thomson's enterprise was aimed at a very small number of customers, as the Press records reveal that only 45 copies were printed, the small letterpress portions alone costing over £7 2*s* to print once the press corrections had been made.[7] An extra copy was produced, and is accounted for in the printing costs, but the only record of it is that on 9 December one E. Fox collected 46 copies of the book from the Stock Room of The Chiswick Press.[8] This extra copy was no doubt for the author himself.[9]

As a piece of book production, *Foochow and the River Min* ranks as one of the most beautiful examples of the photographically-illustrated book. Not only were Thomson's images from a period when he was producing his finest photography, but each element of the book itself was executed by the leading exponents operating in the British book trade at the time. The Chiswick Press, who handled the printing of the letterpress portion, was presided over by the Charles Whittinghams, uncle and nephew, and was one of the most highly regarded and innovative firms of fine printers at a period otherwise undistinguished by the quality of either typography or press-work.[10] Thomson's images were reproduced in the book as carbon prints, and this process was no doubt chosen as it was regarded by contemporaries as being not only fundamentally permanent, but well suited for reproducing images of works of art.[11] The carbon prints were certainly excellent vehicles for photographic reproductions. Although not strictly photomechanical, the carbon process was the first consistently permanent method of printing photographs, which still, however, had to be pasted into volumes like the more familiar albumen prints used in Thomson's volume *Views on the North River*. Thomson, along with many contemporaries, regarded the carbon process 'in its most recent forms [as having] attained to that degree of perfection, certainty, and facility of manipulation which renders it a most formidable rival to silver printing'.[12] The Autotype Fine Art Company was responsible for the commercial production of the carbon prints for his publication, a choice which matched that of The Chiswick Press, as the company, presided over by J. R. Sawyer, had established itself as the leading manufacturer of photomechanical prints in England (the firm of T. & R. Annan being their rivals in Scotland).[13]

'Magnificent Work on China'

Foochow and the River Min, although a magnificently conceived and executed publication, had a very limited circulation, and did not attract the critical attention which Thomson needed to establish his reputation. To achieve this, he needed to disseminate his images as widely as possible, and in the 1870s this meant teaming up with a commercial publisher, and exposing the photographs to critical public attention by the traditional means of publishing. Thomson's first collaboration with a leading commercial publisher came through his contract with Sampson Low, Marston, Searle and Rivington for *Illustrations of China and its People*. It was a relationship that was to last for only five years, but the books published by the company firmly established Thomson as a leading writer, photographer, and authority on China. This major four-volume work was intended to cash in on the insatiable demand for travel literature which was a major feature of British reading habits in the second half of the nineteenth century. The leading figures in the firm no doubt saw the potential of Thomson's superb photographs and his readable text, and the work fitted in well with the firm's long-established publishing profile in the field of travel literature. Edward Marston, a leading figure in the partnership, commented in his memoirs that 'in the course of my life as a publisher I have always been prejudiced in favour of books describing the wanderings of men in remote quarters of this small globe on which we live, and particularly of men who have ventured into lands and seas hitherto unknown and unexplored', adding that 'these works have for many years formed a leading feature of our annual lists'.[14] The firm also had a reputation for publishing books on photography, such as Thomas Sutton's *Dictionary* (published in 1867).

Thomson had approached the firm very soon after making the arrangements for printing *Foochow*, and it may have been on the strength of the images for that volume that the publishers agreed to take on the big job of issuing four large-format volumes of photomechanical prints and accompanying letterpress. Thomson's initial relationship with the firm remains something of an enigma. He alone conducted the negotiations with The Chiswick Press for 500 copies of a Prospectus for *Illustrations of China* in December 1872,[15] indicating that Thomson was keen to have his plan for the project well established before approaching a commercial publisher. By the time the bills for the work of printing the letterpress portions of the individual volumes came around, from February 1873 onwards, Sampson Low were directly involved, having been convinced by this stage that it was the sort of book that would fit well into their own publishing profile, and from which they could make money.

The Publishers' Circular for 1 May 1873 gave the first advance notice of *Illustrations*, under the heading: 'Magnificent Work on China'. The advert announced the work as 'Being photographs from the Author's Negatives, printed in Permanent Pigments by the Autotype Process, and Notes from Personal Observation'. It was offered to subscribers at a substantial discount, particularly if the entire work was subscribed to in advance, when it could be had for £10 10s, still a large sum of money, but significantly less than the £3 3s which each volume would retail for. The first volume actually appeared for sale on 16 May 1873; the second was announced in *The Publishers' Circular* of 16 October. This second volume had the advantage of some of the highly favourable reviews that had begun to appear in the Victorian reviewing journals, especially *The Graphic* and *The Athenaeum*, and as the first two volumes were printed in an edition of 600 copies, the publishers decided to extend the print-run by a further 150 for volumes three and four.[16]

The chosen method for reproducing the images in *Illustrations of China* was the 'Autotype' or collotype.[17] The collotype is a continuous-tone printing process, and was the first practical process for reproducing photographs in ink, being based on the same principles as lithography. The printing of the illustrations for the book was contracted by Sampson Low, Marston, Searle and Rivington to Messrs. Spencer, Sawyer, Bird and Co., who were the principal movers in the Autotype Company, and who had applied successfully for a collotype patent under their own corporate name in 1869, describing their variation of the process as the 'Autotype'. In the preface to *Illustrations of China*, Thomson highlights the reasons for choosing this process: 'It is a novel experiment to attempt to illustrate a book of travels with photographs, a few years back so perishable, and so difficult to reproduce. But the art is now so far advanced, that we can multiply the copies with the same facility, and print them with the same materials as in the case of woodcuts or engravings. I feel somewhat sanguine about the undertaking, and I hope to see the process which I have thus applied adopted by other travellers; for the faithfulness of such pictures affords the nearest approach that can be made towards placing the reader actually before the scene which is represented'.[18] Collotype was regarded by many in the book trade of the 1870s as the pinnacle of photographic reproduction, and to many firms of fine printers today, it still is.[19] In addition to the advantages of permanence, the process also permitted the inexpensive assemblage of more than one image per page, and the complicated montages which are a feature of the book would have been prohibitively expensive by any other process (Fig. 8).[20]

Fig. 8.
Male Heads, Chinese and Mongolian.

Collotype (from *Illustrations of China and Its People.* (1873-74). National Library of Scotland

Among the population of westerners in China itself the work was very well received, and *The Chinese Recorder and Missionary Journal* (edited by Thomson's old friend Justus Doolittle) focussed on the achievements of the enterprise itself rather than on the product alone: 'Five years wandering in China in furtherance of the interest of art, is deserved of a substantial return; and exposed as Mr Thomson has been to numerous perils and difficulties in carrying out his plan, we congratulate him on the successful accomplishment'. Praising the images in particular, the journal continued: 'the plates are sufficient to give a clearer notion of China and the Chinese to a foreigner, than anything that has been published hitherto'.[21]

In Britain the chorus of praise for the work was led by *The Graphic*, which published separate reviews of the first two volumes, both of which were highly favourable. Reminding their readers of Thomson's connections with the magazine, and providing a résumé of his career in China, the reviewer then focussed on the photographs in the first volume, 'which, independently of the interest of their subject, seem to us as specimens of the photographic art of unsurpassable excellence'.[22] The images entitled 'Prince Kung', 'British Consular Yamun at Canton', 'Physic Street', and a 'Mountain Pass, on the Island of Formosa' were singled out as being particularly good, and the accompanying text was also praised for enabling the reader 'to take in all the details of the scene presented'.[23] The second volume was greeted with even stronger language. 'It is only the testimony of our own eyesight that would convince us that photography was capable of yielding such marvellous effects. There is a softness and delicacy about these illustrations that we should have thought unobtainable by any merely mechanical process ... The work is indeed in all ways a perfect miracle of excellence, and Mr Thomson has every claim to be regarded as a public benefactor'. *The Athenaeum*, primarily a reviewing journal, and with a reputation for scathing criticism of books which it did not approve of, was no less fulsome in its praise. Commenting on the photographs in the first volume, it remarked that 'the temptation, either to caricature anything very strange and grotesque, or else to tone down its extravagancies to one's idea of what is right and fitting is almost irresistible.

Photography necessarily avoids both these extremes, and if anyone wishes to verify our assertions in this respect, he cannot do better than compare the sort of illustrations common to works on China with Mr Thomson's photographs'. The journal found the photography in the second volume 'equally good' and in reviewing the final volume concluded by commenting that it was 'fully equal in interest and in execution to any of the preceding ones, and it worthily closes Mr Thomson's truly magnificent panorama of China and its people'.[24] A few years after the publication of *Illustrations of China*, another travel writer was to refer to Thomson as a man 'whose splendid photographic albums of China are deservedly admired'.[25]

The Autotype Company itself was very proud of the collotypes or 'Autotypes' in *Illustrations*, and their advertisements for many years after cited the work as an example of the best material illustrated by their process.[26] So great was the critical acclaim accorded to both that, late in 1874, Sampson Low, Marston, Low and Searle published a second edition, which was basically just a straight reprint, without any emendation to the text or images whatsoever, and with a run of 150 copies.[27] The re-publication was cleverly timed to catch the Christmas market, and the book was listed at three guineas in Sampson Low's advertisements under the heading 'A List of Choice Books for Presents & Prizes'.[28]

After the success of *Illustrations of China*, the work which really established his reputation in the 1870s, Thomson spent the latter half of 1874 concentrating on writing what was to be a popular follow-up to the great work. The trade was given an advance warning that *The Straits of Malacca, Indo-China, and China: Or, Ten Years' Travel, Adventures, and Residence Abroad* was 'nearly ready' in October 1874,[29] and even at this point Thomson was described as 'Author of "Illustrations of China and its People"'. *The Straits of Malacca* was finally published, again just in time for Christmas, in December 1874, although it bears the date 1875 on the titlepage, probably a hedged bet on Sampson Low's part. *The Straits of Malacca* was an octavo with sixty wood-engravings, bound in decorated cloth, and selling at a guinea.[30] It was marketed by Sampson Low as part of 'Low's Library of Travel and Adventure', and rubbed shoulders on the publisher's list with books by the explorer Sir Henry Stanley, and others with titles such as *Warburton's Journey across Australia*, *Remains of Lost Empires*, and *Sub-Tropical Rambles in the Land of the Aphanapteryx*. Thomson's book, with its evocative woodcuts, rode high on the success of *Illustrations of China*, and was aimed at the not inconsiderable portion of the reading public who were unable to afford the luxurious four-volume production. At the published price, it was not a cheap book,[31] but the purchaser got over 550 pages of text and sixty wood-engravings, some of them very close to the original photographs.

The book was a great success, and Edward Marston later remembered *The Straits of Malacca* as 'one of the most important books of travel published by [his] firm in 1875'.[32] The reviewers also thought highly of the book. *The Illustrated London News*, for instance, regarded it as 'one of the best works of its kind lately produced', and, in a lengthy review, praised the book for providing 'a large amount of entertaining knowledge', lauding Thomson for keeping his eyes and photographic lens 'ever wide open to [China's] scenes and manners, of which he sets before us a lively and truthful series of views'.[33] *Nature* highly recommended the work 'to anyone wishing to obtain a fair idea of the social life, scenery, and productions of the districts which he visited', and rounded off the review by commenting that 'the book is a thoroughly creditable and, we believe, credible one, full of the most interesting information, and valuable for the considerable insight it gives into the life of these Eastern Asiaticks. The wood engravings ... from the author's photographs and sketches, add much to the value of the volume'.[34] *The Athenaeum*, however, thought that the work did not really cover any new ground, but the reviewer correctly touched on the volume's real selling point: 'the illustrations are the strong point in this book, and these supply the untravelled public with a better notion of Eastern life and scenery than can be obtained within the same limits from any other source ... some of these engravings have a high claim to praise; they are really beautiful pictures'.[35]

The Photographic Authority

Later in 1875 came the publication of Thomson's translation of Gaston Tissandier's *History and Handbook of Photography*,[36] again published by Sampson Low, Marston, Searle, and Rivington (Fig. 9).[37] Gaston Tissandier (1835–99) published widely on popular scientific subjects, and survived a high-altitude balloon accident. In addition to the translation, Thomson provided the reader with an apparatus of footnotes, which ranged from scholarly defences of Talbot's discoveries to interesting insights into his own techniques, such as vignetting, dry-plate photography, and the carbon process.[38] It was a well-conceived and produced volume, with over seventy woodcut illustrations and a frontispiece produced by Edwards' Photo-Tint process, and retailing at 6*s* bound in green cloth. It evidently sold well, requiring a second edition the following year. Thomson's authority for producing such a work was based on the success of *Illustrations of China*, and *The British Journal of Photography* felt that Thomson 'was himself an accomplished photographer, and well-acquainted with the history of our art-science; hence it is a matter for congratulation that the work of M. Tissandier has been entrusted to such competent hands ... This work should find a place on the shelves of every photographer's library'.[39]

Fig. 9.
Gaston
Tissandier,
*History and
Handbook of
Photography*
(1876).

National Library of
Scotland

More of Thomson's photographs from the Far East began to filter into the public consciousness from this period, no doubt a direct result of the success of both *Illustrations of China* and *The Straits of Malacca*. He was selected to contribute three images to a compendium of the best work by contemporary photographers, compiled by the inventor of the Woodburytype process, Walter Woodbury (1834–85), himself an accomplished and seasoned photographer in the Far East, who had returned to Britain because of ill health and diverted his talents into developing the increasingly important field of photomechanical methods of reproduction.[40] This particular venture, entitled *Treasure Spots of the World,* was conceived as a showcase not only of photographic talent but of the Woodburytype process itself.[41] The other photographers who appeared in the volume included Carlo Naya, Stephen Thompson, Adolphe Braun, and Woodbury himself. Likewise, Thomson's writing on China began to appear outside purely geographic journals, and he wrote several articles for H. W. Bates's *Illustrated Travels*.[42]

Throughout 1875 Thomson continued his busy schedule of lecturing (including venues outside London, like Liverpool), and he was honoured with the Médaille de 2ᵉ Classe at the Congrès International des Sciences Géographiques in Paris. But publishing remained the focus of his energy, and he began to diversify this aspect of his activities, working on a translation of Baron Charles D'Avillier's *Spain*, which was illustrated with over two hundred superb wood-engravings by the prolific illustrator Gustave Doré. The translation must have been a considerable task, as the book runs to over 500 large quarto pages (although, admittedly, the illustrations account for much of the space), and its completion is another testament to Thomson's creative energy. This large-format, handsomely illustrated (half the illustrations were full-page), and literally gilt-edged volume was very much aimed at the well-to-do and bibliophile market, appearing in a lavish gilt-blocked decorated cloth binding by Burn and Co.,[43] and retailing at three guineas. The volume was well received by *The Times*, which credited Thomson for his skills as translator.[44] *The Graphic* and *The Athenaeum* also approved, and a further sign of its success was that the book was reprinted in 1881.

On 2 October 1876 *The Publishers' Circular* announced to the trade the publication by the Society for Promoting Christian Knowledge (SPCK) of a shortened version of *The Straits of Malacca*, priced at 5s and entitled *The Land and People of China*. With a wider, more general audience in mind (no doubt the children of the pious middle classes), the SPCK had had the subject matter arranged around generalised headings such as religion, population, agriculture, and 'Social Condition of the People', and had played down the narrative element that was such a strong and engaging theme throughout both *Illustrations of China* and *Straits of Malacca*. The work, in a decorative cloth binding, was still copiously illustrated with wood-engravings translated from Thomson's photographs, however, and the edition would have had a sizeable circulation, in both North America and Britain. *The Athenaeum* was rather dismissive of it, and missed the point about the intended audience. 'In many respects it is a useful little book, but contains nothing that is really new.'[45] The journal praised the type, illustrations, and the large amount of information, and regarded Thomson's previously published photographs as 'very valuable'. But the most damning criticism was levelled at the numerous errors, which undoubtedly occur throughout Thomson's books on China, the reviewer pointing out that his stay in China was comparatively short. In his home town, *The Scotsman* was rather more generous. 'Mr Thomson has travelled much in China, and has studied [it] – not, perhaps minutely, but with a quick and observant eye', and it observed, echoing the fascination for all things Chinese that underpinned Thomson's successful career as a writer, 'we have compressed into this small volume a great amount of information about an empire and a race which are certainly, in many respects the most interesting and remarkable on the face of the earth'.[46]

In the midst of this energetic round of writing, translating and publishing John Thomson found little time to take photographs. He was not even running a commercial studio in London at this point, something he had managed to operate in tandem with his 'private' photography in China. He did, however, work on one photographic project, from the beginning of November 1876, which resulted in a series of images of the poor of London's streets. These important photographs were to form the basis of a publication known as *Street Life in London*, which many have singled out as his great contribution to photography,[47] and which was announced in *The Publishers' Circular* as follows:

> The first number of a new monthly periodical, entitled *Street Life in London*, the joint production of Mr. J. Thomson, F.R.G.S., author of Illustrations of China and its People &c., and Mr. Adolphe Smith, will be published in a few days by Messrs. Sampson Low & Co. Each number will contain an account of some phases of London life, illustrated by permanent photographs.[48]

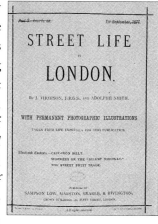

Fig. 10.

Street Life in London.

Part 8
(1 September 1877).
Front wrapper.
National Library of
Scotland

The publication of *Street Life* commenced in February 1877, and a full-page advertisement appeared in the 1 February issue of *The Publishers' Circular*. This promoted the first number to the trade,[49] proclaiming that 'the object of the work is to bring before the public some account of the present condition of the London street folk, and to supply a series of faithful pictures of the people themselves'.[50] The work was issued at 1s 6d (Fig. 10), which compared well with the other illustrated periodicals issued by Sampson Low, such as *Men of Mark* (three Woodburytypes) and *The Picture Gallery* (two Woodburytypes) which also retailed at 1s 6d. Each part contained three of Thomson's photographs, reproduced by the Woodburytype process, and the first part received a number of favourable reviews, which the publishers made much of in various advertisements, no doubt hoping to drum up sales within the trade for the succeeding numbers in the series.[51]

A collected edition of the *Street Life* parts was first announced in October 1877, at 25s, and probably had the Christmas market in mind.[52] This collected edition was published with an elaborately decorative cloth binding, with gilt edges, and was no doubt aimed at the gift-book market. It was described as 'ready' in November.[53] From this we must deduce that the field-work for the parts had been finished by this stage, as the publishers must have had the copy ready for the complete edition, the serial publication being scheduled to continue until December 1877.

All along, the publication of *Street Life* was promoted with the name of Thomson very much to the fore. Not only did the advertisements in the press mention Thomson first, but his name was often in bold capitals whilst that of Smith was often in lower case. The photographs were also the primary element, with the text taking second place in the published advertisements. Thomson's previous books, particularly *Illustrations of China*, were also cited to enhance the reputation of the author, and his Fellowship of the Royal Geographical Society was often used for the same purpose.

Thomson's hectic publishing schedule continued throughout 1877 with work on the second, revised edition of his translation of Gaston Tissandier's *History and*

Handbook of Photography, which *The Publishers' Circular* announced as an autumn book in the early summer, knowing that Thomson was busy collecting the new material.[54] In October the work was given advertising space, the publishers describing it as 'in the Press and will be published shortly'. In fact it was not published until December 1877, delayed by the death of William Henry Fox Talbot, who had been invited to contribute a chapter. The idea of some kind of collaboration with the great photographer and scientist was Thomson's own, first suggested in a letter to his publisher in May of 1877: 'I should like very much if Mr Talbot would tabulate the progress of his discoveries giving a series of facts and dates arranged for reference ... It would supply incontrovertible proof of the great boon which Talbot conferred on the world by the independent discovery of photography in England'.[55] The negotiations were dealt with through the publishers, who approached Talbot at the end of May,[56] and by the first week in June Thomson's new chapter was being proofed, while Sampson Low were pressing Talbot to begin his contribution as soon as he received the proofs of the new edition.[57] The publishers were confident that Talbot's material would add to the value of the book, and they wrote to him that it 'contains the most complete account of the history of photography in existence and on that account, & as a book of reference, it has a value above that of the ordinary "Manual". We are sure that any account from your pen will give the book an additional value in the eyes of all English photographers'.[58] By July Talbot had replied, offering a longer piece of work and another illustration (a photoglyptic plate of a map), which the publishers were keen to accept.[59] A month later Talbot had still not sent his chapter, and Sampson Low wrote to him requesting the material by the following week, as publication was now being held up.[60] During the latter half of August and the beginning of September, Talbot's contribution was eventually delivered, something of an achievement given his failing health. Following the great man's death on 17 September 1877, the task of seeing the remainder of his contribution to the volume through the press was left to his son Charles, who supplied the final portion of his father's contribution.

Talbot's additions were trumpeted loudly by Sampson Low & Co. who had been careful to solicit some enthusiastic reviews to place in the advertisements for the book. *The Spectator* thought it 'the best handbook that we have seen on the subject', while the *Photographic News*, stated that 'in no work previously issued have we an account anything like so minute, perfect, and interesting of the origin and early days of photography'.[61] *The British Journal of Photography* welcomed it particularly for the appendix by Talbot, and predicted that 'the present will be received with quite as much favour as the former edition'.[62]

Despite a workload that was heavy by any standards, Thomson and his family did not lose touch with their roots in Scotland, and managed to find time to return north to visit family; for Thomson this was an opportunity to indulge an interest in painting. Although very little evidence has survived of this side of his artistic life, we do know that he exhibited in the 1877 Annual Exhibition of the Royal Scottish Academy, held between 17 February and 12 May 1877, when his paintings *Homeward* and *A Coming Shower* were shown. Neither work found a buyer.[63] About this time Thomson, clearly making a good living from all these different ventures, bought a handsome seventeenth-century building in the Old Town of

Edinburgh, Cannonball House, close to the Castle, which he kept until 1913, when he sold it to the School Board of Edinburgh, which remodelled it as an annexe to Castlehill School.[64]

SOCIETY MAN, GEOGRAPHY MAN

Apart from the publication of *Street Incidents,* a re-issue in 1881 of unsold sheets of *Street Life in London* (Fig. 11), and several foreign translations and editions of his books (Fig. 12), the last two decades of the nineteenth century and the first two of the twentieth were, for Thomson, years spent largely in photographing the élite of British society, occasionally giving lectures, exhibiting (especially at the Royal Photographic Society) and publishing short papers on his experiences travelling and photographing in Asia. His ever-growing family was a source of much pleasure, and his life centred around Mayfair and St James' in central London, as it was only a short and pleasant walk between his studio, the Royal Societies Club in St James' Street,[65] and the Royal Geographical Society at No. 1 Savile Row,[66] where he continued to enjoy his membership, attending meetings, occasionally speaking, giving instruction in photography, and taking portrait photographs of members.

Fig. 11.
Street Incidents (1881).

National Library of Scotland

Fig. 12.
La China Viaggi di J. Thompson e T. Choutzé (1895).

National Library of Scotland

On 11 May 1881 John Thomson was given the Royal Warrant as 'Photographer to Her Majesty Queen Victoria', the fourteenth photographer or partnership to be so appointed.[67] What the Royal Warrant conferred was more than a mere title to be used as a means of advertising. It conveyed the fact that the Royal Household had called on the photographic services of John Thomson on a regular basis for some time, and that the photographer had successfully applied for the Warrant (as was the procedural custom).[68] We know little of the photographic work that Thomson was doing for the Royal Family prior to 1881, although an informal study of Princess Beatrice playing the harmonium at Osborne in February 1881 survives in the Royal Collection, but this appointment opened up new possibilities for his commercial portrait business.

Later in the same decade Thomson was taking portraits of senior figures in the Royal Household on a more regular basis, and these included Queen Victoria herself, in a group study with two of her young granddaughters in April 1887. In 1889 he photographed the Duke of Rutland, and on a separate occasion Cecilia, Viscountess Downe.[69] The Duchess of York, later to become Queen Mary (1867–1953), also sat for him some time shortly after 1889.[70] His Royal patronage continued in the 1890s, when he photographed Rosario Alba at one of Victoria's favourite retreats in Aberdeenshire, some time in October 1893.[71] Lady Frances Baillie was photographed shortly before her death in August 1894.[72]

Thomson's photographic studio in London attracted the upper echelons of society, keen to be captured for posterity by this famous and successful photographer. In 1884 he moved his premises from 78 Buckingham Palace Road to 70A Grosvenor Street, one of the principal streets of the Grosvenor Estate, in fashionable Mayfair; and in 1905, in partnership with his son John Newlands Thomson, he moved again, although this time only a short distance away to 'The Grosvenor Studios', 141 New Bond Street, close to the most expensive and fashionable shops in London and only a stone's throw from Asprey's (the high-class jeweller's). The relatively few formal portraits by Thomson that survive from this later period indicate that his primary clientele came from the upper classes. Sir Richard Wallace (1819–90), founder of the Wallace Collection in London, was photographed in 1888;[73] the 9th Earl of Cork and Orrery had his portrait taken in the late 1880s;[74] another delicate platinum print which survives is of the four-year-old Walter Grove, the son of a Tory Baronet from the west of England, taken in 1909.[75]

Thomson's connections with the Royal Geographical Society had stood him in good stead during the 1860s and 1870s, as he sought to establish his reputation as a serious photographer and writer, and they proved to be of enormous value during the later stages of his career, providing him with a base from which to write and lecture, and allowing him to make the contacts which would provide him with opportunities to expand his business as a formal portrait photographer. One particularly important contact was Henry Walter Bates (1825–92), a prominent naturalist. Bates had made his name following expeditions to the Brazilian jungle, and had eventually returned to academic life in Britain, editing the *Journal of the Royal Geographical Society* during the late 1860s, and becoming Secretary of the Society between 1864 and 1892. He pulled considerable weight in publishing and geographical circles. He was also a travel writer of some distinction, and edited a successful series called *Illustrated Travels: A Record of Discovery, Geography and Adventure*, in which Thomson published several articles on his experiences in Cambodia and China. Aside from providing Thomson with additional money, these commissions also helped further to establish his reputation as a 'discoverer, geographer and adventurer', as his fellow-contributors to the series were other well-established writers and travellers, many of whom were also Fellows of the Royal Geographical Society. Thomson's portrait of Bates appeared as a frontispiece to *The Naturalist on the River Amazons ... With a Memoir of the Author by Edward Clodd* (London, 1892).

Through his Royal Geographical Society connections Thomson was also asked to take portraits of a number of leading explorers, including the Arctic explorer and navigator Fridtjof Nansen (1861–1930) about 1885;[76] Admiral Sir Albert Hastings Markham (1841–1918), an Arctic explorer who had been awarded the Society's Gold Medal, around 1900;[77] the famous Antarctic explorer Captain Robert Falcon Scott, in 1901;[78] Douglas William Freshfield (1845–1934), who had published *Round Kangchenjunga* in 1903, the same year as the portrait;[79] Carsten Egeborg Borchgrevinck (1864–1934), the Arctic explorer, in 1904;[80] and Sir Douglas Mawson (1882–1958), scientist and explorer, leader of the Australasian Antarctic Expedition 1911–14, whose portrait was taken in 1914.[81] In the late 1880s or possibly 1890 he photographed Sir Roger Casement, a British Consular official in west Africa and Brazil, and at the time an active member of the Royal Geographical Society, but who was to receive the death penalty for his conspiratorial activities on behalf of Irish Nationalism during the First World War.[82] Sir Richard Strachey, who held the Presidency of the Royal Geographical Society from 1887 to 1889, was impressed enough with Thomson's photography to commission a number of portraits of his family, probably around 1888–9, including Lady Jane Strachey herself, and at least three of their ten children, Phillipa (1872–1968), Ralph (1868–1923), and Elinor (1860–1945).[83] Thomson's formal work for the Society also involved him acting as one of the Secretaries at the Sixth International Geographical Congress held in London in 1895, where he also exhibited 'views in Siam, Cambodia, and China'.[84]

In 1886 Thomson was appointed Instructor in Photography to the Society, which seems to have involved him giving basic instruction in his Mayfair Studio to geographers preparing to undertake overseas expeditions.[85] The suggestion for this seems to have come from the Society in January 1886, and Thomson agreed to give the instruction for 10*s* an hour (the fee to include use of instruments and chemicals).[86] A number of leading figures involved with the Society sought out his advice and expertise on this matter, including Sir Henry Stanley[87] and Sir Halford John Mackinder,[88] and in 1906 he contributed a chapter on photography for use on expeditions, which was printed in the ninth edition of the Royal Geographical Society's own publication *Hints to Travellers: Scientific and General*, edited by E. A. Reeves.

Other kinds of photographic work naturally came his way, although almost exclusively from upper- and middle-class customers, and centred on formal portrait work. But there were a few exceptions. In 1884 he made a photographic record of the works of art in the collection of Alfred de Rothschild, which was published as a photographically-illustrated book entitled *A Description of the Works of Art forming the Collection of Alfred de Rothschild*. The work was organised by Charles Davis, and the letterpress was printed at The Chiswick Press, perhaps at the suggestion of Thomson, who by this time had been dealing with the firm for over ten years. It is not clear who handled the reproductions, which appear as beautiful platinum prints[89] of paintings, furniture, porcelain, metal-work, and general views of rooms. Yet although the work has been lavishly executed,[90] the photographs themselves reveal little of Thomson's strengths as a photographic artist.

A similarly lavish volume, entitled *The Devonshire House Fancy Dress Ball,* was another book project that Thomson was involved in at this time, and one which provided greater opportunities to exercise his talents in arranging sitters, organising surroundings, and making pictures. The ball in question was held on 2 July 1897, and was given by the Duchess of Devonshire to celebrate Queen Victoria's Diamond Jubilee. Held at the grand London mansion of the Devonshires, this ebullient *fin-de-siècle* event was one of the most opulent social gatherings of European society before the First World War: most of the *Almanach de Gotha* were present. As a record of the ball, a number of London's leading society photographers, including Bassano, Elliott and Fry, Ellis, Lafayette, and of course Thomson, were commissioned to record the guests in costume, and with appropriate studio backdrops. The resulting images were beautifully reproduced in photogravure by Walker and Boutall, the whole edition printed by The Chiswick Press, and with fifty copies bound in quarter pigskin with vellum sides at a cost of £4 10*s* each.[91] This work was carried out by T. J. Cobden-Sanderson, a leading figure in the private press movement, at the Doves Bindery. The end product is an unusual photographically-illustrated book, and a unique social document.

Thomson took twenty-two of the two hundred and eighty-six portraits, including several of the guests with Scottish associations.

Several compilations of travel accounts, and low-brow geographical books, also made use of Thomson's photographs, using the inexpensive reproductive medium of wood-engraving. Unfortunately, however, Thomson's images often suffered considerably from changes introduced by wood-engravers, and the whims of the editors they worked for. The article on Peking in Edwin Hodder's *Cities of the World*, published in London by Cassell, contained at least six wood-engravings somewhat loosely based on originals which appear to have been taken either from *Illustrations of China* or *Straits of Malacca*. Presumably Thomson would have been paid a fee for the use of his images in this way.[92] Robert Brown's *The Countries of the World*, another Cassell series, was illustrated in the same way, although the wood-engravings in this work are rather more faithful to the originals, and seem to have been culled from the photographs themselves.[93] From Brown's work we can also see how Thomson's reputation as an authority on China had become established after the publication of *Illustrations of China* and *Straits of Malacca*. Thomson's were the images to have if you needed to illustrate your work on China, and his writing was held in equally high esteem: 'Mr Thomson's account of Hong Kong is acknowledged to be one of the best extant'.[94]

His final substantial piece of writing, published in 1898, was *Through China with a Camera*, in effect a distillation of his earlier volumes on China, although this time adding a great many more photographs, reproduced by the relatively new half-tone process. *The Leeds Mercury* thought it 'agreeable and vivid'.[95] *The Daily Telegraph*, in a rather more measured review, gave greater credit for the difficulties Thomson encountered as a photographer in China. Evidently, the time was ripe for another selection of his Chinese images.

Endings

Thomson's reputation and importance as a photographer and writer eventually received high-level recognition as his life and career drew to a close. In 1886 he was awarded a Gold Medal from the Queen for his photography in China, and in 1889 he was awarded a Gold Medal at the Paris International Geographical Exhibition. His work was further rewarded in Paris when, in 1908, he received an award for photography in Cambodia. He no doubt enjoyed the gesture of appreciation proffered by Sir Halford Mackinder, when, in 1900, the latter named one of the peaks of Mount Kenya 'Point Thomson'.[96] Finally, and no doubt most gratifyingly for Thomson, his own beloved Royal Geographical Society made him a Life Fellow in November 1917, 'in consideration of the valuable geographical work you have done during your long connection with the Society'.[97]

The Times on Friday 30 September 1921 announced the sudden, unexpected death of 'John Thomson FRGS of "Moordown", Woodfield Avenue, Streatham and the Royal Societies Club'. His death in fact took place while he was travelling home from the Club in St James' Street, but generally received little attention in the press. *The British Journal Photographic Almanac* noted briefly the death of 'Mr John Thomson, veteran traveller and portrait photographer',[98] whilst in Edinburgh *The Scotsman* reported the 'Death of a Scottish Traveller', and gave a confused but appreciative account of his career, focussing on his travelling rather than his photography.[99] But the account which would have given Thomson the most pleasure was that which appeared in *The Geographical Journal*, the Royal Geographical Society's own publication, and which, whilst appreciating his career as a whole, lauded him in particular as 'the pioneer in the application of photography to travel'.[100]

Having looked at the development of John Thomson's life and career, we now turn to the photographs themselves. This and the following three chapters look in detail at John Thomson's photographs by drawing them together into four main groups: the photography of ruins and other ancient structures; street photography; his more formal portraits of individuals and groups; and, finally, his photography of landscape.

CHAPTER 3

RUINS AND STRUCTURES

... walled cities of vast extent; exquisitely built stone bridges, spanning with a multitude of arches the streams of the interior; temples more curious and extensive than those of Central America, and approaching in their classical appearance the works of the ancient Greeks or Romans.

JOHN THOMSON*

The physical remains of past civilisations have attracted the interest and imagination of the artist and traveller for almost as long as there have been physical remains to discover and travellers to visit them. The ruins of classical Rome had captivated the curious and provided inspiration and information to generations of scholars and travellers, from the early humanists in *quattrocento* Italy, to the sons of the British nobility in the eighteenth and nineteenth centuries. Later, as travel outside Europe became more widespread, visiting artists and writers found their imaginations fired by experiences of a new order. The massive remains of the Egypt of the Pharaohs, for example, had been known about in western Europe through various cultural channels: the Bible, the travel accounts of pilgrims and crusaders, and the reports of traders; but it was the expeditions of the eighteenth century that opened Egypt up for systematic discovery, recording, and interpretation. These expeditions were undertaken by a variety of travellers, including traders and scholars, but especially by wealthy young aristocrats enjoying that privileged experience known as the 'Grand Tour'. Impressed by the size and scale of the ruins, as well as by their historical associations, artists like David Roberts, and writers like Byron, brought their romantically inspired imaginations to bear in portraying the grandeur of ancient Egypt, classical Greece, and imperial Rome.

The European photographers who travelled with their cameras in the first four decades or so following the invention of photography had the benefit, therefore, of a visual and artistic grammar which was already well established. The potential of photography for recording the distant and exotic had been seen at a very early stage. William Henry Fox Talbot (1800–77) himself had taken his camera to France in the 1840s; Alexander Ellis (1814–90) had made daguerreotypes of churches and ruins in Italy in 1841; and Calvert Richard Jones (1804–77) and George Bridges (active in the years 1846–52) had made beautiful images of various archaeological sites around the Mediterranean. The following decade witnessed some rather more thorough and well-planned photographic expeditions, as the business of photography outgrew its amateur origins. The visits to Egypt of Félix Teynard (1817–92), Maxime Du Camp (1822–94), and Francis Frith (1822–98) in the early 1850s led to some of the most accomplished artistic portrayals of that particular location, and the photographic journeys of Desiré Charnay (1828–1915) to the

*John Thomson, *The Antiquities of Cambodia* (Edinburgh, 1867), p.6.

45

Mayan ruins in Mexico provided the first visual depictions of the American continent's past. In Africa, Charnay, Sir John Kirk (1832–1922), and others were beginning to shine the photographer's light on the dark continent, and even the remote regions of northern and eastern Russia were being photographed for the first time. The Far East, perhaps because of its remoteness from Europe, and certainly because of the difficulties of language, climate, and culture, received fewer such visits from ambitious and talented photographers. Those of Samuel Bourne (1834–1912), Eugene Impey (1830–1904), and Linnaeus Tripe (1822–1902) to India, Walter Woodbury (1834–83) to Java, and Felice Beato (1825–1905) to China and Japan, are the best known; but none of these photographers travelled with the sort of motivation that marks Thomson out as different.[1]

John Thomson was essentially a lone traveller, with only his own strength of character and curiosity and desire to travel to spur him on. Occasionally he found added support in the loyalty of the friends and native assistants who travelled with him. His journeys may have been underlined by a commercial imperative (he had a family to support, and almost certainly had a commercial use in mind for many of his images both before and after they were taken), but he was not officially sanctioned or encouraged, nor were his subjects part of the readily and safely commercial British Empire. Thus, whereas most of his contemporaries operated under the protective shield of the British Empire, frequently in some form of official capacity, Thomson was a true freelancer, generally operating alone, without official support, and often on or beyond the boundaries of the British sphere of influence. In this respect he differed significantly from photographers such as Linnaeus Tripe, who was an official Government Photographer in India,[2] Samuel Bourne, who could also be described as an 'official' photographer,[3] and even Felice Beato, who travelled east to document the campaigns of the British Army, first in India (1858), and later in China (1860).[4] There is a sense, therefore, in which Thomson's photographic journeys can be regarded as entrepreneurial, risk-taking ventures; but to see them solely as this would be to mask the true motivating spirit that underpinned this period in his artistic life: his curiosity and desire for adventure and travel. His desire to see at first hand the landscape, people, and monuments of distant and exotic lands came first, and the idea that he could make both money and a reputation from these travels came as a pleasant realisation after his first major undertaking: the journey to Siam and Cambodia.

CAMBODIA

John Thomson's first encounter with the mysterious presence of the past cultures and civilisations of the East was in the jungles of Cambodia, where he visited the vast site known as Angkor *(PLATE 19)*.[5]

Angkor is the name given to the kingdom of the Cambodian peoples established by Jayavarman II in AD 802, and which lasted until the fifteenth century. The heart of this kingdom, which at its height stretched over much of South East Asia, was the complex of religious structures and court buildings at Angkor Thom (which name itself translates as 'great city'). The culture of the kingdom was heavily influenced by Indian concepts, particularly those of

Hinduism and Buddhism, and the main structures of the city, such as the great temple of Angkor Wat (built by Jayavarnam II, 1181–1218), were dedicated to Vishnu. The city remained in use, sporadically, as a religious, civic, and to some extent commercial centre, into the nineteenth century. But by Thomson's time the city's heyday was nothing more than a distant memory, preserved in the stones.[6]

The city of Angkor Thom and the temple of Angkor Wat had been visited by numerous delegations, missionaries, and travellers throughout the period between the last flowering of cultural activity in the sixteenth century, and the mid-nineteenth century. Portuguese and Spanish travellers (such as Diogo do Couto) visited the area in the late sixteenth and early seventeenth centuries, and, on one visit, by a group of Japanese merchants in the seventeenth century, a member of their party made a detailed plan of the great temple. Yet despite these periodic visits, the increasingly ambitious Europe of the nineteenth century knew very little about Angkor. The task of expanding the meagre knowledge of this great site fell first to Henri Mouhot, a writer and artist, and second to John Thomson, the first photographer to visit Angkor.

From 1863, Cambodia became a French protectorate. Although the British Consulate had been established in Bangkok in 1856, the French influence in Indo-China, which was to last until the tragic events of the 1970s, was of crucial importance for opening up the entire region, and Cambodia in particular, to the knowledge of the west. The Frenchman Henri Mouhot (1826–61) had travelled extensively throughout Europe and Russia (he had also married the niece of the famous Scots explorer Mungo Park) by the time the Royal Geographical Society gave him a commission to travel to Thailand on a botanical expedition in 1858. Although primarily a naturalist, Mouhout's mind was as voraciously inquisitive as any in this age of the polymathic genius, and his

Fig. 13.

Henri Mouhot, *Façade of the Temple of Ongcor Wat. c. 1858-1860.*

Wood-engraving (from Mouhot, *Travels in the Central Parts of Indo-China* (1864)). National Library of Scotland

posthumous account, *Travels in Indo-China, Cambodia, and Laos,* first published in France in 1863 and in an English translation the following year, vividly describes his experiences, and is illustrated with woodcuts made from his own drawings (Fig. 13).[7] Significantly, Mouhot likened the ruins to those of Ancient Egypt, immediately attaching to them the sort of romantic associations to which mid-century readers in France and Britain were particularly susceptible. Mouhot's prose (albeit in translation) was certainly evocative:

> The work of Giants! The expression would be very just, if used figuratively, in speaking of these prodigious works, of which no one who has not seen them can form any adequate idea; and in the construction of which patience, strength, and genius appear to have done their utmost in order to leave future generations proofs of their power and civilisation.[8]

If Thomson took this passage as an invitation to see for himself, the woodcuts found in the English edition which he read, although clearly several stages removed from the originals, may well have prompted him to point his camera lens, and record the site with the sort of clarity and accuracy that he clearly felt it deserved.

The journey that brought John Thomson and his companion, H. G. Kennedy, to the same ruins visited by Mouhot, was as arduous as it was exciting for both men. Travelling with only two ox-carts and two ponies, the men and their Chinese porters spent over a month traversing the vast expanse of jungles and plains between Siam and Cambodia. With food running low, Thomson had an attack of an unspecified jungle fever, and had to be carried by bullock-cart for some days, whilst Kennedy nursed him with quinine, an act which probably saved his life.[9]

What Thomson found when the men finally reached the ruined temple of Angkor Wat made a deep impression on him:

> We found our progress materially arrested by huge blocks of freestone, which were now half buried in the soil. A few minutes more, and we came upon a broad flight of stone steps, guarded by colossal stone lions, one of which had been overthrown, and lay among the *débris*. My pony cleared this obstacle, and then with a series of scrambling leaps brought me to the long cruciform terrace which is carried on arches across the moat ... The view from the stone platform far surpassed my expectations. The vast proportions of the temple filled me with a feeling of profound awe, such as I experienced some years afterwards when sailing beneath the shade of the gigantic precipices of the Upper Yang-tsze. The secret of my emotion lay in the extreme contrast between Nakhon Wat – rising with all the power which magnitude of proportions can give, a sculptured giant pyramid amid forests and jungle-clad plains – and the grass-thatched huts, the rude primitive structures which are all that present inhabitants have either wish or ability to set up.[10]

The main elements of the romantic appeal of ruins to the nineteenth-century artistic imagination can be conveniently found in this description: vastness, extremes of size, confusion and disarray. And the same elements were to be given eloquent expression in Thomson's images. Take the image 'Prea Sat Ling Poun' *(PLATE 20)*. Here we see a 'massive' edifice, one of the face-towers at the centre of Angkor Thom, made from precisely cut blocks of stone, with the face of the Buddha carefully sculpted onto each of the four sides of the central tower. The entire structure has been consumed by the jungle, and signs of decay are shown in the foreground of the image. Even more startling is the panorama which makes up plates 10–12 of *The Antiquities of Cambodia* and is entitled 'Westward View from the Central Tower' *(PLATE 21)*. Here Thomson makes use of a high viewpoint (presumably achieved with a great deal of effort), from the central tower of Angkor Wat, overlooking the stone roofs of the upper galleries of the temple. The towers of other parts of the vast site are just visible in the distance, the whole rising 'amid forests and jungle-clad plains' the scale of which could only dimly be perceived from ground level. The high viewpoint was to become one of Thomson's trademarks as a photographer, and some of his finest images taken in China utilised this technique. Thomson's text refers to the 'magnitude' and 'rock-like stability' of the structure, and to the fact that medieval plunderers of the temple were 'as ignorant as we of the nineteenth century are of the mechanical appliances by which the ancients were enabled to transport the masses of stone from the distant quarries and to raise them in the form of this stupendous monument'.[11] The astonishment which Thomson felt when he first saw Angkor was shared by other western visitors. Louis de Carné, a French scientist, clearly expressed the effect: 'I shall ever recall the profound impression this spectacle excited. Pompous descriptions had been given me; I had just re-read the pages of M. Mouhot on Angcor; but in spite of all, I felt overcome. I had, as it were, a shock of astonishment'.[12]

Thomson stayed to record in greater detail the interior architecture, sculpture, inscriptions, and carvings that litter the site. Of the sixty or more images that Thomson made at Angkor, some show clear stylistic connections with the work of other photographers active in the East at this time. The work of mid-century travel photographers was remarkably conservative, and as his first major photographic project, his individual aesthetic was still developing, and therefore at this stage the influence of other photographers on his work was marked.[13] Take the image 'Interior of the Western Gallery' *(PLATE 22)*. This shows a long row of columns on the left disappearing into the distance, with a seated figure placed, for scale, at a mid-point. Thomson was deeply impressed, as we have seen, by the achievements of the original builders of the site, and in this image he tries to convey 'the mechanical arrangements of the galleries or colonnades [which] are as perfect as their design is artistic'. Apart from being successful technically, the image closely resembles others of Asian temple architecture taken by British photographers. Linnaeus Tripe's photograph 'Aisle on the South Side of the Puthu Mundapum, from the Western Portico' *(PLATE 23)* and the image by Eugene Clutterbuck Impey entitled 'The Kootub, near Delhi'[14] both employ a similar depth of perspective to convey scale, with columns retreating into the centre of the image, adding drama to the visual impact of the battle between light and shade.[15]

The detail of the artistic remains to be found throughout Angkor deeply interested Thomson. Several images of carvings and reliefs appear in *Antiquities of Cambodia*, and other examples of unpublished photographs survive. The image 'Interior Ornaments of the Temple' *(PLATE 24)* shows groups of female dancers which are represented on pillars either side of the inner gateways of Angkor Wat. Here the scale of these reliefs, 'nearly life-size', particularly appealed to him.[16] The carefully lit relief of a hunting-scene with elephants, 'Palace of the Leprous King' *(PLATE 25)*, a beautiful image from the 'elephant terrace' at Angkor Thom, was no doubt of interest as an example of ancient Cambodian art, but it may also reflect Thomson's awareness – gained from personal experience – of the importance of the elephant to life in the jungle of South-East Asia. In fact, more than half of the photographs taken at Angkor formed a kind of visual catalogue of artistic remains. Images like 'Stone Figures' *(PLATE 26)*, 'Ornaments on the Wall of the Outer Gallery' *(PLATE 27)*, and 'Sculpture, Nakhon Wat' *(PLATE 28)*, are typical of this type of documentation, with human interest introduced purely to provide scale, as in 'Snake, Seven Headed' *(PLATE 29)*. Similar use of the camera for detailed documentation was being made by other photographers in the East, as we can see from Linnaeus Tripe's 'Basement of a Monolith in the Raya Gopuram' *(PLATE 30)*. Alone of Thomson's images taken at Angkor, 'Unfinished Pillars, Nakhon Wat'

(PLATE 31) makes use of a different aesthetic approach. Thomson always chose his viewpoint carefully. But on this occasion he utilised the pictorial device of isolating part of the structure to render it almost abstract. Combined with the quality of the light available at the time, this technique enabled Thomson to create an image which evokes senses of time and loss in a surprisingly modern way.

In focussing on ruins, Thomson was following the tradition in British art, beginning with the illustrations of Wenceslaus Hollar in John Weever's *Ancient Funeral Monuments* (1630), and continuing through to the work of landscape artists of the eighteenth century like Sandby, Turner, and Crome. Like them he was capitalising on the power of ruins and the effects of nature upon them to engender feelings of melancholy, and to highlight the transience of human achievement in the face of nature. Such an unsettling reminder of the impermanence of empires and their trappings must have had a marked impact on Thomson, travelling, as he was, at a time when the British Empire was at its zenith.

BRONZE TEMPLES, AND BUDDHIST ARCHES

Angkor undoubtedly made a deep impression on Thomson, and it is not surprising that many of the themes which are treated in his Cambodian photographs recur throughout his later photographic journeys. Although he points out in his writings that the ancient buildings remaining in China were of little interest, many of his later photographs there, particularly those in Peking, return to the theme of the picturesque past. In no image is this more eloquently expressed than in 'Bronze Temple, Wan-Show-Shan' (PLATE 32). Located in the grounds of the Imperial Summer Palace, the Wanshoushan (Hill of Longevity) was situated in the garden in the Qingyiyuan (Garden of Rippling Waters), part of the old Summer Palace complex built by the Emperor Qianlong between 1749 and 1751, six miles from Peking (but now part of the city). It had largely escaped the worst of the damage inflicted during Lord Elgin's siege in 1860, although the main part of the Old Summer Palace, Yuanmingyuan (Garden of Perfect Brightness) had been destroyed at that time by the Franco-British force. The bronze temple, which Thomson regarded as 'a very perfect example of Chinese temple architecture', appears to rise out of the undergrowth, like the temple structures of Angkor, and seems to fight against the ravages of nature and of time itself, preserving a hint of what it once was. Thomson's image encourages a sense of that loss. This was quite deliberate on his part, as he readily admits in the letterpress text which accompanies the published version of the image. He comments: 'the picture is taken with the instrument facing the sun, or against the light, in order thus to obtain for the temple a bold and clear outline, and at the same time to give a soft, and unobtrusive pencilling to the objects of the distant landscape, and by this means heighten the pictorial effect'.[17] Although the published collotype reproduced here does little justice to the context of the building – a distant, hazy landscape, which the soft tones of the photomechanical process have all but rendered invisible – one can nevertheless see that the image's main power comes from the detail of the clutter of rubble around the marble base of the temple, and the cumulative effect of years of nature overgrowing the entire structure. Thomson's lyrical comments on another building in the area seem to fit this image particularly well: 'ivy had cast a mantle of green over the charred and battered walls, creeping in and out of the broken balustrades and wreathing many a marble ornament with its tender leaves'.[18]

At Juyungguan, at the Pass of Nankou (Nankow), several miles to the north of Peking, is an ancient archway, octagonal in form, bearing stone carvings and an inscription inspired by Buddhist mythologies which Thomson immediately recognised as bearing a close resemblance to the inscriptions he had witnessed at Angkor Wat. In fact, Thomson was not the first European to notice the importance of this structure, and in the text accompanying his image *(PLATE 33)* in *Illustrations of China* he cites the work of Alexander Wylie, the eminent Sinologist who had first brought the inscriptions to the attention of the scholarly public in papers in the *Journal of the North China Branch of the Royal Asiatic Society*.[19] Thomson, as a member of the North China Branch of the Royal Asiatic Society, would certainly have been informed of the discoveries, and as he knew Wylie well, his visit to the arch may well have been prompted by his friend. The comments accompanying the image do not give any hint of Thomson's reaction to the building other than that of intellectual curiosity, but it is likely that his interest lay especially in the light that the discovery sheds on the early history of the Cambodian kingdoms.

BRIDGES

Ruins aside, ancient structures and the remnants of past civilisations were to remain important subjects for Thomson's camera throughout the rest of his journeys in Asia, and, to a lesser extent, that to Cyprus. The structures of antiquity which Thomson encountered in China may have lacked the effects of centuries of jungle encroachment, but the 'spoiling hand of time' nevertheless had made its mark, and the hardships and dangers which he had to endure were no less than those experienced in the jungles of Cambodia. Many sites which Thomson visited in China were still in everyday use, an aspect which appealed to his sense of the passage of time. Take the image 'Chao-Chow-Fu Bridge' *(PLATE 34)*, an image of a bridge which spans the Han River at Zhaozhou-Fu, the city to which Swatow (Shantou) forms the port. When the image was published in *Illustrations of China*[20] it was closely cropped, and in this it contrasts with other bridge-pictures, where the structures are placed firmly in the context of the landscape, as in 'A Rustic Bridge' *(PLATE 35)*. The sense of the past being closely connected with the present captured Thomson's interest at Zhaozhou-Fu, but his attempts to take a picture of the bridge nearly resulted in disaster, as his account of the reaction of the local populace makes clear:

> Seeing my strange instrument pointed cannonwise towards their shaky dwellings, they at once decided that I was practising some outlandish witchcraft against the old bridge and its inhabitants. The market stalls were abandoned, and for aught I know the shops were shut, and the barbarian who had come to brew mischief for them all might be properly pelted. The roughs and market people came heart and soul to the task, armed with mud and missiles, which were soon flying in a shower about my head. I made a plunge for the boat, which was fortunately close at hand, and, once on board, it told to my advantage when I charged a ruffian with the pointed tripod as he

attempted to stop my progress. My camera lost its cap, and received a black eye of mud in exchange. For myself I sustained but little damage, while it may be fairly said that the bridge was taken at the point of the tripod.[21]

By chance, the glass plate, which was in the camera when this incident occurred, has survived among the Thomson Collection at the Wellcome Institute for the History of Medicine: significantly, it is in two pieces.[22] Another bridge which attracted Thomson because of its combination of great age and present use had been seen by him in the previous year, during his visit to Fuzhau:

> This bridge was erected, it is said, about 900 years ago, and displays no pretensions to ornamentation except in its stone balustrade. It is indeed evident that its builders had convenience and durability alone in view; and the masses of solid granite then employed, still but little injured by the lapse of time, bear high testimony, in their colossal proportions, to the skill of the ancient engineers who raised them up out of the water and placed them in position on the stone piers above. The bridge is fully a quarter of a mile in length, and the granite blocks which stretch from pier to pier are, some of them, forty feet long.[23]

This particular image, 'Part of Lower Bridge' *(PLATE 36)*, provides us with a rather more searching exploration of the relationship between the past and the present. The image has been taken from a very low viewpoint, like the later Zhauzhou-Fu picture, although here Thomson has chosen to get closer to the structure, and the people have allowed him to photograph them standing on the parapet of the bridge, overlooking the photographer and the river. The structure of the bridge itself has been used to divide the image, and its narrative structure, in two. What Thomson is stressing again here is the tremendous antiquity of the bridge which is still in everyday use, and he uses the structure of the ancient bridge to contrast the teeming life above with the stillness of the water below.

YUEN-FU (YONGFU) MONASTERY

At Yongfu Monastery, during this same trip to Fuzhau in Fujian province (perhaps the most artistically accomplished of all Thomson's photographic journeys), the romantic appeal of ancient sites struck him particularly hard. Yongfu monastery, he felt, was 'in point of romantic situation ... finer than anything [he had] seen in China',[24] and he regarded it as the most interesting of all the sites near the city of Fuzhau.[25] Sited high in the grand and imposing mountains to the north of Fuzhau, this remote and ancient monastery required, in 1871, considerable logistical planning, not to mention physical effort, to reach. A long river journey, overland treks, and the ascent of the mountain itself (which Thomson was fortunately able to undertake in the comfort of a chair, in which he and his dog were carried by Chinese porters) were endured until 'ascending a ledge of rock the view of the Monastery burst upon us. There it stood perched upon a huge pointed boulder and beneath an overhanging mass of rock whose stalactites fall like the pointed ornaments of a cathedral roof. It looks like nothing I have ever seen or dreamed of seeing, with its broad eves, carved roofs and ornamented railing painted in the brightest hues'.[26] Understandably, given the profound impact which this building and its location made on Thomson, he took several photographs, and two of these in particular stand out as worthy of close attention.

Thomson stayed several (very cold) nights in the Monastery, taking photographs during the day, often involving the monks, asking them to remove foliage and branches which obstructed his viewpoints. One of these images may well have been 'Yuenfu Monastery' *(PLATE 37)*, a startling glimpse of the building's fragile wooden construction from an elevated vantage-point, high up on a dangerous walkway. The buildings appear almost organic, growing out of the rock-cave itself. The spindly stilts which support the structure echo the long, thin trunks of the trees which rise up from the ledges around the base of the monastery. The commentary supplied with this image indicates the location as being 'in a dark recess, resting on a ledge of solid stone, with a frowning precipice of great depth in front'. Inside the recess Thomson took another view, 'Yuen-Fu Monastery Cave' *(PLATE 38)*, which is technically a highly-accomplished image, recording the 'dark recesses' of the cave without losing the detail of the roofs of the monastery buildings or of the stalactites. Here, Thomson shows his feelings of awe more for the 'grand simplicity' of the cavern which he felt made the feeble efforts of the greatest human architecture (and the frail monastery buildings in the image clearly do not come close to this category) pale into insignificance. This attitude to the effects of human occupation over a long period of time recurred during Thomson's journey around Cyprus in 1878. In 'Greek Monks, St Pantalemoni' *(PLATE 39)*, the long-held adherence to tradition, which provides one of the rocks upon which the Greek Orthodox Church is based, is brought to the fore, and the experiences shared by the monks at the Monastery of St Pantalemoni, and their ancient building, transforms a group study into an essay on time and human occupation.

STONE ANIMALS, MING TOMBS

A further element of John Thomson's fascination with the physical remnants of past oriental civilisations was that of mystery. Sacred and monumental structures such as temples and tombs, often adorned with carvings and statuary depicting scenes from sacred texts and ancient myths, were the source of considerable fascination for the western traveller in the nineteenth century, and for Thomson the statuary on the 'Spirit Roads' to the Ming Tombs, outside Nanjing, and those found at the site twenty-six miles to the north of Peking, held particular interest.[27]

The tomb (Xiaoling) of Zhu Yuanzhang (or Hongwu) is found just to the east of Nanjing at the foot of a range of hills. The mausoleum itself is an imposing structure dating from just before the Emperor's death in 1398. The site is laid out with a gateway, pavilion, beacons, and a road flanked by statues representing animals and humans, all of which precede the area devoted to the tomb, although the 'Spirit Alley' was not erected until 1413. Yet he disparaged the work of the original carvers, both sites evidently appealed to him on a more aesthetic level, as they occupied his attentions for several photographs, both whole plate and stereoscopic. At Nanjing the 'Spirit Alley' contains a series of animals in pairs, which are shown both sitting and standing, although the human figures are all standing, as it was forbidden for men to sit in the presence of an Emperor. In terms of artistic expression, Thomson thought they were quite poor examples of their genre, but in his appreciation he missed a vital point of ancient Chinese art: statues were not intended to be appreciated in isolation; rather, they held the place of the general as opposed to the particular idea of the animal, and thus the sort of individualistic, expressive statements that mark out western sculpture from classical antiquity to the end of the nineteenth century cannot be compared to ancient Chinese art.

Established by the Emperor Zhu Di (1360–1424), the site of the Peking tombs is marked first by two large beacons, placed judiciously to guide the errant soul (as they are at Nanjing). The road to the tombs itself is some 1,100 metres long, and, again as at Nanjing, the road is flanked by twenty-four stone animals. Twelve stone men, placed in pairs facing each other, guard the way at the Peking site, whereas only eight are found at Nanjing. The animals are the same in both sites: lions, camels, elephants, and horses, and the mythical Chinese creatures Xiezhai, and Qilin, all carved from single blocks of stone. The human figures consist of a mixture of warriors and civilians, the former clad in armour and wielding fearsome weapons befitting their status as the guardians of the souls of Emperors. Of the images he took at Nanjing, perhaps the most striking is that of the warrior-guardians *(PLATE 40)*. Although it is reproduced in *Illustrations of China and its People*,[28] the published image has been heavily cropped, and the original negative reveals much more of Thomson's impression of the site. Two stone figures have been isolated in the foreground, with two Chinese men (possibly Thomson's assistants) chatting nonchalantly in their shadow. The chosen viewpoint shows the alley winding towards the tomb with other figures shown in between, and with the hills as a backdrop conveying the feeling that the souls of Hongwu and his wife rest in the heavenly hills themselves.

At the Ming Tombs to the north of Peking, the most dramatic image of all in the Nanjing/Ming tomb series is that which appears in *Illustrations of China*[29] as 'Stone Animals, Ming Tombs' *(PLATE 41)*. As in the Nanjing image, Thomson selected a low viewpoint to capture the 'Spirit Road' which emerges from the bottom of the frame, with the seated camel, noble and yet time-worn, occupying the right foreground and given scale by a Chinese man holding a pipe. Other animal statues (standing camels, and elephants) can be seen at further points along the road, which itself winds into the distance: a mysterious place only hinted at by the direction of the path, but which evidently lies in the direction of the distant hills (and which in the published collotype are only vaguely perceivable). The image invites the viewer to take the next step towards the Emperor's resting place (part of which is itself depicted in a beautiful image, the succeeding plate in *Illustrations of China*), and the image was perhaps intended as a comment on man's inevitable mortality.

CYPRUS

By the time of his last major photographic expedition, that to Cyprus in 1878, Thomson's main photographic interests had moved towards social documentary work. His time since returning from the Far East had largely been occupied in working his surviving negatives into publications, and in lecturing and otherwise establishing himself as a travel writer. His photographic journey to Cyprus, therefore, stands alone as an overseas project in this period, and the published record of his visit concentrated equally on the topography of the island and on the native population, with little attention being paid to antiquities and early architecture. One of the exceptions is the image 'A Rock-Cut Tomb, Famagusta' *(PLATE 42)*. The striking Woodburytype is accompanied by a short text which reveals little of Thomson's feelings at this site, but the visual arrangement of light and shadow, and the placing of the solitary human figure, combine to create an atmosphere in which notions of antiquity, morbidity, and solitude are powerfully suggested. Given the strength of this image (heightened, it must be said, by the rich tones made possible by the Woodburytype process), it is somewhat disappointing that Thomson's only comments are that 'these tombs probably mark the site of the burial-ground of a settlement even more ancient than Arsinoë, and carry us back to a time when Cyprus was under Phoenician rule'.[30] With the image 'Church of St. Lazarus, Larnaca' *(PLATE 43)*, Thomson remains with the subject of death and mortality, and this location, a churchyard with its British 'inhabitants', was no doubt of particular appeal to Thomson's readers for its associations (as revealed in the accompanying text). However, the search for the picturesque had not been abandoned by Thomson at this date, and the image 'St Nicholas, Nicosia' *(PLATE 44)* is another good example of it. For the combination of the building's great age, its monumental and architectural significance, and the depredations it had undergone through the actions of time and nature, has produced an image very much in tune with his Far Eastern work.[31]

19.

20.

19. *Part of the Western Gallery, Exterior.* 1865. 288 x 182 mm.
Albumen print from wet-collodion negative. Royal Asiatic Society

20. *Prea Sat Ling Poun.* 1865. 254 x 202 mm.
Modern albumen print from wet-collodion negative. National Library of Scotland/ Wellcome Institute Library, London

21.

22.

21. *Westward View from the Central Tower.* 1865.
Panorama formed by three images, together 180 x 712 mm.
Albumen prints from two wet-collodion negatives. Royal Asiatic Society

22. *Interior of the Western Gallery.* 1865. 228 x 182 mm.
Albumen print from wet-collodion negative. Royal Asiatic Society

23.

23. Linnaeus Tripe, *Aisle on the South Side of the Puthu Mundapum,*
from the Western Portico. 1858. 335 x 294 mm.
Albumenised salted-paper print from wet-collodion negative. National Library of Scotland

24.

24. *Interior Ornaments of the Temple.* 1865. 228 x 182 mm.
Albumen print from wet-collodion negative. Royal Asiatic Society

25.

26.

27.

25. *Palace of the Leprous King.* 1865. 163 x 204 mm.
Modern albumen print from wet-collodion negative. National Library of Scotland/Wellcome Institute Library, London

26. *Stone Figures.* 1865. 187 x 233 mm.
Albumen print from wet-collodion negative. Courtesy of the Trustees of the Victoria & Albert Museum

27. *Ornaments on the Wall of the Outer Gallery, Nakhon Wat Temple.* 1865. 100 x 92 mm.
Albumen print from wet-collodion negative. Courtesy of the Trustees of the Victoria & Albert Museum

28.

29.

28. *Sculpture, Nakhon Wat, Cambodia.* 1865. 188 x 238 mm.
Platinum print. Royal Geographical Society

29. *Snake, Seven Headed.* 1865. 98 x 90 mm.
Albumen print from wet-collodion negative. Courtesy of the Trustees of the Victoria & Albert Museum

30.

31.

30. Linnaeus Tripe, *Basement of a Monolith in the Raya Gopuram*. 1858. 354 x 287 mm.
Albumenised salted-paper print from wet-collodion negative. National Library of Scotland

31. *Unfinished Pillars at Nakhon Wat*. 1865. 98 x 92 mm.
Albumen print from wet-collodion negative. Courtesy of the Trustees of the Victoria & Albert Museum

32.

32. *Bronze Temple, Wan-Show-Shan. c.* 1871–72. 287 x 242 mm.
Collotype. National Library of Scotland

33.

34.

35.

36.

33. *Ancient Buddhist Arch at Kew-Yung-Kwan, Nankow Pass.* c. 1871–72. 190 x 237 mm.
Collotype. National Library of Scotland

34. *Chao-Chow-Fu Bridge.* c. 1870–71. 254 x 305 mm.
Modern albumen print from wet-collodion negative. National Library of Scotland/Wellcome Institute Library, London

35. *A Rustic Bridge.* c. 1870–71. 235 x 290 mm.
Modern albumen print from wet-collodion negative. National Library of Scotland/Wellcome Institute Library, London

36. *Part of Lower Bridge.* c. 1870–71. 124 x 98 mm.
Carbon Print. National Museum of Photography, Film, and Television

37.

38.

37. *Yuenfu Monastery. c.* 1870–71. 298 x 246 mm.
Collotype. National Library of Scotland

38. *Yuen-Fu Monastery Cave. c.* 1870–71. 250 x 303 mm.
Modern albumen print from wet-collodion negative. National Library of Scotland/Wellcome Institute Library, London

39.

39.*Greek Monks, St Pantelemoni.* 1878. 120 x 180 mm.
Woodburytype. National Library of Scotland

40.

41.

40. *Ming Tombs of Emporers, Nanking. c. 1871–72. 200 x 255 mm.*
Modern albumen print from wet-collodion negative. National Library of Scotland/Wellcome Institute Library, London

41. *Stone Animals, Ming Tombs. c. 1871–72. 200 x 255 mm.*
Modern albumen print from wet-collodion negative. National Library of Scotland/Wellcome Institute Library, London

42.

42. *A Rock-Cut Tomb, Famagusta.* 1878. 110 x 174 mm.
Woodburytype. National Library of Scotland

43.

44.

43. *Church of St. Lazarus, Larnaca.* 1878. 115 x 180 mm.
Woodburytype. National Library of Scotland

44. *St Nicholas, Nicosia.* 1878. 115 x 175 mm.
Woodburytype. National Library of Scotland

70

CHAPTER 4

HEARTS OF DARKNESS

We have, we need scarcely say, great sympathy in all efforts put forth to throw light on the haunts and ways of life, the hardships and struggles, of the lower strata of society.

THE LANCET*

The street, that open area of interaction between man and his fellows, remained a place of fascination for John Thomson from the time of his first encounters with the street life of Asia. It subsequently became the sphere for what is arguably his most influential photographic journey: that around the 'teeming streets' of London in the late 1870s. Thomson's photography of the street encompassed several connotations of that term: he photographed the street, in the most straightforward sense, as a paved road or highway, and as a number of buildings in a double line with a road in the middle; but his camera also documented the inhabitants of the street, viewing it in particular as the realm of the common people. His vision also encompassed the street's less appealing aspects, and he depicted it as a byword for unemployment, homelessness, and destitution.

The 'street' did not dominate Thomson's photography, but it came to occupy a central place in his work, to judge by the large proportion of his surviving material that is devoted either to the physical environment of the street, or to the people who occupy it. Thomson's primary interest was not the physical but the human geography of the street, and it is here that we are confronted with the principal problem in viewing this aspect of his photography from a late twentieth-century perspective: the extent to which his photographic survey of individuals on the streets of the cities of Asia and London represents an accurate and realistic documentation.

Central to Thomson's street photography was his use of 'types' as a means of visual documentation. The concept of types (as it applied to society) attempted to categorise and order the 'lower' social classes by assigning generalisations to the varieties of occupations – criminals, vendors, beggars, and so forth – that made up the poor.[1] The 'type' therefore provided a vehicle for exhibiting the 'characteristic qualities of a class', as the *Oxford English Dictionary* puts it, in the guise of 'a representative specimen'. Victorian painting had taken up this idea in order to tackle social themes (most effectively treated by Ford Madox Ford in his painting *Work*), and photography soon followed suit. The concept of 'type' in the nineteenth century was a realm in which the disciplines of physiognomy, anthropology, and art could come together, and, as one recent commentator has pointed out, art and illustration (and, by implication, photography) 'played an essential part in the public exchange of ideas and assumptions about human types'.[2] The question that

---

*Anon, 'London Street Life', *The Lancet* (10 February, 1877), p. 213.

now confronts our appreciation of Thomson's street photography is whether his use of the 'type' allowed his photography directly to engage with the individuals he photographed, thus producing a realistic documentation of his subjects, or whether his treatment has resulted merely in superficial generalisations.

EARLY ENCOUNTERS WITH THE STREET

Singapore was the first town of any size in which Thomson stayed during his time in the Far East, and naturally enough the Singapore streets were the first to interest him photographically. The handful of images which survive from this early period of his artistic life find him viewing the hustle of central Singapore from the safety of a high vantage point. From this same early period we also see the streets of Penang captured in the heat of mid-day, since the challenges of photographing the same scene during the bustle of the more temperate early evening would have been beyond the technical possibilities of the time.[3] The streets of Penang (Figs 14–15) were also the arena for Thomson's first interaction with different races, and he betrays in his written accounts what appears to the modern reader a distastefully superior attitude to the racial and cultural groups which he encountered. In one passage, for example, he explains that he had hired Malayan assistants because, at the time, the Chinese population had

refused to lend themselves to such devilry as taking likenesses of objects without the touch of human hands. Moreover they, as 'Orang puti' or 'White men,' shrunk from having their fingers and much-prized long nails stained black, like those of the blackest of 'Orang etam' or black men. My Klings, on the other hand, were of the colour of a well-sunned nitrate of silver stain all over; and had they, who even pride themselves on their fairness of skin, objected to the discoloration of their fingers, I should have had no difficulty in obtaining negroes of an ivory black in this small island.[4]

This reveals a racial and cultural insensitivity which was typical among western visitors to the Far East in this period, and many similar statements can be found throughout his writing. Another of Thomson's preoccupations was that the Chinese were virtuous, whilst the Malayan people, which he thought did 'as little work as possible', were not. He even thought that 'it is impossible to say how one-twentieth part of the Malay population occupies itself', again a viewpoint commonly held among western commentators on the region during the nineteenth century, but based on mis-assumptions about the type of work in which Malays engaged.[5] Some of these early photographs, although technically and visually accomplished, portray their subjects as stereotypes. A classic 'type', a Siamese boatman *(PLATE 45)*, must have been one of the first images taken by Thomson during his visit to Siam in 1865.

These rather straightforward and simplistic treatments were to become deeper and more sophisticated as Thomson's journeys around the Far East continued and his experience as both photographer and traveller grew. The concern for the welfare and the social and economic conditions of the people he encountered – and which characterised his later output – stemmed directly from his involvement with the individuals. But this process of development inevitably took time.

As with most photographers, Thomson's personal interests did not always coincide with the commercial work that he was obliged to undertake for financial reasons. The photographs he took for publication in the book *Visit of His Royal Highness the Duke of Edinburgh ... to Hong Kong* (1869) demonstrate this tendency. Most of the images are straightforward topographical views, with little to distinguish them from the work of other photographers. One image, 'Chinese Street (prepared for Illumination)' *(PLATE 46)*, stands out from the rest and conveys something of the atmosphere of the Royal visit. The emphasis of the image is firmly on the elaborate street decorations, but the viewer nevertheless glimpses the Chinese populace lining the streets preparing for the festival. A Royal visit was a major social highlight for any British colony in the days of Empire, and the visit of the Duke encouraged Hong Kong society, both British and Chinese, to engage in 'incessant festivities'.[6] This image hints at the revelry to come.

Thomson's early journeys on mainland China, on the other hand, came, in time, to concentrate more closely on 'the street'. A group of images taken in Canton (1868–70) show his interest in the 'labouring poor' of China, and social concern becomes more and more marked in his photography from this time on. This concern does, however, treat the 'lower orders' as a distinct group, apart from the rest of society, and to be regarded, studied, and commented upon accordingly. Thus the portions of the Cantonese population who lived and earned their living on boats tend to be treated as 'types' rather than individuals.

In Amoy (Xiamen) Thomson turned his attention to what he saw as a universal predilection of old women. Although the image is labelled 'Amoy Women' *(PLATE 47)*, its real subject is gossip. And it is another example of the particular standing for the general. However, Thomson's written account of this photograph in *Illustrations of China* gives considerable detail of his encounter with these women, treating them very much as individuals. The photograph also provides the sort of seemingly unobtrusive observation nineteenth-century photography was unaccustomed to dealing with.

In contrast with these old women, the men who posed for Thomson in 'Street Gamblers' *(PLATE 48)* show considerable vitality, albeit combined with a hint of menace. Although the image was obviously posed, it powerfully conveys the atmosphere of a private gambling house. Gambling, a universal pastime, was particularly prevalent in nineteenth-century China, and at one point in Hong Kong it came under government supervision designed to control what had become a serious social problem. Thomson has captured the faces of men obsessed with this vice: their faces determined to 'carry on, at all hazards, until fortune smiles once more, or leaves them beggared at the board'.[7] The principal figure, full of youthful *braggadocio*, commands our attention.

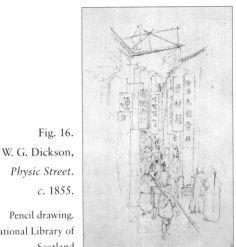

Although Thomson's street photography emphasised the people who lived and worked on the street, he by no means ignored the street's physical realities. In Canton, he halted his journey to capture 'Physic Street' *(PLATE 49)*. It was a scene which presented 'an appearance no less interesting than picturesque', and the frame has been filled with Chinese banners and the brick and wood of the shops themselves. The curve and direction of the street leads the viewer into a never-ending distance of banners and shops. The long exposure time necessary for such a narrow and confined space (even at one of the more open, brighter parts of the street, no doubt taken early in the morning, before the street has filled with trade), has left only a few of the shopkeepers and other individuals time to register on the emulsion. Others have left only a trace of their passing, blurry monuments to the life of one of China's busiest cities. The individual dressed in white to the left of the image seems to have been recorded several times, probably as he crept out of his shop to keep an eye on what was going on. This particular thoroughfare had caught the eye of other visiting artists before Thomson arrived in Canton, and the street was therefore already marked out, to an extent, as being a pictorial landmark, acquiring the sort of visual status that many of the classical structures in cities like Rome and Athens had acquired by the early nineteenth century. W. G. Dickson (1821–94), an Edinburgh doctor working in China in the 1850s, also sketched the street (Fig. 16), capturing the same atmosphere as Thomson.[8] Felice Beato also made pictures in the streets of Canton, although his image 'The Street of Sweet Harmony' *(PLATE 50)*, captures a darker, more brooding space, with a busy crowd looming in the centre of the image. Ten years later, Thomson's 'A Street in Larnaca' *(PLATE 51)* was to capture a slightly different atmosphere from that in 'Physic Street, Canton'. In this case, the Woodburytype print by which this image is known has a much stronger tonal density, emphasising not only the street's physical dimensions, but its emptiness, contrasting with the lighter atmosphere of the Canton image.

The waterways of China also fired his imagination. Those of the boat-city of Canton, for example, he regarded as the real 'streets' of this 'aquatic Babel'.[9] The water-borne life of river workers was of particular interest to Thomson, as in his depiction of a junk in Hong Kong harbour (Fig. 17).[10] The focus is on the deck, the working domain of the crew. Later, a similar scene reveals the captain of a junk plying its way up the Yangzi ('Chinese Skipper, Yangtze' *(PLATE 52)*). The portrait again shows the individual in his normal working (and living) environment, and, although obviously posed, the subject shows Thomson engaging more directly with the life and condition of those whom he encountered than was current in contemporary book illustration.[11] The romantic image of the native boatman is still alive in Thomson's mind, and he gets the viewer much closer to the reality of the working

waterman's life than earlier visual representations found possible (Fig. 18). Five years and three thousand miles later, Thomson returned to the theme of water-workers, this time working with the traffic on London's alternative street, the river Thames. 'Workers on "The Silent Highway"' (PLATE 53), shows two men posed on the deck of a Thames

Fig. 18.
J. T. Thomson,
Hussain, a Malay of Malacca.
c. 1864.

Coloured lithograph (from *Sequel to some Glimpses into Life in the Far East* (1865)).
National Library of Scotland

barge, with the characteristic tools of their profession, heavy ropes, very much to the fore, as they are in the image 'Chinese Skipper, Yangtze' (where the Captain is also holding a coiled rope). The accompanying text shows considerable sympathy towards the plight of this section of the London working classes, recounting the decline in importance of the Thames watermen, and proposing several reforms, whilst commenting favourably on the ability of the watermen's trade union to agitate for decent wages and conditions. Thomson shows the heroic quality of the men: noble, strong, and commanding the passage of their vessel down the Thames. Here he captured in visual terms what Joseph Conrad expressed in *Heart of Darkness*:

> The tidal currents run to and fro in its unceasing service, crowded with memories of men and ships it had borne to the rest of home or to the battles of the sea ... What greatness had not floated on the ebb of that river into the mystery of an unknown earth! ... The dreams of men, the seed of commonwealths, the germs of empires.[12]

FORMOSA (TAIWAN)

The island of Formosa was only a few days' sailing from Amoy (Xiamen), on the south China coast, and John Thomson saw an opportunity to make a short journey there. The photographs which he took on that occasion form one of the earliest photographic records of the island. His preoccupation whilst on Formosa was to document the native Pepohoan peoples, about which very little was known, and of whom there were as yet no extant photographic studies. Thomson's photographic work ranged from views of the native dwellings, as in 'A Pepohoan Dwelling' (PLATE 54), to the Pepohoan people themselves. His portrayal of the individual villagers of Baksu (where a group of images was taken) returns to the concept of 'types', treating the people somewhat simplistically as representative of non-Pepohoan tribes. His ethnographic interests are given fuller scope in the interior of Formosa than on any of the other journeys. The language of his later discourses emphasises his interest in the life of the tribes-people, but here again we encounter a typically Victorian attitude towards other races. Although the Pepohoans are 'savages', he concedes that they are 'tolerably clean',[13] and goes on in his discussion of the 'types' to describe and account for their traditions and customs, taking some pains to explain their context to his British readers. He acknowledges, in one image, that of a woman smoking a pipe,[14] that the sight 'may appear a violation of good taste', but he continues to point out that 'a pipe is among them as acceptable a love token as a jewelled ring would be with us'. Stereo photographs taken at this time also deal with the methods adopted by the Pepohoans when carrying children

(PLATES 55–56), and the costume of Baksa Women *(PLATE 57)*. These images, with the camera placed head-on to the subject, fall very much into the bracket of photography as a tool for ethnographic documentation, a style which Thomson resorts to on only a few occasions, but particularly when he is unable to relate on a one-to-one basis to his subjects, as the linguistic and cultural barriers between the Pepohoans and himself were no doubt too great for him to break down during such a short visit.[15] The Formosa studies therefore lack the characteristic individuality which is otherwise one of the most enduring hallmarks of Thomson's photography.

PEKING (BEIJING)

By the time Thomson reached Peking, which can be regarded in some senses as the culmination of his photographic journeys on mainland China, the city had reached a population of over two million, and was very much the legal, cultural, and political capital of Qing Dynasty China. The streets of Peking had been an object of fascination for western visitors for centuries before Thomson first glimpsed the colours, or caught the strong smells which characterised them. Baron de Hübner, who visited the city in 1871 (probably just before Thomson reached there), found it 'not an easy task to walk about in Pekin [sic]. Whether or not you are on foot or on horseback, you have not the time to look about you; and yet, if everything is not beautiful, all is curious, new, and interesting'.[16] He found the thoroughfares in a poor state of repair, with little bridges of planks covering 'stinking streams', and the streets clogged with camel trains and hundreds of hack-cabs.[17] But far from being put off by the overpowering crowds, the smells, traffic, and numerous other difficulties, Baron de Hübner, like many western visitors, liked walking about Peking: 'for here everything is different from what one sees elsewhere'.[18] Thomson's accounts of the principal Peking streets give a very similar impression, and the 'great concourse and traffic', the stagnant and polluted mud pools, and the bustle of street traders and shops are all commented on at some length.[19]

Thomson described the Peking streets as 'highly picturesque and interesting',[20] and holding 'great fascination'. His writings on Peking betray a great deal of sympathy with the poor, referring to the 'fearful signs of squalor and misery ... apparent everywhere in the unwelcome and uncared-for poor', especially when contrasted with the 'tokens of wealth and refinement' which he found elsewhere.[21]

But how did these opinions translate into Thomson's photographic representation of China in general and Peking in particular, for consumption by a largely ignorant British reading public?

For Thomson, the people formed an essential part of this picturesque charm, particularly the traders who plied their skills and wares along these streets. But was his vision merely a repetition, in photographic form, of the kind of superficial representation that is evident in the work of many of the western artists who had visited China, and who really had gone little beyond depicting the curious 'otherness' that they perceived? The treatment of Pu-Qua's 'A Pedlar' (Fig. 19), by the English

Fig. 19.
Pu-Qua,
A Pedlar.
1799.

Coloured
stipple engraving
(from J. H. Mason,
*The Costume of
China* (1800)).
National Library of
Scotland

Fig. 20.
Auguste Borget,
*Pont près de
Canton.*
1842.

Tinted lithograph
(from *Sketches of
China and the
Chinese* (1842)).
National Library of
Scotland

lithographer Dadley, for example, and that of Auguste Borget's 'Pont près de Canton' (Fig. 20), are typical of western artists' obsession with the novelty of the Chinese streets and street people, with little interest in the context in which both exist.

The Peking street photographs are among the freshest of Thomson's *al fresco* subjects, particularly the series that includes 'The Chiropodist', 'The Mender of Broken Glassware', and 'The Peep-Show, Peking' (PLATES 58–60). A group of similar images was bracketed under the heading 'Street Amusements and Occupations, Peking' in *Illustrations of China*. Printed four to a page, they present a coherent group of street 'types', which was no doubt his intention. The chiropodist in the image of the same name was an itinerant practitioner, and treats a patient in an obviously posed scene, albeit a very relaxed one. This image would have struck the contemporary European reader as strange, and the apparent ease with which both patient and practitioner are willing to allow a stranger to observe and photograph what Europeans would regard as a very private act, necessitated an accompanying text. 'The Mender of Broken Glassware', posed like the previous image, is, however, rather more wooden in its arrangement, the subjects having obviously been gathered together and told to keep still, whereas in the previous photograph Thomson has used considerably more guile in getting the participants to behave as if the photographer were not present.

However, not many of Thomson's street photographs betray the restrictions of the wet-collodion process as obviously as 'The Mender of Broken Glassware'. The delightfully voyeuristic image entitled 'The Peep-Show, Peking', gives us something of the feel of the great twentieth-century masters of street photography like André Kertész, Henri Cartier-Bresson, or Robert Doisneau. A large device stands in the centre of a Peking street, its box-like structure clearly having an optical element, as two (or possibly three) figures can be seen peering into apertures in the front, whilst another figure stands by, possibly operating moveable elements at the rear. Figures to the far left of the frame register only partially, and, barely visible (they have been almost cropped out of the published version), they reveal more of Thomson's technique: crowd control and persuasion must have been used to keep the curious onlookers from venturing into the crucial zones of the image.

Thomson's books *Foochow and the River Min* and *Illustrations of China* presented this great land in a way that had not been attempted hitherto. Between them they provided a kind of visual encyclopaedia which conveyed images of the land, architecture, industry, and commerce of China, as well as something of the people that populated the land. Seen in this context, his photography of the street people was innovatory. By contrasting the superb landscape photographs with images of urban social problems like begging (PLATE 61), Thomson was trying to portray the whole of China as faithfully as possible. He succeeded in combining traditional representation of different types with personal investigations into the life and experiences of some of the *individuals*, a technique which he exploited more fully in *Street Life in London*.

LONDON

Although the journeys made by Thomson throughout Asia were of immense importance, both in terms of his own artistic development and of his legacy to the history of photography, the one journey that remains the most discussed and most frequently cited (by historians of photography, and other cultural critics) is that which he made around the streets of London, in 1876 and 1877, in the company of a journalist named Adolphe Smith. This group of thirty-six images, published in serial form as *Street Life in London,* has been among the most widely reproduced of any of Thomson's photographic *oeuvre,* and it is all too easy to see it in isolation from the rest of his output. These images are also among the most frequently misunderstood of his photographs.[22] It is therefore important to view them in the context of the street-orientated photography in the Far East that preceded the series. They must also be viewed in the context of the significant interest in inner-city social problems that was a feature of British culture from the 1830s onwards.

In fact Thomson's photography in the London streets can be seen as growing naturally out of his Far Eastern expeditions. His published books reflect these changing interests. From the architectural and landscape work issued at the beginning of his career (*Antiquities of Cambodia, Views on the North River*) to the later, more widely-based studies (*Foochow and the River Min, Illustrations of China*), the focus on 'the street' became more and more important. Having tested his stamina, health, and skills as a traveller and photographer in the difficult conditions of Asia, and having experienced some of the most striking phenomena of what were regarded by his British contemporaries as the very fringes of the Empire's civilised influence, what could be more natural than to turn inward, and use the same skills and experience to examine the very 'heart of Empire', London? The industrial and social developments of the nineteenth century were having dramatic effects on the physical and social map of the great city, and, indeed, some visitors and observers likened London to ancient Rome.[23] We have seen how the massive physical remains of ancient Eastern civilisations were of profound interest to Thomson; how natural, therefore, for Thomson to be interested in the powerful effects of the world's greatest civilisation on the 'magnificent and powerful' city of London.

Thomson was not alone in his interest in the street folk of the metropolis; in fact, throughout the nineteenth century the poor in Britain were the subject of detailed study, analysis, classification, and categorisation. Government passed legislation; journalists wrote articles in the élite as well as the popular press; reformers published tracts and lobbied parliament; philanthropists sought to improve conditions; and priests, doctors, socialists and others strove to raise awareness of the life of the poor. By the time Thomson and Smith came to make their journey around the streets of London, in search of the street life of the lowest classes, the poor had become one of the most studied sectors of British society. What was new about the approach of Thomson and Smith was the use of photography as a specific medium for conveying the information they found and the problems to which they wished to attract attention.

Fortunately, we know something of the background to the publication. Thomson's co-author, Adolphe Smith, although nine years his junior, was an experienced and established journalist, and had earned a reputation for himself for his work in Paris during the Franco-Prussian War of 1870–71. Not only were his own credentials impressive, but his connections were among the most influential in the social reform movements of the British press at the time. His father-in-law, Blanchard Jerrold, edited the liberal journal *Lloyd's Weekly London Newspaper*, and Jerrold himself was the brother-in-law of Henry Mayhew, the redoubtable reforming journalist responsible for the enormously influential *London Labour and the London Poor*, which was itself the model for Thomson and Smith's project.[24] Smith was also active in left-wing political movements, acting as interpreter at the International Trade Union Congresses held at Paris and London in 1886 and 1889 respectively,[25] and continuing to agitate in the British press on political matters long after the *Street Life* project was completed.[26]

Another influence on Smith and Thomson's project was the remarkable publication *London: A Pilgrimage* (London, 1872), which was a collaboration between Blanchard Jerrold and Gustave Doré (1832–83), the highly influential illustrator. The two had known each other since the days of the Franco-Prussian War, and when Doré arrived in London in 1869 a partnership began whereby Doré's illustrations were paired with Jerrold's journalistic musings, forming what they intended to be a comprehensive study of the metropolis. Unfortunately, the resultant volume falls far short of that ideal. The 'excursions' that are presented in the book are described as quests for the 'picturesque and typical', but although the approach takes the form of case-studies of the everyday existence of people from all classes and regions of the city, much of the narrative in fact deals with interesting and unusual events and scenes. The result is a rich, although fanciful, account of metropolitan life, rather than the all-embracing study which the authors intended. There are parallels between *London: A Pilgrimage* and *Street Life in London*: both were part works; both combined the talents of a visual artist with a journalist; and both were concerned with the underprivileged and dispossessed (although Jerrold and Doré's work also examined the middle and upper classes). Given the family connections between Jerrold and Smith, it is possible that the earlier work may have given the authors of *Street Life in London* some pointers as to approach and methodology.[27]

'Outdoor Pauperism', as homelessness and poverty were euphemistically referred to by the middle classes, was certainly a nagging problem for the controlling powers of London in the 1870s, with the middle-class papers constantly airing opinion on matters of this kind.[28] The intervening period between the publication of Mayhew's *London Labour and the London Poor* and *Street Life in London* certainly witnessed a prolonged bout of Parliamentary activity aimed at tackling London's pressing social problems. Between 1850 and 1880 there were over forty major Acts dealing with public health in London alone, but by 1876 many of the social problems evident on London's streets had failed to disappear. Those in positions of influence and authority clearly required further evidence, in Thomson's and Smith's opinion, that a more widely-based programme of urban renewal was required.[29]

The work of Smith and Thomson was prefigured, to an extent, by Mayhew's *London Labour and the London Poor*. This massive compendium about the working classes aimed at gathering large quantities of information so as to make scientific analysis of the situation possible. Although many writers, most notably

Charles Dickens, had written about the street 'types' of London in the eighteenth and early nineteenth centuries, Mayhew's was the most extensive and influential survey. His work has retained a reputation as the most detailed of all the chronicles of the London poor, and this reputation was certainly strong enough in 1876 for Thomson and Smith to restate its importance to their own work in the preface to *Street Life*. The principal area of overlap between *Street Life* and *London Labour* is the overriding interest in the street traders and their respective trades. Mayhew's interest in recording case studies is echoed by the numerous images and articles in *Street Life*. The vast body of individuals who made up the street-trading fraternity (albeit divided into categories and sub-categories by Mayhew) had not previously received detailed study *en bloc*, and Smith and Thomson justified *their* project by pointing out that twelve years had passed since the publication of *London Labour*, and that the conditions of the street-folk therefore deserved another close examination. Mayhew, Thomson, and Smith realised that the importance of the trades went beyond the services that were provided to Londoners, for the trades had their own customs and loyalties, and operated for the working classes in a way analogous to that of the London livery companies. Another feature common to the two studies is the continual affirmation of the damaging effects of modernisation on the lives, trades, and traditions of the London poor. Thomson and Smith, for example, obviously working with a copy of *London Labour* close at hand, repeated the complaints of the London water-workers,[30] who had had their position and numbers materially affected by the steam boats which had begun to ply their trade up and down the Thames. There were numerous reasons for this breakdown in traditional working-class structures and their replacement with new ones, but, whatever the causes, the effects were marked.[31] What should also be pointed out is that Thomson and Smith, like Mayhew before them, continually place the London street-folk apart from the rest of the society in which they lived. Mayhew defined street-folk as 'a wandering horde intermingled with, and preying upon ... civilised or settled tribes', and he continues to refer to them as 'nomadic', and goes on to point out physiological and psychological characteristics which set them apart from their fellow citizens. This prompted one writer to comment that 'Thomson's eyes were as keen as Mayhew's ears, but both did far more than record, and both were outsiders looking and listening in'.[32]

Life and Labour was illustrated with twenty-eight wood-engravings after daguerreotypes by Richard Beard. One of the earliest photographers operating the French process in London (from 1841), Beard continued making photographs until the late 1850s,[33] and his *Criminal Prisons of London and Scenes of Prison Life* (1862) was also illustrated with woodcuts based on photographs. What Thomson's images manage to do is not only give the street-folk a visual identity, but ascribe to them a place (as he saw it) within the physical and social geography of London. To Thomson and Smith, like Mayhew before them, the streets and their occupants were an essential part of London, and a crucial element of the 'Londonness' of London. What both Mayhew and Thomson and Smith were (ultimately un-successfully) moving towards was a realisation that the street people of London possessed a distinct culture of their own, and one that did not converge with that of the middle and upper classes.

By 1867, the impact of the knowledge of the poor made available through the work of Mayhew and others was beginning to bear fruit in terms of social change: the Reform Act of that year gave the vote to working men, although there was little enthusiasm for change among the middle and upper classes, who feared that political power had been given to the ignorant multitudes, a danger that the Education Act of 1870 was later intended to combat.[34] There was therefore a great deal of middle-class unease about the 'lower' social orders,[35] and *Street Life in London* had a specific role to play in providing a more balanced and accurate portrayal of urban street life, hence the comments by Smith and Thomson admitting that they were not the first to treat this subject, but that it is 'so vast and undergoes such rapid variations that it can never be exhausted; nor, as our national wealth increases, can we be too frequently reminded of the poverty that nevertheless still exists in our midst'.[36]

What was also important was that *Street Life* challenged the dominance of the graphic artists who had made a living working up similar themes for weekly illustrated papers such as *The Graphic* and *The Illustrated London News*. In effect it radically challenged the nature of social documentation. As a seasoned contributor to both *The Graphic* and *The Illustrated London News*, Thomson knew both the style and subject matter that appealed to the middle-class reading public that bought them, and he was able to exploit photography's novel features to maximise the effect of these periodicals' particular combination of image and text.

As we have seen, the emergence of *The Graphic* onto the mid-Victorian publishing scene coincided with Thomson's most active period as a photographer. By the time of his return to Britain in 1872, and his ensuing search for a paying vehicle for his images, *The Graphic* had established itself as one of Britain's most important illustrated journals, and its reputation for covering subject matter like working-class life would no doubt have been quickly noticed by Thomson. The publisher W. L. Thomas had a reputation for being open to the work of all artists, no matter in what medium they worked, as he provided the skilled wood-engravers needed to work up the illustrations at a time when mass-produced photographic images were not yet financially feasible in the periodical press.[37] Many of *The Graphic*'s images examined classic working-class themes. Thus we see working-class markets, charitable institutions, the fallen middle classes, and the amusements of the poor. The dramatic played a key part in the graphic representation of these themes, with images often stylised to create human interest in what were pervasive social problems. Luke Fildes's powerful 'Houseless and Hungry' (Fig. 21) was one of the first images in this style to appear in the journal, or indeed in any British Victorian publication of its type. One commentator has observed that this style presented working-class themes 'with a vivid sense of actuality',[38] and dealt with the painful aspects of working-class life in the great city through compelling (although highly romanticised) narrative studies. The series of 'London Sketches' in particular

Fig. 21.
Luke Fildes,
*Houseless
and Hungry.*
1869.

Wood-engraving
(from *The Graphic*,
1 November 1873).
National Library of
Scotland

(Figs. 22–23) was intended to convey visually the drama of the streets which 'is being perpetually performed by a continuous succession of helpless actors'.[39] Because the subject matter was new, primary observation played a stronger element than with other graphic themes (such as the 'olde English' Christmas themes that dominated the December numbers of *The Graphic* and its competitors), and this element made the use of photographic images like those presented by Thomson in his series 'Sketches of Life in China' fit easily into *The Graphic*'s house style. It is not known, however, whether the way in which Thomson's images were used met with his approval, for they were very heavily 'interpreted' by the artists and professional wood-engravers who worked on them prior to publication. The dressing-up of Thomson's originals was not, on the whole, handled very sympathetically, although the series lasted for sixteen parts, and so must have found favour with the editor and, it must be assumed, the readers. The insertion of people who are not in the original images, the exaggeration of facial features, such as those in 'A Gambling House at Macao' (Fig. 24), and the dressing-up of the narrative element of the images by the wood-engravers seems at odds with Thomson's photographic aesthetic, with its emphasis on photography's unquestionable veracity.

Probably the first, and what is now regarded as one of the most successful attempts to document the working classes in the street was a series of images known as the Newhaven Project, undertaken by the Edinburgh photographers David Octavius Hill and Robert Adamson. These posed but strikingly fresh photographs are regarded, rightly, as being well ahead of their time.[40] Images like 'Willie Liston Redding the Line' and 'Newhaven Fishwives' (PLATES 62–63), are the earliest attempts to use photography to provide new insights into the lives of ordinary working people. But, on the whole, early photographic representations of British streets emphasised the physical structures over the people who inhabited them. We see in Thomas Annan's *Old Closes and Streets* a view of some of Glasgow's worst inner-city slums,[41] but the people who lived in them and who had to endure appalling conditions register only as fleeting ghosts, the photographer allowing them to wander in and out of the camera's range at will (PLATE 64). In other images, where the people play a more central role in the photographic narrative, they are grouped together, without establishing a coherent social context, although in Annan's case this approach was taken for good reasons.[42] At a more extreme level, the photographs taken by Archibald Burns (active around 1858–80) of Edinburgh's slums, less well known than Annan's influential series, are another profound group of images of the urban landscape. Here the photographs were taken after the population had been relocated, but before the buildings themselves were pulled down in 1871. The streets, devoid of human activity, as in 'Corner of Horse Wynd and Cowgate Looking East' *(PLATE 65)*, are presented almost as if they were ancient ruins, the melancholic charm of the structures, as in 'Simson the Printers House in the Cowgate' *(PLATE 66)*, replacing the awful realities of the lives of the people who had had to live and work in them only weeks previously.[43]

Few photographs of the London streets had been taken before Thomson's journey around them, and even fewer were published with the intent of informing public opinion. William Henry Fox Talbot had used his new calotype process to record the London streets in the 1840s, but people did not feature in any prominent way in these mainly architectural documents. In 1875 Henry Dixon and Alfred and John Bool had founded the Society for Photographing the Relics of Old London, prompted by the threatened demolition of a sixteenth-century coach house, the Oxford Arms in Warwick Lane *(PLATES 67–68)*. Like *Street Life*, these portfolios of carbon prints were specific publications, with a specific purpose, in this case to document old buildings in London before their destruction. What the two projects also share is the same desire to point out the problems that have come hand in hand with the industrial transformation of 'old London'; in Bool's and Dixon's case it was the physical structures that were under threat; in Smith's and Thomson's it was the social and community structures which were breaking down.[44]

To combine photographs of the London streets, and to place the poor, the working classes, criminals, and the homeless at the centre of the images, was a new departure in the photographic documentation of the social topography of London, and Thomson's innovative use of photomechanical technology heightened the effects of this portrayal.

Perhaps the most striking feature of *Street Life in London* is that the images have been reproduced photomechanically by the Woodburytype process from the photographer's original dry-plate negatives. The resultant prints give a strikingly sharp, almost three-dimensional representation. The Woodburytype process was still relatively new in 1877 (its heyday was really the 1880s, and the process was used right up until the early years of the twentieth century). The principal benefits of the Woodburytype were seen by the contemporary photographic establishment as being primarily the permanence of the images, and the consistency of image quality throughout a print-run.[45] Contemporary advertisements stressed the permanence of the prints and the cheapness for such high quality, a result of large print-runs. An advertisement for *Men of Mark*, for instance (another illustrated weekly, also published by Sampson Low, Marston Searle, and Rivington), declared that 'but for the invention of the Woodbury process, the work now contemplated would be hopeless, not only for the reasons above stated [that is, the impermanence of the prints], but from the inadequacy of the ordinary process of photographic printing to supply with sufficient rapidity the number of proofs required ... at all seasons of the year'.[46] The aesthetic qualities of the process, on the other hand, received very little appreciation in the contemporary photographic literature, although Thomson himself remarked that the 'delicacy and beauty of the proofs' was the chief reason for their use in book illustration.[47] The rich black tones, the slight relief visible where light and dark areas of the image meet, and the dramatic sharpness, particularly in the highlights, make any image reproduced as a Woodburytype seem particularly 'real'. This verity was all the more heightened for the Victorian viewer, whose eye had been trained, at least in terms of photography, to expect images to be characterised by a plummy-red hue (found in high quality gold-toned albumen prints) or a rather muddy yellowy-brown (in the less well made prints). Thomson's dramatic social observations were intended, as the preface to the second part states, to capitalise on photography's 'unquestionable accuracy' and to present to the viewer 'true types of the London poor', by 'bringing to bear the precision of photography'. This can be seen particularly clearly in the image 'The Cheap Fish of St Giles's' *(PLATE 69)*. The Costermongers at the centre of this dramatic scene, with their suits and hats, have been frozen in the exposure, no doubt carefully instructed by the photographer to remain still, whilst the crowd of customers and onlookers that has gathered has been unaffected by any such restriction, consequently registering somewhat blurred. The process has permitted the texture of the Costermongers' clothes to be clearly visible, and even such details as the name on the rim of the cart-wheel can be seen. In contrast to the deep textures of the figures, the fish cart itself leaps out at the viewer, the barrel, the detritus on the cart, and the dirt on the floor beneath making clear that although this scene is a *tableau*, it is no studio contrivance.[48] The smell of the fish almost hits the nostrils.

This photograph also brings out another aspect of Thomson's *Street Life* work, namely the fact that the images have been 'staged', and that far from observing the subjects unobtrusively, they have a tendency to confront them directly. Some critics have objected to Thomson's use of the *tableau* in staging the photographs, pointing out that this undermines the boast of 'accuracy' claimed by Smith and Thomson in the Preface.[49] In fact, the restrictions which prompted Thomson to 'stage' these images, and indeed which affected the physical placing of his camera, would have left him little option but to make the photographs in the way that he did. To the inhabitants of the London streets in the mid-1870s, the sight of a photographer with a tripod-based camera, plate boxes, and other equipment – and possibly with an assistant (and Adolphe Smith himself?) in tow – would have been a decidedly uncommon sight, and one therefore that would have aroused considerable interest. The technology of photography as it stood in 1876 simply would not have permitted the sort of unobtrusive, discreet observation that is a hallmark of the great era of photojournalism from the 1920s to the present. In order to shorten exposure times as much as possible for rapid photography on a busy street, photographers like Thomson have always chosen 'fast' lenses. The use of this equipment results in a drastically shortened depth of field – as evidenced in some of Thomson's *Street Life* images. But John Thomson had to bring to bear skills other than those of the landscape, architectural, or formal portrait photographer. Crowd control, choreography, persuasion, and the sort of personal skills that were not commonly practised by photographers would have been needed to operate in London's busy thoroughfares, and with the pressures of a crowd which would no doubt have been naturally suspicious of such a strange phenomenon. A photographer would be faced with the challenge of coping with the distractions of a noisy, bustling crowd whilst trying to concentrate on making a photograph: hardly conditions conducive to spontaneity. Thus what we cannot see from the images are the onlookers, hustlers, and the curious, the original audience in the drama of the photographic act. We do catch an element of this in the faces of the anonymous individuals who gather on the fringes of the image, staring directly at the camera, observing the observer (photographer) with a reflected intensity. The men standing in the background in '"Hookey Alf" of Whitechapel' *(PLATE 70)*, for instance, show this quality, while the individual who is only a hazy silhouette in 'The Seller of Shell-Fish' *(PLATE 71)* also seems to have a keen interest in what was going on. Two men peer in curiosity at the photographer in 'Recruiting Sergeants at Westminster' *(PLATE 72)*, trying to appear nonchalant as they gather at the corner of Whitehall and Parliament Square; and a uniformed policeman lurks, somewhat menacingly, half out of frame, on the fringes of 'The Street Locksmith' *(PLATE 73)*.[50]

The actual representation of the people in the images has also resulted in criticism of the way in which Smith and Thomson handled this aspect of their project. The criticism focuses in particular on the use of the general to represent the particular.[51] But in this respect Smith and Thomson were merely following a theme in visual representation that had its origins in 'The Cries of London',[52] and which was eagerly employed by a large number of important photographic artists well into the twentieth century. William Carrick's 'Russian Types' were among the earliest conscious use of this concept in photographic terms.[53] E. Alice Austen's photographs taken in New York in the 1890s were still primarily concerned with types.[54] The work of Sigmund Krausze among the street folk of Chicago also dealt with 'Street Types' in 1891.[55] The concept was still prevalent in the twentieth century with Emil Hoppé's 'American Types',[56] and European photographers were also using this concept well into the twentieth century, including Waldermar Titzenhaler with his 'Types of German Workers'.[57] The great German photographer August Sander even felt that viewed by the photographer in a certain way, the peculiarities of individuals would cease to exist.[58]

In fact, Smith and Thomson did not ignore the individual by any means, and the thirty-six separate essays in *Street Life* mention numerous individuals. The first of the images to appear in the first part, 'London Nomades' *(PLATE 74)*, is typical in this respect. Dominated by the structure of the caravan, the image, taken at Battersea, reveals six travelling people, the 'Nomades' of the title, who are posed with the vehicle, the adults outside and two children inside (and protected) but looking out. One of the children, like most energetic young persons, was unable to remain still for the duration of the exposure. Thomson's text names the principal character as one William Hampton, of whom he reveals a high opinion, describing him as 'a man of fair intelligence and good natural ability'.[59] The old woman at the centre of the image, Mary Pradd, was murdered a month after the photograph was made, and Thomson recounts Hampton's tale of the crime in great detail, even preserving the flavour of his language in the belief that 'this unvarnished story would at least be more characteristic and true to life'.[60]

Such wealth of detail, and the desire (at least) to provide a realistic portrayal of the individuals recurs in many of the textual accounts, as well as in the images themselves. '"Caney" The Clown' *(PLATE 75)* is a particularly unusual portrait, and the individuality of the image is reflected in the text by Smith which accompanies it. 'Caney' himself is posed seated on a small chair, making repairs to another, outside a window at which can be seen a maid who is watering flowers in a window-box, quite oblivious to either the clown, or the photographer. The clown has fallen on hard times, and Smith recounts in detail his tragic life story, in the course of which it is revealed that he is now forced to repair umbrellas and chairs to avoid starvation and the workhouse. Smith then moves on to describe the 'trade' of repairing chairs in London, the tiny profits that are to be made, and the precarious nature of this corner of the British economy.

With 'The Street Locksmith' *(PLATE 73)*, Thomson and Smith devote attention to the street traders of London's East End, in much the same way as the Peking street traders had been observed by Thomson, and dealt with photographically in *Illustrations of China*. Thomson observes the locksmith at work at his stall on the Whitechapel Road, watched by a customer, a young boy, and (barely visible) a policeman. Adolphe Smith's parallel text accords the street traders considerable business acumen: 'The trade ... gives employment to a great number of persons who are gifted with a little ingenuity. It is first necessary to recognize what are good and useful articles, then, by an observant study of human nature, to learn which is the best means of selling'. The moral tone of much of Smith's case-studies emerges later in the narrative, as the individual in the photograph is singled out as a paragon of honest, sober, hard work.[61] The '"Mush-Fakers" and Ginger-Beer Makers' *(PLATE 76)*, a familiar group on the London streets, are contrasted with their brisk-trading rivals, the vendors of ice-cream *(PLATE 77)*, a delicacy 'for which the juvenile population exhibit astonishing voracity, in all the poor districts of the metropolis'.[62] It is clear that the sympathies of Thomson and Smith lay with the traditional trader, the ginger-beer maker, rather than the brash new-comer onto the London streets, the ice-cream seller.

One of the most striking features of the *Street Life* images becomes apparent when they are contrasted with the treatment of similar themes by the contemporary illustrated weekly magazines. The Covent Garden Market, now a distant memory, replaced by cafes, wine bars, and boutiques, was London's best known fruit and vegetable market for over three hundred years, following its foundation in 1656. The workers at the Market became a familiar sight for Londoners, and *The Graphic*'s treatment of them (Fig. 25) gives a fanciful, idealised impression of jolly men, cheerfully going about their business in the early morning: their colourful nature matching the hues of the flowers they trade in, and with children happily playing at their feet. Such sentimentality is not found in Thomson's photograph 'Covent Garden Labourers' *(PLATE 78)*, nor does Adolphe Smith's text do anything other than attempt to portray the men in the context of the trade in which they are engaged, informing the reading public rather more accurately about their working lives and the hardships which they face. Similarly, the image 'Covent Garden Flower Women' *(PLATE 79)*, with its accompanying text (which goes into even more

Fig. 25. Anon, *Early Morning in Covent Garden Market*. 1871.

Wood-engraving (from *The Graphic*, 16 September 1871). National Library of Scotland

detail about the women in the picture), closely follows the style first adopted by Mayhew, and captured by Richard Beard in 'The Wallflower Girl' (Fig. 26) for *Life and Labour and the London Poor*. Again this is an image which does not trivialise the individuals or their occupations by ascribing to them unrealistic qualities. Even Gustave Doré's illustration 'The Old Clothesman's Children' (Fig. 27), showing the children 'rolling about on his greasy treasure', conveys the spirit of Jerrold's text in a rather sanitised and appealing cartoon, whereas Thomson's depiction of a similar subject in 'An Old Clothes Shop, Seven Dials' (PLATE 80), where 'the poorest inhabitants of a district, renowned for its poverty' both buy and sell used clothing, attempts to convey the realities of the shop and its proprietor.[63]

Fig. 26. Richard Beard, *The Wallflower Girl. c.* 1850.

Wood-engraving after a Daguerrotype (from Henry Mayhew, *London Labour and the London Poor* (1851)). National Library of Scotland

Perhaps the most moving of all the portraits in the series, and certainly the best known, is 'The Crawlers' (PLATE 81). It is also one of the most frequently misunderstood of Thomson's photographs.[64] Getting very close into the subject, Thomson has made an image which very clearly conveys the misery and hopelessness of urban poverty. The contrast between the old woman and the young baby; between the haggard lines on her face, and the smooth skin of the baby's; and between the darkness of the dirty stone doorway and the white face of the child (heightened by the tendency of the Woodburytype process to enhance contrast) stand as a metaphor for the gap

Fig. 27. Gustave Doré, *The Old Clothesman's Children. c.* 1872.

Wood-engraving (from Blanchard Jerrold and Gustave Doré, *London: A Pilgrimage* (1872)). National Library of Scotland

between the rich and poor of London society. Smith's text delivers the same message in language which hits just as hard. The women, described by Smith as 'wrecks of humanity', have so little energy that they can only crawl to take advantage of the sympathy of shopkeepers and others that look out for them (in what is now fashionable Covent Garden). In the words of Smith, they have 'been reduced by vice and poverty to that degree of wretchedness that destroys even the energy to beg'.[65]

The publication of *Street Life in London* evoked mixed responses from contemporary reviewers. Some modern commentators have taken the critical review that appeared in *The Athenaeum* as evidence of Thomson's failure accurately to portray the realities of life on the London streets.[66] The review certainly was critical: 'the idea of illustrating life in the metropolis by photographs seems, on the face of it, excellent', but the idea of using photography for this purpose is fatally flawed from the outset as 'the camera is not of itself an artist'. Thomson is singled out as an 'intelligent operator' rather than an 'able artist'. The crucial problem identified was the lack of spontaneity, but this criticism is levelled more at photography in general than Thomson in particular, as the review finishes by commenting that 'the photographs are in themselves good, and the text is simple, straightforward, rich in curious details, and readable'. Far from being a 'scathing' attack on Thomson, the journal was articulating a general feeling about the shortcomings of photography for such subject matter.[67] But not all reviews and notices of *Street Life* were so negative. *The Graphic*, reviewing the collected edition, noted how 'the manifold industries of the poor of our great City are transferred from the street to the drawing-room' by the 'photographs and word pictures' which 'ably illustrate the curious callings of our poorer brethren'. It goes on to talk of Thomson's portrayal of 'familiar scenes, most of them to be met with on an everyday walk, but each carefully drawn from life and the history of the models faithfully recounted'.[68] *The Lancet* went further, welcoming the first part as a worthy and 'more ambitious' successor to Mayhew's *London Labour and the London Poor*. The 'effective treatment' of the subjects of the first part is praised, and the journal records its sympathy with 'all efforts put forth to throw light on the haunts and ways of life, the hardships and struggles, of the lower strata of society', wishing the project success in diffusing information important to the 'sanitarian, the citizen, and the philanthropist'.[69] *Street Life in London* sought from the outset to raise awareness of social conditions, and an anonymous commentator in *The Westminster Review* praised the series for 'bringing into notice byways of social life which are as little thought of as they may prove to be transient. It is well for us to get such vivid little pictures of how whole classes of our fellow-citizens live, while we are considering how to spread comfort and health and moral light around ... It is to be remarked as worthy of all praise that these pictures of London life are free from the patronising caricaturist spirit so repulsively pervading even popular and useful writers on such matters'.[70] Thomson and Smith were seen by contemporaries as bringing fresh evidence to bear on a problem that had not gone away since the publication of Mayhew's *Life and Labour*, and *Street Life* therefore gained its relevance to contemporaries from this renewal of emphasis.

The reason *Street Life* has ultimately succeeded as the first social documentary photography is, therefore, because its primary aim was to inform: it was never the intention of Smith or Thomson to claim the sort of literary and artistic high ground that the reviewer in *The Athenaeum* criticised the project for not attaining. Rather, they aimed to transfer the experiences of the poor into the homes of the comfortable middle class, and to make them aware of a different, harsher reality.

45.

46.

45. *Siamese Boatman*. 1866. 254 x 102 mm.
Modern albumen print from wet-collodion negative. National Library of Scotland/Wellcome Institute Library, London

46. *Chinese Street (prepared for illumination)*. 1869. 242 x 180 mm.
Albumen print from wet-collodion negative. National Library of Scotland

47.

48.

47. *Amoy Women.* 1871. 100 x 204 mm.
Modern albumen stereograph from wet-collodion negative. National Library of Scotland/Wellcome Institute Library, London

48. *Street Gamblers. c.* 1868-71. 215 x 165 mm.
Modern albumen print from wet-collodion negative. National Library of Scotland/Wellcome Institute Library, London

49.

50.

49. *Physic Street, Canton. c.* 1869–71. 270 x 215 mm.
Collotype. National Library of Scotland

50. Felice Beato, *Canton Street (Street of Sweet Harmony). c.* 1860–61. 235 x 232 mm.
Albumen print from wet-collodion negative. Courtesy of the Trustees of the Victoria & Albert Museum

51.

51. A *Street in Larnaca*. 1878. 115 x 176 mm.
Woodburytype. National Library of Scotland

52.

53.

52. *Chinese Skipper, Yangtze*. 1872. 100 x 190 mm.
Modern albumen stereograph from wet-collodion negative. National Library of Scotland/Wellcome Institute Library, London

53. *Workers on 'The Silent Highway'* . 1876–77. 114 x 90 mm.
Woodburytype. National Library of Scotland

54.

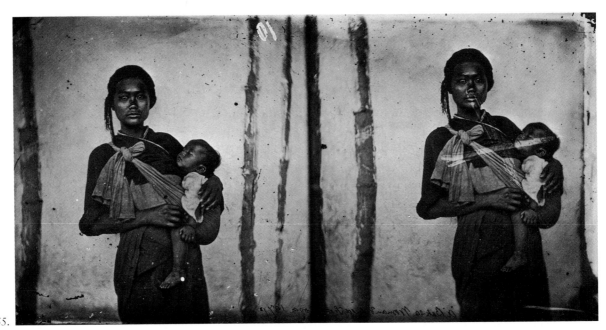

55.

54. *A Pepohoan Dwelling.* 1871. 250 x 303 mm.
Modern albumen print from wet-collodion negative. National Library of Scotland/Wellcome Institute Library, London

55. *Mode of Carrying Child.* 1871. 103 x 203 mm.
Modern albumen stereograph from wet-collodion negative. National Library of Scotland/Wellcome Institute Library, London

56.

57.

56. *Baksa Woman, Seated*. 1871. 103 x 203 mm.
Modern albumen stereograph from wet-collodion negative. National Library of Scotland/Wellcome Institute Library, London

57. *Costume of Baksa Women*. 1871. 103 x 203 mm.
Modern albumen stereograph from wet-collodion negative. National Library of Scotland/Wellcome Institute Library, London

58.

59.

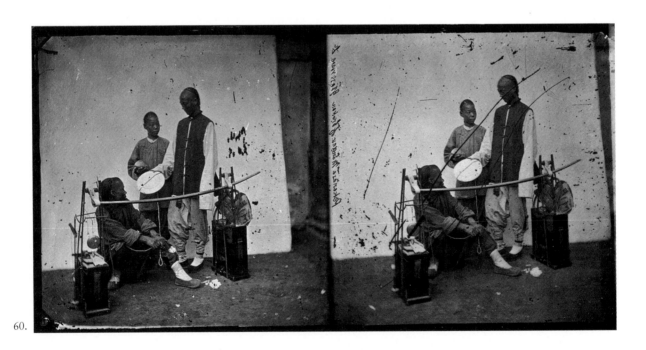

60.

58. *A Pekingese Chiropodist.* 1871–72. 100 x 103 mm.
Modern albumen print from wet-collodion negative. National Library of Scotland/Wellcome Institute Library, London

59. *The Peep-Show, Peking.* 1871–72. 100 x 103 mm.
Modern albumen print from wet-collodion negative. National Library of Scotland/Wellcome Institute Library, London

60. *The Mender of Broken Glassware.* 1871–72. 101 x 205 mm.
Modern albumen stereograph from wet-collodion negative. National Library of Scotland/Wellcome Institute Library, London

61.

61. *Beggars. c.* 1871. 123 x 97 mm.
Carbon print. National Museum of Photography, Film, and Television

62.

63.

64.

62. David Octavius Hill and Robert Adamson, *Willie Liston Redding the Line*. 1843. 202 x 144 mm.
Salted paper print from calotype negative. National Library of Scotland

63. David Octavius Hill and Robert Adamson, *Newhaven Fishwives*. 1843. 190 x 130 mm.
Salted paper print from calotype negative. National Library of Scotland

64. Thomas Annan, *Old Vennel off the High Street. c.* 1878–79. 281 x 230 mm.
Albumen print from wet-collodion negative. National Galleries of Scotland

65.

66.

65. Archibald Burns, *Corner of Horse Wynd and Cowgate Looking East*. 1871. 185 x 237 mm.
Lightly albumenised salted paper print from wet-collodion negative. National Library of Scotland

66. Archibald Burns, *Simson the Printers House in the Cowgate*. 1871. 185 x 226 mm.
Lightly albumenised salted paper print from wet-collodion negative. National Library of Scotland

67.   68.

67. Henry Dixon and Alfred and John Bool, *Oxford Arms*. 1875. 236 x 185 mm.
Carbon Print. Courtesy of the Trustees of the Victoria & Albert Museum

68. Henry Dixon and Alfred and John Bool, *St Bartholomews the Great, Smithfield*. 1875. 236 x 185 mm.
Carbon Print. Courtesy of the Trustees of the Victoria & Albert Museum

69.

70.

69. *The Cheap Fish of St. Giles's*. 1876–77. 112 x 90 mm.
Woodburytype. National Library of Scotland

70. *'Hookey Alf' of Whitechapel*. 1876–77. 111 x 85 mm.
Woodburytype. National Library of Scotland

71.

72.

71. *The Seller of ShellFish*. 1876–77. 87 x 112 mm.
Woodburytype. National Library of Scotland

72. *Recruiting Sergeants at Westminster*. 1876–77. 113 x 90 mm.
Woodburytype. National Library of Scotland

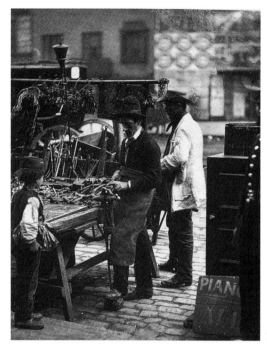

73.

74.

73. *The Street Locksmith*. 1876–77. 114 x 90 mm.
Woodburytype. National Library of Scotland

74. *London Nomades*. 1876–77. 110 x 86 mm.
Woodburytype. National Library of Scotland

75.

75. *'Caney' The Clown*. 1876–77. 116 x 88 mm.
Woodburytype. National Library of Scotland

76.

77.

78.

79.

76. *'Mush-Fakers' and Ginger-Beer Makers*. 1876–77. 107 x 82 mm.
Woodburytype. National Library of Scotland

77. *Halfpenny Ices*. 1876–77. 115 x 90 mm.
Woodburytype. National Library of Scotland

78. *Covent Garden Labourers*. 1876–77. 115 x 86 mm.
Woodburytype. National Library of Scotland

79. *Covent Garden Flower Women*. 1876–1877. 112 x 82 mm.
Woodburytype. National Library of Scotland

80.

80. *An Old Clothes Shop, Seven Dials*. 1876–77. 116 x 90 mm.
Woodburytype. National Library of Scotland

81.

81. *The Crawlers*. 1876–77. 115 x 87 mm.
Woodburytype. National Library of Scotland

CHAPTER 5

FORMAL PORTRAITS

Tighten the head rest; dont spare the sitter –
it acts as a tonic to brace one's jaded energy.

JOHN THOMSON*

There is no single object presented to our senses which engrosses so large a share of our thoughts, emotions, and associations as that small portion of flesh and blood a hand may cover, which constitutes the human face. There is nothing we gaze upon with such admiration, think of with so much fondness, long for with such yearning, and remember with such fidelity – nothing that gladdens us with such magic power, haunts us with such fearful pertinacity – common as it is, meeting us at every turn, there is nothing we peer into with such unflagging curiosity, or study with such insatiate interest. Nor is there anything surprising in the effect thus produced. For the face is not, like the hand or foot, a mere portion of ourself or of our neighbour; it is the very representative of our race – the one synonym of humanity.[1]

Lady Eastlake's characteristically astute observations on the human face provide us with a convenient summary of the reasons why, throughout the history of photography, more photographs of the human face have been taken than any other kind of image. The human necessity to have a 'likeness', for a whole variety of reasons, has driven photography in a number of diverse directions. Its commercial aspects focussed on the portrait (albeit in a multitude of guises) from the time of the earliest daguerreotype studios in Britain and France, through the carte-de-visite 'craze' of the 1860s, to the mass culture of the 'snapshot' in the late twentieth century. It should therefore come as no surprise that taking photographs of the human face formed the most constant aspect of John Thomson's photographic output throughout his entire career.

Thomson first began to make money from photography by taking the portraits of the western merchants and others living and working in the fast-growing commercial centre of Singapore in the early 1860s. From this point onwards, the photographic portrait was to be the mainstay of his career, a regular source of income, and something to fall back on when other, perhaps more interesting, but often more risky projects were yet to realise their rewards.

One of the most important aspects to bear in mind when examining the work of any commercial portrait photographer is that the choice of subjects is very often outside his or her control, and in this respect Thomson is no exception, being reluctant, as any sensible photographer would be, to turn away business. But throughout his career there were occasions when he was able to make the choice of

*John Thomson, 'Proverbial Photographic Philosophy', *British Journal Photographic Almanac* (1875), p. 129.

sitter and location, and any appreciation of his portrait photography as a whole must take these two different circumstances into consideration.

The royal portraits he took in Siam bring out clearly these two elements of his work. Whilst it is unclear whether or not the opportunity to make the photographs was a direct commission, it seems from his own writing that he made the initial approaches, making contact with the court soon after arriving in Bangkok. After having established his presence and his profession, the court may have asked him to make the photographs. Thomson would have realised that such a group of interesting and unusual portraits would prove to be of considerable interest to his British audience. The actual sittings were, however, orchestrated very effectively by his principal sitter, the King of Siam, and he found himself unable to control the situation.

Freed from the constraints of having to manage the day-to-day running of his commercial studio, John Thomson's sojourn in Bangkok gave him a greater freedom to explore his own photographic ideas and interests. Thus he had the opportunity to arrange, direct, and otherwise pose, the upper elements of the Siamese Government and Court for the purposes of formal portrait photography. The likenesses which he made on this occasion, with few exceptions, have a slightly confusing quality about them. The poses, props and look of the pictures bear a close resemblance to work issuing from many of the higher-quality portrait studios in Paris or London in the 1860s and 1870s: they have the feel of Nadar, or Elliott & Fry. The curiously European backdrops and poses tend to disorientate, but this concentrates attention on the expressions and countenances of the sitters, those aspects which, Lady Eastlake argued, reveal the essence of our humanity. Moreover, it must be remembered that the spirit prevalent at the Siamese Court during the late 1850s and 1860s was influenced by the desires of the reigning monarch, His Majesty Prabat Somdet Pra parameñdr Mahà Mongkut, who dedicated himself upon taking the throne to bringing Siam into closer relations with the great western powers of the day, encouraging trade, commerce, and culture, all with the intention of modernising his country.

The historical figure of Mongkut has permeated western culture, without the west really realising it. His fame has been spread by myriad books, novels, plays, musicals and motion pictures, with major actors such as Yul Brynner and Rex Harrison cast in the role of the King. The famous films *The King and I*, and *Anna and the King of Siam*, are based somewhat loosely on his character as depicted in Anna Leonowens's book *English Governess at the Court of Siam*, and Margaret Landon's *Anna and the King of Siam*. However these give a highly misleading impression of what Mongkut was actually like. Not surprisingly he bore little physical resemblance to Yul Brynner. He had suffered a partial paralysis of the facial muscles as a teenager, and had lost all his teeth long before he became King.[2] 'He had a very homely as well as old face', wrote one westerner who came into contact with him,[3] and the British diplomat Sir John Bowring remembered him as 'of middle height, thin, with a somewhat austere countenance'.[4] For his part, John Thomson wrote of the King's 'erect and commanding figure' and also of the 'expression of severe gravity' which had settled on his 'somewhat haggard face'.[5]

Mongkut was forty-seven years old in 1851, the year of his elevation to the Siamese throne, and had spent the previous twenty-seven in the habit of a Buddhist monk, during which time he had forsaken the wealth, power, and excesses of the court for a life of poverty, chastity, and democracy in a community of Buddhist priests where he was known as 'Mongkut the beggar'.[6] During this period he had devoted himself to prayer and learning, becoming familiar with all the major languages of South-East Asia, as well as French and English. His interests had also expanded into areas such as history and archaeology, and he had become particularly devoted to the study of astronomy. He also cultivated western visitors to Siam, especially missionaries like the French Jesuit Pallegoix, and the American Daniel Beach Bradley. His reign as monarch, however, came at a difficult moment for Siam, which was trapped between the colonial ambitions of several western powers, those of Britain and France in particular. This delicate situation tended to act against Mongkut's instincts, which generally favoured improving contact with the west, as a means of assisting the internal programme of modernisation which he had started, and to give Siam a role on the international stage. This process had begun in earnest in 1855, with the mission of Sir John Bowring, which resulted in a treaty giving favourable conditions to British merchants operating in Siam, and which was soon followed by treaties with other western powers.[7]

Among the western inventions which appealed most to Mongkut was photography. In 1856 and 1857 he had sent daguerreotypes (by an unknown photographer) of himself and the Queen Consort to both Queen Victoria and President Pierce of America (the latter photograph was in the Smithsonian, but is now lost). In 1856, by way of return, Queen Victoria had sent Mongkut a camera and other photographic apparatus, and he had received help from the British Consulate (and an unnamed Swede) in how to use it.[8] Shortly afterwards, he sent photographs to Pope Pius IX (these are still in the Vatican), and from Thomson's account of his time in Bangkok we know that the King's brother was the primary enthusiast for photography at the court.[9]

Soon after he was elevated to the throne, Mongkut began placing his favourites around him as advisors and ministers at court and in the Government. Friends were rewarded, and members of his own family in particular were favoured. Thomson's portraits of some of these individuals may well have been commissions, in particular his 'Siamese Noble, 1866' (PLATE 82), and his photograph 'Prime Minister in 1865, the late Kralahom' (PLATE 83) (showing the former Minister of Defence who had benefitted from Mongkut's patronage),[10] and his 'Siamese Lady of Title, Wife of the Prime Minister, 1866' (PLATE 84). These are all taken with European furniture, carpets, and poses, following the westernising lead provided by the King himself; but, with the exception of the nobleman, the sitters seem ill at ease in these surroundings.

THE TWO MONGKUTS

Two pictures in particular stand as evidence of the contradictory signals which inevitably issued from the Siamese Court under Mongkut (PLATES 85–86). They are both portraits of the great King himself, and although, in both, the old man sits placidly, his eyes fixed intently on the camera, yet remaining distant and aloof, the two images emit differing messages. In this respect there is a sense in which the two portraits sum up the western experience in Asia in the nineteenth century. On the one hand, countries like Siam attracted western powers anxious to exchange the attitudes and techniques of the modern world for commercial and political power. Countries like Siam also undertook steps to modernise – or more accurately westernise – their own countries, taking advice from outside in how to bring this about. Yet Siam, China, and countries like them also maintained a cultural and political distance, so that the west could only gaze at them and admire them from afar, never really participating in or fully comprehending them. So we have the two portraits of Mongkut. On the one hand we have the modern monarch, dressed as a French Field Marshal, posed amid furniture and clothing which could easily have been made in Paris or Birmingham. This is Mongkut the moderniser, who corresponded with most of the great European monarchs (and even the Pope himself), in their own languages, and who insisted on Siam playing a conspicuous part in the Paris Exhibition of 1867.[11] On the other we have the Siamese King as religious leader, defender of the faith, in the traditional court regalia expected of his status. The statement he makes in this image is: 'thus far and no further'. It was the King, rather than Thomson, who controlled these sittings. Mongkut's first choice had been an unfamiliar pose dressed in a 'robe of spotless white', and taking a prayerful aspect.[12] Thomson had carpeted and canopied a space ready for the photograph, but Mongkut left the room just before the picture could be made, without explanation. Thomson was understandably perplexed, but the Prince, the King's brother, interpreting for him, remarked: 'the King does everything which is right, and if I were to accost him now, he might conclude this morning's work by cutting off my head!'.[13] The King quickly returned, however, and Thomson had no option but to hold his ground, remain calm, and expose the plates:

> [The King was] dressed this time in a sort of French Field Marshal's uniform. There was no cotton stuff visible about his person now, not even stockings. The portrait was a great success, and his majesty afterwards sat in his court robes, requesting me to place him where and how I pleased. I consulted the Prince, who said – 'Yes, place him, but do not for the life of you lay hands on him, more especially on his thrice sacred head'. Here was a difficulty. How to pose an Oriental potentate who has ideas of his own as to propriety in attitude, and that too, without touching a fold of his garments? I told the King, in plain English, what I wanted to do, and he said, 'Mr Town-shun, do what you require for the excellency of your photograph.' He enquired my nationality. I told him I was born in Edinburgh. 'Ah! You are Scotchman, and speak English I can understand; there are Englishmen here who have not understanding of their own language when I speak.'[14]

This second portrait, with the King dressed in his silk court robes, wearing traditional headgear, and surrounded by other trappings of his status, was only partially achieved through the skills of the photographer. Mongkut was in control throughout the sitting, and shows his knowledge of how important photography was in forming attitudes in the west. He was an assiduous reader of western newspapers, had a substantial private library of western books, and clearly wished to send the message back, through Thomson's portraits, that Siam was both a modern, outward-looking power, and one with traditions, dignity, and a *gravitas* of its own. Mongkut was clearly worried that an image of himself dressed in the simple white robes of a Buddhist at prayer might have encouraged the west to regard Siam as a simple country, devoted to religion, and knowing nothing of politics, diplomacy, and the other 'arts' which the western powers were practising in South-East Asia.

MANDARINS AND PRINCES

Despite his growing interest in the life of ordinary people in China, and the expression of that interest through his photography, John Thomson by no means abandoned the formal portrait during his later journeys. No doubt this was partly a matter of expediency. To photograph members of the governing classes might, as he had found in Siam and Cambodia, help to open doors and smooth passages around a country which otherwise posed enormous difficulties for the lone traveller. Thomson also knew from previous experience that images of important statesmen and members of royal families were marketable commodities in the west, and the middle-class readers of *The Illustrated London News* and *The Graphic* in particular were enormously interested in the holders of wealth and power, no matter over what country they presided.

The Chinese statesman that the British reading public was best acquainted with was Yixin, Prince of Kung (Gong). The Prince held enormous influence in China, and had been responsible for negotiating the peace treaty with General Gordon and the allied powers in 1860 during the Taiping Rebellion (1851–64). His actions during this episode, and in particular during the internecine political manoeuvring that followed this crisis in Chinese politics, had resulted in a *coup d'état* by which Prince Kung dissolved the anti-western Council of Regency, and cleverly assumed powers himself, acting on behalf of the Dowager Empress. His time in power was not easy by any means, although he managed to remain immensely popular with the Chinese people: a popular hero whom many in China at the time believed to be the only man capable of governing the immense country.

The Baron de Hübner, travelling in China in 1871, more or less at the same time as Thomson, encountered Prince Kung, and wrote a lengthy description of the man, which is worth repeating in its entirety:

> Yih-sin, Prince of Kung, is about forty years of age. He has, for a Mandjou, wonderfully regular features, and a languishing look; he is short-sighted, and has a way of winking his eyes. A gracious and rather sarcastic smile precedes his pleasantries. Before speaking to you, he looks at you fixedly, full in the face; but when he begins to speak, he looks down. His figure is slender and above the ordinary height. His complexion is sallow and his features are drawn, as if from over-fatigue. On the whole he has the indifference, the *laissez-aller* and the simplicity of a man of high birth. One sees also that he is a man who is rather *blasé* with everything; and who has enjoyed power long enough to be surfeited with it; which, however, does not mean that he would willingly give it up or let it be taken from him. His hands, which are rather effeminate, are remarkable, according to the custom of the country, for the enormous length of the nails ... The left hand of the prince was ornamented with a fine ring of green jade. The rest of his dress was remarkable for its simplicity; a dark blue tunic, with the collar and the turning up of the sleeves,

of a lighter blue; on his cap a single button with a tassle of crimson silk. 'This statesman' I was told, 'Is not a man of very superior intellect; but he possesses in the highest degree the precious talent of knowing how to choose able men, and to employ each one according to his capabilities. He is brave and courageous.'[15]

Thomson for his part regarded him as 'quick of apprehension, open to advice, and comparatively liberal in his views', adding: 'He is the acknowledged leader of that small division among Chinese politicians who are known as the party of progress'.[16] The Prince and the other leading members of the government 'wisely availed themselves of my presence to have their portraits taken' at the Chinese Foreign Office, as Thomson modestly recalled in *The Straits of Malacca*. 'The Prince for a few minutes kept me in a pleasant talk, enquiring about my travels and about photography, and manifesting considerable interest in the process of taking a likeness', wrote Thomson, and it may well have been one of Thomson's photographs that the Prince promised to give to the Baron de Hübner.[17] The two portraits of the Prince *(PLATES 87–88)* not only show us his physical characteristics, his long finger-nails, and his simple attire, but they powerfully transmit the sense of the man that the Baron captured in his recollections: especially the 'penetrating' eyes of which Thomson spoke.[18]

Thomson chose one of his portraits of the Prince *(PLATE 88)* as the first plate in the first volume of *Illustrations of China*, a decision dictated in part no doubt by the undoubted curiosity among the British middle classes concerning the Prince. But the portrait also stands as a kind of *imprimatur*. Featuring a moderniser, and pro-western figure at the top of the Chinese Government, it introduces the reader to the spirit of the entire work from the outset: imperial China is revealed, in detail, with the approving participation of those who governed it. This image also has a further significance. The background of rocks and foliage in the garden of the Foreign Office in Peking betrays nothing of the orient, unlike the other portrait of the Prince *(PLATE 87)*, where the distinctive wooden structure framing the sitter could be more easily located geographically. The first image therefore, lacking an oriental reference, calls the reader to focus attention on the man in the picture as an individual, rather than distracting the viewer with the context in which he sits.

Other senior members of the current Chinese political élite were photographed at the same time as Prince Kung. All were members of the Zongli Yamen, or Foreign Board, which was responsible for co-ordinating all relations with the west, and of which Prince Kung was the senior minister (Fig. 28). The Zongli Yamen held a crucial strategic position in the Chinese political set-up, as it closely advised the throne (which in practice at this time meant the Empress Dowager). In fact, the Zongli Yamen remained the most pro-western force in Chinese politics up until Prince Kung's death in 1884,[19] and Thomson himself felt that 'it affords one of the few signs of progress in the present state of China ... it is not too much to say that to the enlightened policy of the distinguished members of this

Fig. 28

The Foreign Office, Peking. 1872.

Wood-engraving (from *The Graphic*, 18 October 1873). National Library of Scotland

Council and to their chief, we owe our present peaceful and comparatively advantageous relations with the Chinese Empire'.[20]

Dong Xun (Yung Tajin), President of the Board of Finance *(PLATE 89)*, was a noted author and a particular authority on hydrography who had impressed Thomson with his plans to improve irrigation and drainage throughout China. Shen Guifen, President of the Board of War *(PLATE 90)*, had been governor of the province of Shanxi, where he had been determined to limit the trade in opium. They were photographed in their satin robes and boots, Thomson clearly trying to capture something of the 'air of quiet, dignified repose' which he had detected in them.[21] There is a sense in which, by photographing these individuals in particular, and by selecting the study of Prince Kung and the group portrait of the three members of the Zongli Yamen for inclusion as plates in *Illustrations of China*, Thomson was attempting to portray China in a favourable light to his western, middle-class readers. As they sipped their China tea, or admired their Chinese porcelain, Thomson hoped his readers would regard China not only as a country of great beauty, fascination, and interest, but also one which was in the hands of men trying to modernise (that is to say westernise) it.

The Chinese preferred to be photographed straight on, and Thomson learned to adapt his own portrait techniques to suit these formal traditions. A Chinese photographer in Hong Kong explained to him that: 'men of taste' in China, 'must look straight at the camera so as to show their friends at a distance that they have two eyes and two ears. They won't have shadows about their faces, because, you see, shadow forms no part of the face. It is'nt [sic] one's nose, or any other feature; therefore it should not be there. The camera, you see, is defective. It won't work up to that point; it won't recognise our laws of art'.[22] Despite the somewhat disparaging tone which Thomson adopted when he wrote about the techniques of Hong Kong photographers, he knew that to be successful he had to be flexible with his own traditions of picture making, and the series of formal portraits of mandarins in Canton conform to the rules firmly established within Chinese portraiture. Thus the sitters are posed square-on to the camera, seated next to a small table of neat geometrical design, simply ornamented, and with simple backdrops *(PLATE 91)*. The pyramidal style of image construction dominates the arrangement of the sitters and props within the frame, each figure being positioned in the centre of the frame, flanked by a table on one side, and perhaps a child on the other. In the case of the three Cantonese mandarins *(PLATE 92)*, they have been arranged with one standing in the middle, the two elder men seated in front, on either side, again forming a triangle or pyramid. The position of the mandarin in Chinese society was evidently the subject of a great deal of ill-informed speculation in Britain, and Thomson's photographs can be seen as attempts to provide a lifelike portrayal to help correct these views. 'The general impression out of China is that a mandarin spends his days in idleness and luxury, whilst he battens upon the booty wrung by himself and followers from the unhappy people over whom he is placed; but this is not altogether a correct view', wrote a contemporary of Thomson in China, for 'the Chinese officials lead a laborious life, and instances are not wanting of individuals winning the esteem and even devotion of the people'.[23] The chief cause of these erroneous opinions seems to have been the secluded lives which the mandarins led. Thomson's ability to get inside the *yamen* (the mandarin's official residence) and take photographs as strikingly fresh and immediate as 'Mandarin of the Late Empire' *(PLATE 93)* shows his skills in breaking through barriers of convention and propriety. This image in particular, albeit taken within the constraints of the Chinese portrait tradition, testifies to his desire to give as accurate a record of as wide a range of Chinese life and society as possible.

Thomson also succeeded in gaining the confidence of a young Manchu bride in Peking, and his photograph of her *(PLATE 94)* is an almost perfect example of the discreet and intimate style that was entirely appropriate to the sitter. Another Manchu woman was photographed head on and from the rear *(PLATES 95–96)*, and each time the backdrop renders her almost two-dimensional. We are drawn to admire her coiffure and her jewelry, but viewing the images together encourages an air of mystery to surround the sitter.

FROM THE STREET TO THE STUDIO

There is also a sense in which some of the photographs of humbler folk taken during Thomson's great photographic journeys form part of the formal portrait tradition. Images like 'Old Woman, Canton' *(PLATE 97:* probably taken in 1868) could be regarded as 'street' photography, as the photographer treated it as one of a series of 'types of the labouring class', but it could also be considered a fine example of his *formal* portraiture. The photograph of this woman, and another of her husband, were reproduced by Thomson in *Illustrations of China*.[24] In the text which accompanies these images he likens the couple to Darby and Joan, their lives having been 'a uniform scene of hardships and toil'. The version of the image reproduced here, however, reveals more of the effects of such a life upon her features than can be discerned from the published version. Thomson describes her as still active, and working on lighter domestic duties, adding that 'her hair has grown thin and white, but she still dresses it with neatness and care'.[25] But both this photograph and another closely related image, taken ten years later on Cyprus and entitled 'Selling Bread' *(PLATE 98)*, can also be regarded as formal portraits, in that they take these working women out of their normal context, the street or workplace. Here again, the emphasis on the effects that the passage of time had on the lines of the face is particularly marked, although 'Selling Bread' sought also to discern the 'traces of youthful comeliness' which Thomson felt still lingered about his subject. The choice of mottled backdrop, presumably a whitewashed wall which had become dirtied with age, suggests a studio session, and the image conveys more of the atmosphere of an Irving Penn sitting (from a much later era), than of the intimacy of a Cypriot dwelling.

Occasionally, as we have seen in other areas of his work, Thomson's photography breaks with the formal chronology of photography's development, and introduces ways of making pictures which are far ahead of their time. This can be seen in his stereograph of a boatwoman wearing a patterned headscarf, probably taken in Canton, *c.*1868–71 *(PLATE 99)*. This appealingly simple photograph, using only a makeshift canvas sheet as a backdrop, contrasts greatly with the formal constructs of his Siamese portraits. It is not only the simplicity of the image which comes across as particularly modern. The sitter's knowing glance, directed firmly at the photographer, is an instance of both informality and familiarity, both extraordinarily rare occurrences in nineteenth-century photography by Europeans in Asia.

Thomson's group photographs such as 'Tartar Soldiers' *(PLATE 100)*, 'Buddhist Monks' *(PLATE 101)*, 'Native Group, Nicosia' *(PLATE 102)*, and 'Group at Avgoru' *(PLATE 103)*, although taken over a ten-year period, approach the problem of the group portrait from the same perspective. Thomson's achievement is in conveying the dynamic of the collection of individuals, who are united by some characteristic, be it membership of a religious order, or military cadre, or simply by being part of the same family, whilst also capturing something of the moment in which he found them, utilising the immediacy of photography to great effect. The soldiers who are the subjects of the photograph variously called 'Tartar Soldiers' and the 'Banner Men of Canton' formed the guard of the British Consul in Canton, and impressed Thomson for 'their fine manly build, and soldierly appearance'.[26] But the complex arrangement of the eleven men, ordered so that they all face different directions and reveal different dynamic poses, has created an effective sense of movement. The 'Buddhist Monks' at the Ku-Shan Monastery near Foochow all sit in contemplation, their faces reverently facing the floor, and Thomson has organised them so that their bodies all face towards the middle of an undefined circle. The spirituality of the monks is brought alive as vividly as the energy of the Tartar soldiers. The photograph 'Native Group, Nicosia' was created by the photographer out of a 'friendly-disposed crowd of spectators' who had gathered to observe him photographing the local mosque. Thomson seized upon the moment, and turned his attention from one kind of picture-making to another. The group was organised and choreographed by the photographer in a way that not only follows the architecture of the building they are posed against, but introduces the same rhythm and action that worked so successfully in 'Tartar Soldiers'. The line formed by the variations in the relative heights of the heads of the sitters leads the eye through the group, ending at the figure of a turbaned Turk who had wandered into exactly the right position in the frame at the 'decisive moment' when the image was taken.

SOCIETY PORTRAITS

The portrait studio that bore Thomson's name in London was first established in the late 1870s, after the years of frenetic activity following his return from the Far East, and during which he had firmly established his reputation as 'China Thomson'. This was achieved, as we have seen, through a combination of publishing, lecturing, and making other photographs in London and Cyprus which enhanced his status as one of Britain's most innovative and important photographers.

London high society has always been susceptible to the attractions of the successful artist, particularly those who have led an adventurous life, and Thomson was able to capitalise on the fame which his books and photographs of China had generated. He chose to site his studio in London to be close to the 'upper' echelons of British society. He moved from Buckingham Palace Road to Mayfair, a part of the city which has been at the heart of aristocratic London since the eighteenth century. During the latter half of the nineteenth century Mayfair was the most fashionable part of the city, and naturally enough the residents of the *beau monde* demanded the presence of services of a quality to match their pretensions, and so, as a result, Thomson's portrait business thrived.

The key to this success was undoubtedly his reputation as a traveller and adventurer, but the addition of the title 'Photographer to the Queen', which he was entitled to stamp onto his mounts and place on his advertisements after he had been awarded the Royal Warrant in May 1881, no doubt gave an additional boost to his photographic career. His Royal commissions included a portrait of Queen Victoria in 1887 (PLATE 104), which portrayed her as aloof and remote, still pensive in her mourning. It was an image which helped to establish the received iconography of Victoria. But in 'Queen Victoria with Two Grand-daughters' (PLATE 105) he was able to portray another side of her, one that showed her deep involvement with her family, revealing tenderness and warmth that were rarely seen in the photographs and images that were more widely circulated. The upper classes, anxious to follow the Queen's lead, and the aspirant portions of the upper-middle class, eager to show that they shared the same tastes and judgment as the Royal family, gave Thomson their patronage – the geographic location of his studio no doubt having confirmed in their eyes just how refined and respectable his services were. Other society photographs falling into this category are the portrait of Rosario Alba (PLATE 106), the wife of Carlos, 16th Duke of Alba and 9th Duke of Berwick, at Abergeldie (the Highland residence of the Prince of Wales) and the image of the Duke of Rutland in 1889 (PLATE 107), now in the Royal Photographic Collection.[27] Other commissioned work at this time related more closely to Thomson's own interests as a traveller and geographer, and, as we have seen, it was generated to some extent through his contacts at the Royal Geographical Society. Portraits such as those of the arctic explorer Admiral A. H. Markham (PLATE 108) and of the Secretary of the Royal Geographical Society, Henry Walter Bates (PLATE 109), were pictorially very similar to the 'straight' work done for the Royal family. The conservative nature of Thomson's commercial portraiture was no doubt forced on him by the constraints of taste and fashion current at the time, but one project stands out as an opportunity for experimentation and photographic sophistication.

The Devonshire House Ball

The Devonshire House Fancy Dress Ball was a dazzling social event given by the Duke and Duchess of Devonshire at their London Mansion on Piccadilly, in celebration of Queen Victoria's Jubilee. The press reports published the following day described it as a 'brilliant gathering', in the sense that all of the brightest jewels in the crown of European aristocracy were present. It was perhaps the last flowering of the *belle époque* which would be washed away by the Great War. The idea behind the event was to celebrate aristocracy's historic past. This was achieved by the present holders of the most important noble titles dressing themselves up as their illustrious predecessors or some other equally important figure from European history. The atmosphere of decadence is captured in contemporary accounts: 'The fine old house, itself a historical relic, with its state rooms, with heavy gildings, its old fashioned crystal chandeliers, its marble staircase, and its illuminated garden, an oasis of peace and verdure in the centre of one of the busiest

London streets, lent itself admirably to the brilliant scene in which the servants, some attired as Egyptian footmen, some, negroes themselves, in their own quaint and barbaric Eastern dress, carried out the illusion of antiquity to their knee breeches and white wigs'.[28] John Thomson, as we have seen, was one of the photographers chosen to document this extraordinary idea by translating these flights of fancy into a visual record, preserved in printed form via the agency of The Chiswick Press and Emery Walker's process-engraving business, and made available to a number of the guests as a lavish memento volume. In a sense, the work of the official photographers to this event resembles the approach of those modern practitioners whose business is based around translating the whims of advertising agencies into compelling and believable photographic images. The photographs from the Devonshire House Ball did much the same: they had to be well crafted photographically, in order to 'sell' a particular product, in this case an idea of the role and history of one small but enormously influential and powerful sector of European society. This 'product' was sold largely to members of the same society (the eventual owners of the book), but some of the images had a wider circulation in the illustrated weeklies of the middle-class press. *The Graphic*, for example, published a two-page account of the Ball by Lady Violet Greville, illustrated with five images taken by the firm of Lafayette.[29]

Although we cannot be sure how much freedom the photographers had on this project, the twenty-two images which are credited to Thomson clearly involved a remarkable bout of complicated studio work, involving the painting and construction of sets, the acquisition of props, and the selection of costumes and accoutrements worn by the sitters and which were required to coordinate with the backdrops and stage-sets. All of this would have required considerable planning and logistical capabilities, no doubt made all the more difficult by having to conduct this business through the formalities of the British class system which made communication between a middle-class photographer and the leading figures of the upper classes slow and difficult. The preparations were considerable.

> Never in our time has so much attention been paid to old family pictures, never have the masterpieces of portraiture in the National Gallery been so carefully studied, while for weeks past the Print-room at the British Museum, commonly given up to quiet students, has been invaded by smart ladies and gentlemen anxious to search the prints and drawings of the 16th, 17th, and 18th centuries for something in which they could obey the Duchess's summons to appear 'in an allegorical or historical costume dated earlier than 1820'. Never in our time have the costumiers been so busy, and the houses so well-known to everybody who has ever organized private theatricals, such as Messrs. John Simmons, of the Haymarket, Messrs. Nathan and Messrs. Alias, have been driven distracted with orders and counter-orders.[30]

One journalist, observing the event as if it were itself a stage-play, remarked that the majority of the guests 'wore their costumes as if they had lived in them, instead of having them home this week from the costumiers. With the ladies this was not surprising. A woman is never ill at ease in a beautiful dress. But the men! Many of them did not look as if they were masquerading; there was an ease, a self-possession about them which was quite admirable'.[31]

Thomson's contributions to *The Devonshire House Fancy Dress Ball* provide some interesting insights into his formal portrait work. He had to coordinate an immense variety of stage-sets and costumes, balancing them with the various ages and sizes of the sitters. More importantly, he had to adjust his work to accommodate the wide range of stylistic effects which his sitters desired to achieve. Thomson showed considerable versatility in creating these diverse atmospheres, and four of his photographs in particular display the range of effects he was capable of achieving. The slightly severe and straight 'Marie Stuart' *(PLATE 110)* as posed by Lady Katherine Scott, the daughter of the Duke and Duchess of Buccleuch, shows off to great effect the glorious texture of her white silk dress, shining against the dark backdrop. The voluptuous and erotically-charged 'Scheherezäde' *(PLATE 114)* of Miss Ogden Goelet, the daughter of Robert and Ogden Goelet (who owned much of the mid-town East Side of New York, and who were among the guiding spirits behind the foundation of the Metropolitan opera in New York[32]) shows the young woman 'attired in a beautiful robe of golden gauze, glittering with multi-coloured jewels, and draped at the waist with the soft sashes of *crepe de chine* in pale shades of mauve, pink, and blue'.[33] It is an image very much in the tradition of Ingres Odalisques, or of Roger Fenton's *Seated Odalisque*, taken in 1858.[34] Similar variation was required in the formal photographic techniques to provide the painterly effects of oil-on-canvas for Lady Sarah Wilson's Madame de Pompadour *(PLATE 112)*,[35] and there is evidence of considerable manipulation of the photogravure plate to achieve this. Two images especially conjure up the illusory qualities of the event, with two of Thomson's sitters acting out the roles taken by their forebears. Lady Louisa Jane Montague-Douglas-Scott (d. 1912) chose to assert her family's age and status by dressing herself as her own ancestor, Elizabeth, Duchess of Buccleuch, and wife of Henry, the 3rd Duke, after a painting in the family collection *(PLATE 113)*.[36] Janetta Manners, Marchioness of Granby, wife of the 7th Duke of Rutland, posed herself in the guise of Isabella, who had married Charles, the 4th Duke, in 1775 *(PLATE 111)*. The photographer for this image was charged with the task of emulating the delicate effects of Richard Cosway's portrait miniature of Mary Isabella, Duchess of Rutland, painted in 1790 or 1791.[37]

Thomson's portrait photography embraced different classes of subject, and different traditions of portrait-making. The fact that he was equally accomplished at the different varieties of the craft of portrait-making testifies to his professionalism when faced with difficult and challenging commissions. But what is perhaps more remarkable is that Thomson was not just a remarkable maker of photographic portraits. He was also a richly talented photographer actively interested in a number of photographic and artistic genres. It is perhaps this versatility which marks John Thomson out as a truly great photographer.

82.

83.

84.

82. *Siamese Noble*. 1866. 252 x 204 mm.
Modern albumen print from wet-collodion negative. National Library of Scotland/Wellcome Institute Library, London

83. *Prime Minister in 1865, the late Kralahom*. 1865. 252 x 203 mm.
Modern albumen print from wet-collodion negative. National Library of Scotland/Wellcome Institute Library, London

84. *Siamese Lady of Title, Wife of the Prime Minister*. 1866. 254 x 203 mm.
Modern albumen print from wet-collodion negative. National Library of Scotland/Wellcome Institute Library, London

85.

85. *The late 1st king of Siam*. 1866. 254 x 203 mm.
Modern albumen print from wet-collodion negative. National Library of Scotland/Wellcome Institute Library, London

86.

86. *H.R.H. the King of Siam*, 1865. 252 x 202 mm.
Modern albumen print from wet-collodion negative. National Library of Scotland/Wellcome Institute Library, London

87.

87. *Prince of Kung.* 1872. 254 x 204 mm.
Modern albumen print from wet-collodion negative. National Library of Scotland/Wellcome Institute Library, London

88.

88. *Prince Kung* 1872. 254 x 204 mm.
Modern albumen print from wet-collodion negative. National Library of Scotland/Wellcome Institute Library, London

89.

90.

91.

89. *Yung Tajin, Diplomat. c.* 1871–72. 254 x 204 mm.
Modern albumen print from wet-collodion negative. National Library of Scotland/Wellcome Institute Library, London

90. *Shen-kwe-fen. c.* 1871–72. 254 x 204 mm.
Modern albumen print from wet-collodion negative. National Library of Scotland/Wellcome Institute Library, London

91. *Mandarin and his son. c.* 1870. 304 x 254 mm.
Modern albumen print from wet-collodion negative. National Library of Scotland/Wellcome Institute Library, London

92.

93.

92. *Chinese Mandarins. c.* 1870. 302 x 252 mm.
Modern albumen print from wet-collodion negative. National Library of Scotland/Wellcome Institute Library, London

93. *Mandarin of the Late Empire, China. c.* 1870. 304 x 252 mm.
Modern albumen print from wet-collodion negative. National Library of Scotland/Wellcome Institute Library, London

127

94.

94. *Manchu Bride. c.* 1871. 102 x 99 mm.
Modern albumen print from wet-collodion negative. National Library of Scotland/Wellcome Institute Library, London

95. *Manchu woman. c.* 1871. 104 x 102 mm.
Modern albumen print from wet-collodion negative. National Library of Scotland/Wellcome Institute Library, London

96. *Manchu woman. c.* 1871. 101 x 101 mm.
Modern albumen print from wet-collodion negative. National Library of Scotland/Wellcome Institute Library, London

97. Old Woman, Canton. *c.* 1868. 216 x 165 mm.
Modern albumen print from wet-collodion negative. National Library of Scotland/Wellcome Institute Library, London

98. *Selling Bread*. 1878. 108 x 78 mm.
Woodburytype. National Library of Scotland

99.

99. *Chinese Boatwoman. c.* 1868-1871. 103 x 201 mm.
Modern albumen stereograph from wet-collodion negative. National Library of Scotland/Wellcome Institute Library, London

100.

101.

100. *Tartar Soldiers.* *c.* 1868–70. 202 x 262 mm.
Collotype. National Library of Scotland

101. *Buddhist Monks.* *c.* 1870–71. 227 x 290 mm.
Carbon Print. National Museum of Photography, Film, and Television

102.

103.

102. *Native Group, Nicosia*. 1878. 126 x 190 mm.
Modern albumen print from wet-collodion negative. National Library of Scotland/Wellcome Institute Library, London

103. *Group at Avgoru*. 1878. 126 x 190 mm.
Modern albumen print from wet-collodion negative. National Library of Scotland/Wellcome Institute Library, London

104.

105.

104. *Queen Victoria.* 1887. 163 x 119 mm.
Modern silver print from wet-collodion negative. Royal Photographic Collection, Windsor Castle.

105. *Queen Victoria with two Grand-daughters,*
Princess Margaret of Connaught and Princess Alice of Albany 1887. 481 x 360 mm.
Platinum print with overpainting. Royal Photographic Collection, Windsor Castle.

106.

107.

106. *Rosario Alba.* 1893 234 x 159 mm.
Albumen print. Royal Photographic Collection, Windsor Castle

107. *The Duke of Rutland.* 1889. 93 x 141 mm.
Albumen print. Royal Photographic Collection, Windsor Castle

108.

108. *Admiral A. H. Markham.* 1900. 225 x 140 mm.
Platinum Print. Royal Geographical Society

109. *Henry Walter Bates. c.* 1892. 129 x 92 mm.
Photogravure. National Library of Scotland

110.

111.

112.

113.

110. *Lady Katherine Scott as Marie Stuart*. 1897. 185 x 128 mm.
Photogravure. National Library of Scotland

111. *The Marchioness of Granby as Mary Isabella Duchess of Rutland after Cosway*. 1897. 166 x 105 mm.
Photogravure. National Library of Scotland

112. *Lady Sarah Wilson as Madame de Pompadour*. 1897. 184 x 128 mm.
Photogravure. National Library of Scotland

113. *Duchess of Buccleuch as Elizabeth, Duchess of Buccleuch*. 1897. 186 x 125 mm.
Photogravure. National Library of Scotland

114. *Miss Goelet as Scheherezäde*. 1897. 143 x 165 mm.
Photogravure. National Library of Scotland

CHAPTER 6

MAN AND NATURE

... there is one picture of a forest scene which struck us as rivalling some of the grandest Highland scenery of MacCulloch.

ANON*

The motivating forces behind Thomson's landscape photography were both practical and idealistic. He knew that the armchair travellers of Victorian Britain had a ready appetite for picturesque 'views', 'scenes', and 'bits' of the Orient; but he was far from a picture-making machine, relentlessly churning out stock views for the memento albums of westerners with an interest in the East. Not for him were the 'distinct but lifeless charts of the mechanical proportions of nature' produced by other photographers of landscape;[1] for behind his photography was an essentially artistic motivation which dictated not only his choice of subject matter, but the way in which he portrayed the land.

This personal response was born of the same guiding spirit that influenced his photography of the ancient architectural structures of Cambodia and China, and the strong hold which this romantic view of nature had over his landscape photography had as much to do with received notions of the picturesque as with the nature of the physical geography of Asia.

The direct influence of other picture makers on Thomson's work is hard to establish, but we do know that he had exhibited work alongside that of photographers such as Francis Bedford and Francis Frith,[2] and admired the work of the Chinese photographer Afong Lai (see below pp. 142–44). He also thought the photographs taken in Java by Walter Woodbury worthy of emulation.[3] The influence of contemporary painters is even harder to determine, but it is certainly possible to discern in his response to the picturesque a debt to the broad tradition of British pictorial landscape art with its origins in the eighteenth century. This tradition centred on the search for the ideal form of nature. In the eighteenth century, British artists began to travel around Britain and Europe on this quest, sketching and painting what they began to term the 'picturesque'. Through this process, the portrayal of nature in art underwent a transformation, particularly within the context of compositions of the ideal landscape, which were heavily influenced by French artists of the previous century such as Claude and Poussin.[4] Gradually, as this new interest in nature and the landscape took hold, the notion of the sublime entered into the artistic formula, as an important constituent of the picturesque, where the dangerous elements of nature became the focus of artistic attention.

*Anon, 'Mr Thomson's Illustrations of China', *North China Herald and Supreme Court Consular Gazette* (11 January, 1872), referring to PLATE 122.

But Thomson's own landscape vision did not simply translate the tradition of the artistic traveller into a new, exotic, oriental sphere of activity. The camera itself helped to change the way in which the landscape was portrayed, and Thomson's contribution was to help the transition from the distanced, largely objective recording of the natural order during the wet-collodion era, to the self-consciously artistic and subjective photography of the pictorialist movement of the turn of the century. Thomson held that photography had an obligation to do more than passively record. He felt that the photographer had to act as an artist both before and after the camera has played its part, and in this sense he can be seen as bridging the gap between the artistic amateurs of photography's first two decades, and innovative expressionists like Emerson, Coburn, and Stieglitz. This can be seen best in work like 'Hoi-How, The Proposed New Treaty Port, Island of Hainan' (PLATE *115*), which reveals almost nothing of the landscape itself, relying entirely on the pictorial effects achieved by reducing the image to a long rectangle, and emphasising the dominance of the sky over the landscape of this coastal region. The resulting image, almost abstract in its reduction of form to strips of black and white, echoes the work of John Beasley Greene[5] from an earlier era, and pre-empts some of Peter Henry Emerson's Norfolk landscapes.[6]

Several other factors influenced this aspect of his picture making. In common with other landscape artists working in the 1860s and 1870s, the progress of industrialisation and urbanisation, and the inevitable human consequences that followed in their wake, created a renewed fascination with nature. To some extent Thomson's Chinese landscape photographs answered this quest for the purity, beauty, and majesty of the natural world, the oriental locations heightening the experience of viewing his work from the perspective of the Victorian city.

Whereas affinities exist between Thomson's aesthetic response to the ancient ruins and structures of the Far East and those of other European photographers who dealt with similar subjects, Thomson's treatment of the landscape differed in several ways from that of his contemporaries. The great photographer of British India, Samuel Bourne, for example, often looked for similarities between the Indian and European landscape, such as the Alpine feel to 'View in Wanga Valley' (PLATE *116*), and where they could not be found in nature, he sought them in man-made structures, as in his image of the colonial town of Simla (PLATE *117*), with its neo-gothic Church building dominating the view.[7] Other British photographers working outside Europe at this time were often part of official expeditions, and their work frequently had a particular focus. James MacDonald's photographs taken in the near East in the 1860s and early 1870s, like 'Convent of St Katherine' (PLATE *118*), and 'Hermitage, Wády Ed Deir' (PLATE *119*), for example, examined the impact of classical and early Christian settlements on the landscape of Palestine and Sinai.[8] Thomson, unlike MacDonald and other photographers working for official purposes, had free reign to explore his own vision of China.

Long before that of the west, Chinese painting had developed a remarkably accomplished landscape tradition, and it remained the pre-eminent subject in Chinese art until the end of the Qing dynasty (1911). There is a sense in which Thomson's work echoes some of the major themes of this native pictorial aesthetic. The emphasis placed by Confucianism on the importance of 'mountains and water' (Shan-shui) in the portrayal of the beauty of landscape can be seen in much of his work. Rivers are a recurring focus, although his interest in hills and mountains may also owe something to the land of his birth (a constant source of comparison in his writing). The verdant mountains of southern China, bathed in the soft clouds of its sympathetic climate, were a consistent theme in the Chinese landscape tradition, and despite the technical difficulties associated with wet-plate photography in such conditions, much of Thomson's work here bears comparison with the softness of Chinese scroll-painting. His interest in the relationship between man and nature also finds its precursors in the often touching portrayal of the connection between man and his environment entrenched in Chinese art by the philosophical beliefs of Confucianism and Taoism. The fact that Thomson collected early Chinese scroll-paintings adds weight to the probable influence of native artistic traditions on this aspect of his photography.[9]

Early Landscape Work

Although Thomson's photographic response to the landscape of Asia does not feature prominently in his early work (where his interests seem to have been primarily the people and their cities, towns, and buildings), occasionally a glimpse of the qualities which were to shine so eloquently from his later output can be discerned. The photograph 'Palmyra Palms' *(Plate 120)*, which he photographed in Siam in 1865, for instance, is almost filled with a dense array of pattern and texture formed by the long grasses at the foot of the image and the explosion of foliage at the top of the trees themselves. The figure seen climbing one of the trees to the left of the image takes on an almost incidental role, where other, more conventional photographers at this time might have afforded it a greater status within the composition. Thomson was to return to the use of pattern and texture as a device in later work such as 'Mountain Pass on the Island of Formosa' *(Plate 121)*.

The temperate terrain of southern China, easily accessible from the ports and cities on the coast, had attracted a number of western artists, eager to draw or paint the landscape, buildings, and people of this beautiful region of the 'Flowery Land'. Talented artists like George Chinnery painted and sketched beautiful and often charming scenes of this region, although he, and other artists like him, rarely penetrated to the interior.[10] Thomson's first major journey on mainland China therefore began to break new ground, as it followed a route up the north branch of the Pearl River.

The trip took him where 'the scenery changes from cultivated lowland, with its farm houses and villages, to the rugged and mountainous, with picturesque hamlets scattered among the bamboo brakes',[11] and he likened the area to the Scottish Lowlands.[12] The journey took in the monastery of Feilaisi, and he then travelled further up river to the Qingyuan pass, to the Boluohang Temple, and, finally, to the Grotto of Guanyu, some 200 miles above Canton. The images taken on this journey, although blighted to some extent by the difficult weather conditions (haze and mist did not suit the collodion process), reveal a pastoral vision of the gentle, fertile landscape which became more dramatic the further north he travelled. Thus, images like 'North Branch of the Pearl River' *(Plate 122)* and 'Looking North From the Pau-Lo-Hang Temple' *(Plate 123)* were 'intended to give some idea of the grandeur of the inland scenery. The vast plain covered with the graceful bamboo or the luxurious green of the paddy fields, and studded with picturesque villages, contrasted abruptly with the background of 'Crags knolls and mounds confusedly hurled/The fragments of an earlier world' (a literary reference to the sublime qualities of the landscape, quoted by Thomson to reinforce his visual depiction).[13] The Chinese word which is printed alongside the English caption to this latter image translates as 'painting', a term which is used here to suggest an artistic approach, and one which conforms to the overall style of the image's presentation, which has been vignetted to add to its aesthetic impact. The seated figure resting among the roots of a tree in 'Forest in Formosa' *(PLATE 124)* also rests literally in the folds of nature, and here the inherent aesthetic qualities of the image have been heightened by Thomson's choice of the platinum process in one surviving print (presented to the Royal Geographical Society in 1904). The pastoral theme dominated Thomson's photography at this time, and is seen in images like 'An Up-Country Bridge' *(PLATE 125)*, and in particular, 'Road to the Village of Wong Tong' *(PLATE 126)*. Here, shaded by the massive branches of an old tree, a village path winds its way along a stream towards a distant village, the buildings of which can be glimpsed behind the dense foliage which adds to the layer of textures which the collodion process records in such precise detail. The figure of a child, posed at mid-point on the path, leads the eye to the very centre of the image, along the path itself; the eye is then given the freedom to roam to either side, taking in the 'venerable trees' which Thomson found 'nestling in the most beautiful and secluded spots'.[14] It is a scene displaying the partnership between man and nature: although the figure is dwarfed by the massive branches of the tree, here nature has not overpowered man, but the path, evidence of man's efforts over a long period of time, has become an integral part of the landscape itself.

FUZHAU

By the time his travels brought him to the thriving city of Fuzhau, a little way up the River Min from the south China coast, John Thomson had developed and tuned his photographic aesthetic to respond to the magnificence of the landscape more acutely than before. This engagement of a kind of 'higher gear' in his photography was the result of the previous year's travels through parts of southern China, during the course of which he seems to have regained not only his taste for travel, but the various skills which went hand-in-hand with journeys of this kind: logistical, social, linguistic, and organisational. With the practicalities of travelling taking up less of his time and mental energy, he found greater opportunity to concentrate on taking photographs. All photographers, faced with a fresh location, unfamiliar conditions of light, terrain, and climate, require time to attune themselves technically and aesthetically to meet the demands of the new environment and situations. By the time he reached Fujian province and the city of Fuzhau, he had had a year of travelling under his belt, and his eye had become used to 'seeing China'.

But this process of experience and adjustment may not have been the only factor which helped to produce a corpus of landscape photographs that rivals that of any travel photographer in the nineteenth century. To some extent the landscape here had acquired a kind of visual grammar of its own, thanks to the attentions of visiting artists and photographers, in particular a native Chinese photographer called Afong Lai, attracted to the area not only by the great beauty of the scenery, but also by the proximity of western traders requiring visual records of their stay in one of China's most exquisite regions. John Thomson was well aware of the work of Afong Lai, who from 1859 had a commercial studio in Hong Kong which was very close to Thomson's, on Queen's Road Central,[15] and which maintained a thriving business throughout the latter half of the nineteenth century, and well into the twentieth.[16] Thomson had occasion to praise his work in an article published in England in 1872, and indicated a familiarity with his photography: 'There is one Chinaman living in Hong Kong, of the name of Afong, who has exquisite taste', he eulogised, concluding that the photographer in question was 'an exception to the general run of his countrymen'.[17] Somewhat later, Thomson recalled Afong Lai as 'a plump and good-natured son of Han, a man of civilised taste, and imbued with a wonderful appreciation of art ... judging from his portfolio of photographs he must be an ardent admirer of nature; for some of his pictures, besides being extremely well executed, are remarkable for their artistic choice of position'.[18]

Afong Lai had visited Fuzhau in 1869 and again in 1870, and had taken a series of photographs from which he produced albumen prints intended for sale to the British merchants, bankers and consular officials that he was evidently working for. These images were produced as a commercial enterprise (they have printed captions, indicating that they were intended for a number of customers), and a typical album of this material survives in the National Galleries of Scotland, no doubt brought back by one of the 'Scotch Sirs and Scotchmen' who were the subject of one of the images in this album.[19] His stay (we do not know how long he was there) produced a large body of work, the series being numbered up to 118. The work has some similarities to Thomson's output whilst in Fuzhau. Scenes in the city, such as the Fives' Court and the Foreign Settlement, were chosen by both photographers not on aesthetic grounds, but because the images would have been saleable, as mementos. But subject matter of greater aesthetic interest is also found in common between the two bodies of work. Both men travelled up the Yuen-foo branch of the Min, and climbed the hills to visit the Yuen-foo monastery, and both travelled far up river to visit the tea-plantations just below Yenping. But despite the similarities in subject matter, the resulting images themselves reveal marked differences in approach, and betray two very different responses to the landscape. Although Afong Lai's photographs should be regarded as a highly accomplished, beautiful collection of images, they lack the consistent, intense vision that the Thomson series displays, particularly those images which he selected for inclusion in *Foochow and the River Min*, and which were printed for that book by the carbon process.

Bankers' Glen was a popular haunt for the westerners living in Fuzhau, and it is not surprising that it should form the subject of photographs by both Thomson and Afong Lai. Both men sought to focus on the inherent strength of the landscape at the glen's entrance, showing the rocks as if they were the spine of some great animal. In 'Banker's Glen, River Min' (PLATE 127), Thomson appears to have climbed some way up the mountain-side in order to isolate the rock formation from its wider context, whereas Afong Lai, in 'Entrance to the Bankers' Glen, view to the left looking up Yuen-foo River' *(PLATE 128)*, has chosen a more distant viewpoint, positioning himself to include a group of trees in order to provide scale. The movement of the trees has registered in the long exposure time, giving both a sense of the reality of the scene, and of the power of natural forces. Thomson travelled further up the glen, and in one image from this series *(PLATE 129)* the complex of patterns formed by the trees and bracken is translated into a richly textured photographic image, the collodion process allowing this wealth of detail to register in full. The dappling of the light on the branches of the trees adds to the quiet, pastoral nature of this image. Both photographers have conformed to a general Taoist principle in visual portrayal, concentrating on what the Chinese traditions and beliefs regarded as sacred manifestations of the landscape: mountains. The human presence is reduced to a minimum, in acknowledgement of the subservience of man to the spiritual power of the mountain.[20]

Several photographers are known to have taken photographs of a religious building known as 'The Island Temple', and which was the subject of one of Thomson's most eloquent lyrical studies: 'The Island Pagoda' *(PLATE 130)*. Afong Lai's 'View of Island Temple' *(PLATE 131)* takes a low viewpoint for the same scene, but looks at the subject side-on, in strong, direct light, giving the temple a somewhat regular appearance, although mirrored in the water. This same viewpoint was favoured by other photographers, such as Tung Hing, who also visited the area in the 1860s and 1870s.[21] The Island Temple was not universally regarded as picturesque, however. One Scottish visitor to the area, for instance, Dr J. Ivor Murray, who stayed in Fuzhau in 1854, did not find it especially remarkable.[22] But if Thomson saw the Temple in a different way, what raised his vision above the commonplace? His chosen viewpoint was not quite so low down, or as close to the surface of the river as Afong's, and he retreated slightly so as to create a space in which the Island appears to exist in isolation. The stillness of the water (securing this image on what was a busy stretch of one of China's great rivers must have involved considerable patience) has created a reflection which is not quite perfect enough to suggest that the temple is resting on a sheet of glass, but which conveys the impression that the island is itself a silent, mysterious passenger on the waterway. The climate, which could often be hazy and difficult for taking pictures, has helped the photographer by obliterating the surrounding hills, and the image, of near-perfect serenity, has echoes of the Buddhist-inspired landscape art produced by Japanese and Chinese artists. In fact, the temple could as well be in the clouds, floating towards a celestial harbour, and the tree even appears to be a kind of natural sail: imagery entirely appropriate for a shrine dedicated by the river's boating population to the 'Queen of Heaven'.[23]

This mystical quality is also achieved by another photograph, again one that is redolent with religious imagery, entitled 'The Altar of Heaven' *(PLATE 132)*. The scene is one of high drama: a religious site located in the middle of an open space, perched on a hill-top outside Fuzhau. Here, at the scene of religious worship, were enacted rites and sequences of behaviour that remained a mystery in the west to all but a few of the academic *cognoscenti*. The reader-viewer of this image is presented with mystery in a double sense: in that the rites practised at the site can be conceived as directed towards the spiritual unknown; and in the sense that the very practices themselves were not fully understood by the intended audience. But as the viewpoint stretches out to encompass the wider landscape, the fertile plain, and the hills and fields in the distance joining the cloud-laden sky, we are encouraged to experience the mystery of nature itself, a beauty that cannot be known in the ordinary sense, but which if it is properly to be appreciated, must be experienced, like the religion practised at the 'Altar of Heaven'.

Man and Nature

A number of the photographs taken at this time revolve around the river Min and its tributaries, reflecting the importance of this artery both in terms of the commercial life of the region and, more importantly, in the way it affected the landscape. The tea trade which relied on the river as a means of efficient transportation helped to provide a context in which man's experience of nature, in Thomson's mind, was materially transformed. He did not look upon the river as an arena for man's struggle with the forces of nature. He knew from personal experience that the rapids could be extremely dangerous, as he attempted to show, both in a formal, but strikingly modern-looking view of the river, 'Rapids, Min River' *(PLATE 133)*, and in an implied way in a 'picturesque' study of one of the rapid boats, 'Shui-Kau Rapid Boat' *(PLATE 134)*. But in the image 'Pine Raft, Min River' *(PLATE 135)* Thomson has transformed what must have been a common occurrence into a moment where man and nature are seen functioning in tandem. The same serenity that we find in the image 'A Reach of the Min' *(PLATE 137)*, where man's engagement with nature is purely one of contemplation and appreciation, is repeated in the image 'Yuan-fu Rapid' *(PLATE 136)*. Occasionally Thomson presents a view of nature where man takes a dominant role. Two images in particular present this different emphasis. 'Rocks in the Rapids' *(PLATE 138)* is a particularly powerful photograph, where the human presence is signified by the silhouette of a figure carrying a pole, standing in a symbolically commanding position on top of the mass of rocks, which almost fill the frame. Thomson's chosen viewpoint provides a further dynamic, as the diagonals created by the angle of the pole and the slope of the distant mountain meet to form the apex of an inverted triangle, the downward movement of which continues through the image, dividing it, but investing the figure with even greater power. Conversely, in the image 'Foochow City' *(PLATE 139)*, Thomson has changed his mind. Here the reflective onlooker is dwarfed by a gigantic boulder, which almost seems ready to crush the figure. If nature, in the guise of the rock, broods over Fuzhau, then man can only do so under its umbrella.

The attitude of reverence and contemplation which man should properly direct towards the great waterways of nature, whilst forming a central part of the Chinese landscape aesthetic, seems also to have interlocked with Thomson's own response, as his depiction of this subject matter outside of the Fuzhau region continued to explore similar themes. In the image 'A Canton Junk' *(PLATE 140)*, the sheer 'photographicality' of the scene transcends any purely picturesque qualities: the movement of the water has been turned by the long exposure time into an almost solid mass, upon which the boats and rocks seem to rest, watched only by the two native figures, silent and still in their appreciation. The two figures in 'Lan-long Valley, Formosa' *(PLATE 141)* seem also to be fixed in contemplation, but this time the object of their fascination appears to be their own reflection in the water. The quietness of the river as a means of transport is again highlighted in 'Tam-Shui, Walled Town Seen from an Eminence' *(PLATE 142)*. But occasionally Thomson's photographic vision leaps forward dramatically in time, heralding an essentially twentieth-century aesthetic. In 'Right Bank of the Lakoli River, Formosa' *(PLATE 143)* we have a scene of almost perfect tranquillity, the waterway observed by two onlookers in the morning stillness. But the photographer's eye for pattern and texture has transformed this scene into an essay in tonal gradation, working outwards from the central band formed by the boulders. The abstraction inherent in nature is here called upon by Thomson to aid his depiction of the landscape, an approach destined to become a mainstay of the great American photographers of the mid-twentieth century, like Edward Weston, Minor White, and Ansel Adams (1902–84), whose 'Mount Williamson, Sierra Nevada, from Manzanar' (1945) utilises the same artistic devices.[24]

Thomson was not obsessed with the 'singular' in nature, but often singled out the ordinary for special appreciation.[25] Two of the images he took whilst journeying around the island of Cyprus in 1878, for example, treat very mundane aspects of man's encounter with nature and the land, but these images also operate on a higher level, and in the image 'A Mountain Path, near Mount Troodos' *(PLATE 144)* the photographer shows the timeless problems of mobility around the island for a people whom he clearly regarded almost as museum pieces – their ways of life quaintly preserved by their physical and cultural remoteness. British rule over the island, the photograph is saying, will bring with it all the benefits of civilisation and Empire, and will help, therefore, to 'improve' this way of life. The subject matter tackled by Thomson in 'The Pines of Olympus (Troodos)' *(PLATE 145)* deals with a deeper problem, and one that goes to the heart of the western artistic engagement with the landscape. The deforestation of the ancient woodlands on the Cypriot mountains is dealt with here in much the same way as that in which the social problems of London were tackled in *Street Life*. Thomson's own expedition up Mount Olympus, albeit in terrible weather,[26] revealed the depletion of the 'green mantle of noble trees' by the 'ruthless hands of rough mountaineers'.[27] This destruction took place in order to extract resin and pitch from the trees, which the loggers were able to sell at local markets, but the hills were being drastically denuded at the time of Thomson's visit, and he called for 'stringent laws for their preservation'.[28] 'The Pines of Olympus' shows us the ancient trees themselves, with the shape of the twisted trunk of one reflected in the stooping figure of Thomson's guide. But the scene is also littered with the stumps and remnants of trees which have succumbed to the axe, and Thomson's figure, examining the trunk of a recent victim, appears like a policeman crouched over a victim, or a doctor tending a patient. Thomson's reaction seems at first glance surprisingly modern. But his deep attachment to the forest was shared by many European writers and artists, and Thomson's views are in fact another manifestation of what is a deep-rooted response to the ancient European woodlands.[29]

The Wu-Shan Gorge

Thomson's epic voyage from Shanghai up the Yangzi river was probably the longest photographic journey he ever made.[30] The most dramatic part of it took place in the stretch north of the city of Yichang, where the terrain changes markedly from relatively open countryside to a region of hills and mountains. 'Here the river narrows from half a mile to a few hundred yards across, and pours through the rocky defile with a velocity that makes it difficult to enter', wrote Thomson.[31] His interests here ranged from the purely scientific to the practical. The somewhat precarious nature of human existence certainly caught his attention in 'City of Kwei, Upper Yangtze' *(PLATE 146)*. The age of the stones also fascinated Thomson; but most of all the sheer scale of the mountains, and the power of the natural forces that formed the gorge, had a profound affect:

> The further we entered the gorges the more desolate and dark became the scene, the narrow barren defile presenting a striking contrast to the wide cultivated plains, through which we had been making our way from the sea, for more than 1,000 miles.[32]

The grandeur of the landscape, whilst not totally unexpected on Thomson's part, nevertheless assailed his visual sense at several key points on the journey. Perhaps the most dramatic scene he photographed was that taken at the mouth of the Wushan Gorge. The conditions were ideal:

> The river here was perfectly placid, and the view which met our gaze at the mouth of the gorge was perhaps the finest of the kind that we had encountered. The mountains rose in confused masses to a great altitude, while the most distant peak at the extremity of the reach resembled a cut sapphire, its snow lines sparkling in the sun like the gleams of light on the facets of a gem. The other cliffs and precipices gradually deepened in hue until they reached the bold lights and shadows of the rocky foreground.[33]

The image taken at this time, known principally from the collotype reproduction in *Illustrations of China*, presents a remarkable combination of visual effects and devices to convey this grandeur *(PLATE 147)*. Thomson chose a viewpoint which produced an aerial perspective, where the mountains disappear into the distance in a series of layers, each one registering a different tone, getting progressively lighter the further from the photographer. The viewpoint allowed the effects of this tonal layering to be combined with a geometric overlay created by the patterns formed by the diagonal edges of the mountain-ridges. This abstraction is heightened by the mirroring created by the unusually still waters of the gorge itself. This careful construction leads the viewer straight to the centre of the image, where a way through the confusion can just be discerned, the viewer taking on the role of navigator through the picture. The tranquillity of the scene is not disturbed by a single reference to man, but the very act of photographing, and the parallel act of viewing the picture, implies human involvement.

The romanticism of the natural world was alive to Thomson in the same way that the ruins of the Cambodian jungle captured his imagination. The role of nature was central to both. 'The feeling, the ideality, the soul with which all nature is flooded'[34] were all of central importance to Thomson, and the formal topographic forms of the landscape, together with the effects of light, combined to make the crucial elements of his photography of the land. His visual appreciation did not derive power from a passive appreciation of the form of the landscape, but from the feelings generated by his *experience* of the landscape itself. This aspect of his photography therefore rests on man's involvement with, and response to, nature; a connection which unites his approach with those of the great landscape photographers of the twentieth century.

115. *Hoi-How, The Proposed Treaty Port, Island of Hainan. c.* 1868–71. 75 x 315 mm.
Collotype. National Library of Scotland

149

116.

117.

118.

119.

116. Samuel Bourne, *View in Wanga Valley. c.* 1863–64. 283 x 240 mm.
Albumen Print. National Library of Scotland

117. Samuel Bourne, *Simla. c.* 1863–64. 237 x 290 mm.
Albumen Print. National Library of Scotland

118. James MacDonald, *Convent of St Katherine.* 1868. 170 x 214 mm.
Albumen Print. National Library of Scotland

119. James MacDonald, *Hermitage, Wády Ed Deir.* 1868. 170 x 210 mm.
Albumen Print. National Library of Scotland

120.

120. *Palmyra Palms, Siam.* 1865. 250 x 204 mm.
Modern albumen print from wet-collodion negative. National Library of Scotland/Wellcome Institute Library, London

121.

122.

121. *Mountain Pass on the Island of Formosa.* 1871. 306 x 253 mm.
Collotype. National Library of Scotland

122. *North Branch of the Pearl River. c.* 1869-70. 255 x 222 mm.
Modern albumen print from wet-collodion negative. National Library of Scotland/Wellcome Institute Library, London

123.

124.

123. *Looking North from the Pau-Lo-Hang Temple. c. 1869–70. 167 x 236 mm.*
Albumen Print. National Library of Scotland

124. *Forest in Formosa. 1871. 220 x 290 mm.*
Platinum Print. Royal Geographical Society

125.

126.

125. *An Up-Country Bridge. c.* 1870–71. 154 x 230 mm.
Albumen Print. National Library of Scotland

126. *Road to the Village of Wong Tong. c.* 1869–70. 202 x 253 mm.
Modern albumen print from wet-collodion negative. National Library of Scotland/Wellcome Institute Library, London

127.

128.

129.

127. *Bankers' Glen, River Min. c.* 1870–71. 303 x 255 mm.
Modern albumen print from wet-collodion negative. National Library of Scotland/Wellcome Institute Library, London

128. Afong Lai, *Entrance to the Bankers' Glen, view to the left looking up Yuen-foo river. c.* 1869-70. 227 x 272 mm.
Albumen Print. National Galleries of Scotland

129. *Banker's Glen. c.* 1870–71. 302 x 238 mm.
Carbon Print. National Museum of Photography, Film, and Television

130.

131.

130. *Island Pagoda. c.* 1870–71. 253 x 304 mm.
Modern albumen print from wet-collodion negative. National Library of Scotland/Wellcome Institute Library, London

131. Afong Lai, *View of Island Temple (above Upper Bridge Foochow) c.* 1868–70. 175 x 234 mm.
Albumen print. National Galleries of Scotland

132.

132. *The Altar of Heaven. c.* 1870–71. 236 x 300 mm.
Carbon Print. National Museum of Photography, Film, and Television

133.

134.

133. *Rapids, Min River. c.* 1870–71. 256 x 300 mm.
Modern albumen print from wet-collodion negative. National Library of Scotland/Wellcome Institute Library, London

134. *Shui-Kau Rapid Boat. c.* 1870–71. 252 x 305 mm.
Modern albumen print from wet-collodion negative. National Library of Scotland/Wellcome Institute Library, London

135.

135. *Pine Raft, Min River. c.* 1870–71. 255 x 305 mm.
Modern albumen print from wet-collodion negative. National Library of Scotland/Wellcome Institute Library, London

136.

137.

136. *Yuan-fu Rapid. c.* 1870–71. 253 x 303 mm.
Modern albumen print from wet-collodion negative. National Library of Scotland/Wellcome Institute Library, London

137. *A Reach of the Min. c.* 1870–71. 270 x 235 mm.
Carbon Print. National Museum of Photography, Film, and Television

138.

139.

138. *Rocks in the Rapids. c.* 1870–71. 242 x 294 mm.
Carbon Print. National Museum of Photography, Film, and Television

139. *Foochow City. c.* 1870–71. 222 x 292 mm.
Carbon Print. National Museum of Photography, Film, and Television

140.

140. *A Canton Junk. c.* 1868–71. 145 x 292 mm.
Collotype. National Library of Scotland

141.

142.

141. *Lan-long Valley, Formosa.* 1871. 252 x 300 mm.
Modern albumen print from wet-collodion negative. National Library of Scotland/Wellcome Institute Library, London

142. *Tam-Shui, Walled Town Seen from an Eminence.* 1872. 250 x 303 mm.
Modern albumen print from wet-collodion negative. National Library of Scotland/Wellcome Institute Library, London

143. *Right Bank of Lakoli River, Formosa.* 1871. 254 x 304 mm.
Modern albumen print from wet-collodion negative. National Library of Scotland/Wellcome Institute Library, London

144.

145.

146.

144. *Mountain Path, Near Mount Troodos*. 1878. 110 x 175 mm.
Woodburytype. National Library of Scotland

145. *The Pines of Olympus*. 1878. 115 x 180 mm.
Woodburytype. National Library of Scotland

146. *City of Kwei, Upper Yangtze*. 1872. 390 x 490 mm.
Gelatin Silver Print. Royal Geographical Society

147.

147. *Wu-Shan Gorge.* 1872. 208 x 280 mm.
Collotype. National Library of Scotland

149.

149. *Photography on the Common. c.* 1876–77. 57 x 84 mm.
Woodburytype. National Library of Scotland

Chapter 7

John Thomson and Photography

Michael Gray

What occult science confers on this mystic apparatus the power of picturing objects placed before it, producing an image so perfect that alike no point of beauty, no spot or blemish, escapes its microscopic observation?

The 'look' of a photograph is the result of both aesthetic and technical factors. The aesthetic sensibilities of the photographer may be the crucial determinants in the entire creative process, but even the most innovative photographer has to work within the technical constraints imposed by the materials and methods available to him. In this respect, Thomson was no exception. Moreover, for a photographer like Thomson, who actively marketed his work through publication, technical constraints were not confined to his photographic procedures, since at the very end of the creative process came the actions of the publishers and printers who manipulated the photographic images to suit the chosen means of reproduction. This chapter examines both of these aspects of Thomson's photographic work – the photographic processes he used to create his images, and the methods he and his publishers chose to reproduce them in printed publications – and sets both in the context of the development of photography and of the photographically-illustrated book during Thomson's lifetime.

For over 150 years – from the first discoveries of William Henry Fox Talbot in the 1830s to the dawning of the electronic age – the essential components of photography have remained unchanged. Light-sensitive chemicals on a support (normally paper, glass, or film) are exposed to light (normally in a camera). After further chemical development this creates a negative image (the 'negative') which can later be used to replicate an infinite number of positive prints. These prints are made by shining light through the negative onto a sheet of paper which has also been coated in light-sensitive chemicals. Development 'brings out' the resultant positive image, which is then made permanent by a further chemical process known as 'fixing'.

The majority of Thomson's photographs – and certainly the bulk of those reproduced and discussed in this book – were created using a photographic process known as the wet-collodion process, the most widely used process of its kind during the second half of the nineteenth century. The wet-collodion process had distinctive characteristics. It was cumbersome in operation, requiring a considerable quantity of chemicals as well as expertise in their handling. The resultant image could be created, however, using shorter exposure times than

---

[*]John Thomson, 'Taking a Photograph' in *Science for All* (London, 1877), p. 258.

previous processes had required, and the negatives created by the wet-collodion process produced images of very high resolution, able to record the finest detail, even in areas of shadow. The Thomson negatives at the Wellcome Institute for the History of Medicine were created using this process, and in order to understand how Thomson created his images, and why they look the way they do, some understanding of the development of the technology of photography during the first fifty years of its history is necessary.

Calotype to Collodion: Paper to Glass

John Thomson took up photography at a time when the medium was undergoing its first vital transformation: when the support for the light-sensitive chemicals used at the negative stage changed from paper to glass. Photography had progressively evolved and improved from its basic form, as first practised by William Henry Fox Talbot and his circle between 1840 and 1847 and subsequently developed in Scotland by Sir David Brewster and his circle over the following decade.[1]

The chemistry of the wet-collodion process was, at its inception, identical to that of its predecessor, the calotype, from which it had evolved, although, superficially, the two appear to be quite different. With the calotype, the light-sensitive chemicals were retained within the upper and surface layers of a sheet of paper which had been sized with gelatin. With the wet-collodion process however, the photo-sensitive chemical layer was formed on a glass support (or 'plate') and appeared to be transparent and virtually invisible, especially after receiving after-treatment with copal varnish.

Both processes used the salts of silver to form their light-sensitive layer. Both utilised potassium iodide to form silver iodide by a process known as double decomposition. Exposed wet in the camera,[2] both were, for a time, 'brought out' by using the same organic developing agent,[3] and they were then fixed with sodium thiosulphate, known as 'hypo'.[4] Manipulation of the process was complicated enough in a purpose-built darkroom, and even more difficult in the field, as Thomson discovered.[5]

Collodion and the Wet-Collodion Process

The collodion process, in its essentials, took the following form. A solution of iodised collodion (that is, pyroxylin containing potassium iodide, previously dissolved in alcohol and ether) was poured centrally onto a glass sheet (or 'plate'),[6] which was rocked and manipulated by the photographer or his assistant until the milky viscous solution had been distributed evenly over it (Fig. 29) and the solution had coagulated but not dried.[7] At this point the glass was smoothly but swiftly immersed in a dipping bath containing silver nitrate, which formed – by a process termed double de-composition[8] – a light-sensitive layer of silver iodide within the transparent milky cellulose membrane. It was absolutely vital that all operations up to and

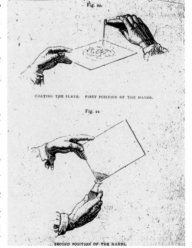

Fig. 29

Coating the Plate.

Wood-engraving (from Gaston Tissandier, *History and Handbook of Photography* (1876)). National Library of Scotland

168

including development be carried out whilst the sensitised plate was still moist. Photographers of Thomson's calibre used a variety or combination of developing agents, carefully selecting and modifying the formulae of each according to the circumstances at the time of the exposure and the contrast range that they wished to secure in their negatives.[9] Because it was almost impossible to control or vary image contrast at the stage of making the positive print – true for both of the two main silver-based printing-out processes used at the time – it was essential to make negatives which, in terms of contrast, matched precisely the inherent tonal characteristics of the printing papers used.[10]

With the minimum of delay, the wet, sensitised plate was then inserted into a single darkslide,[11] placed in the camera back, and exposed for a period of between 5 and 30 seconds. Immediately afterwards, the operator would return to the darkroom or tent (if working in the field), and immerse the plate – sensitive side up – in a tray made from gutta-percha and containing either an ammonio-sulphate of iron, or a

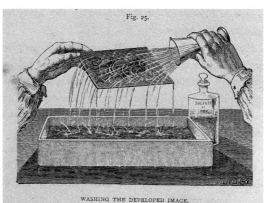

Fig. 25.

WASHING THE DEVELOPED IMAGE.

Fig. 30

Washing the Developed Image.

Wood-engraving (from: Gaston Tissandier, *History and Handbook of Photography* (1876)). National Library of Scotland

pyrogallol developing solution.[12] When the shadow detail had fully been brought out, the plate was given an initial wash (Fig. 30) to clear any residual developer, and was then fixed with a strong solution of potassium cyanide, before being washed again to remove all residual traces. At this point the manipulative processes were not yet fully complete, but the image was sufficiently stable to allow the photographer to delay further treatment until circumstances were more convenient for later manipulation and refinement of the chemical processes. When a photographer, like Thomson, had been working in the field, he or she would have to wait until able to return to a well-equipped and more permanent darkroom facility (Fig. 31) to select, prepare, and utilise a wide range of chemical and mechanical redeveloping techniques, for either reduction or intensification of the negative image. Thomson would undoubtedly have used such techniques in order to enable all his various negative images to obtain the levels of excellence which characterise his work. Given the complexity of the process, Thomson advised amateurs against making their own collodion unless fully acquainted with the chemistry of the operation.[13]

Fig. 31

The Dark Room.

Wood-engraving (from Gaston Tissandier, *History and Handbook of Photography* (1876)). National Library of Scotland

The Discovery of Collodion (or Pyroxylin): an Early Example of Technology Transfer

According to most authorities, Henri Braconnot (1780–1855) was responsible for the discovery, in 1833, of xyloidin,[14] a highly flammable substance produced by the action of nitric acid on starch.

Two years before, he had also synthesised pyrogallic acid,[15] which later became important as a photographic developer.[16] It was, however, Christian Friedrich Schönbein (1799–1868), who was also interested in the properties of nitric acid operating on organic substances, who discovered pyroxylin (also known as guncotton) early in 1846. Böttger, working in Frankfurt am Main, also heard of this preparation, and in August 1846 arrived independently at the same process.[17] Further research into the characteristics and properties of this new compound were explored by a number of other chemists including Knop, Kamarsch, Herren, Millon and Gaudin,[18] who all found that a mixture of potassium or sodium nitrate with sulphuric acid could be used, and that other similar cellulose compounds could assist in synthesising pyroxylin.[19]

Baudin is credited with having discovered, in 1846, that pyroxylin was soluble in alcohol and ether, but he evidently took the work no further. The following year, Flores Domente, working with Louis Ménard and Bégelow, discovered that this cellulose complex took a variety of forms, a number of which were soluble in a solution of ether and alcohol. In 1847, these two chemists discovered a type of pyroxylin which became known as collodion. The importance of this discovery for photography was that when poured onto a sheet of glass it produced a transparent film which could serve as a carrier for the photographic image. This idea was successfully utilised by Gustave Le Gray (1820–82) in France, and by Frederick Scott Archer (1813–57) in England, who both made wet collodion negatives during the period 1849–51, although Archer was the first to publish details, which first appeared in the March 1851 issue of *The Chemist*. Ordinary guncotton is not soluble in an ether-alcohol solution, but Domente and Ménard were able to produce it in a form which was. Neither, however, could analyse or identify the chemical differences between the soluble and the non-soluble forms, but did deduce that the former differed in possessing a higher nitrogen content.

For a time, the wet-collodion process was even more problematical and unreliable in practice than the calotype process, especially when used in the field and at remote locations. In the early 1850s it was an option that few could as yet contemplate or pursue. Nevertheless, there were some remarkable individuals who pressed on regardless, and for every success there were undoubtedly many abysmal failures. As early as 1854 the Reverend William Ellis had returned with images taken in Madagascar.[20] Reports of his achievements at this early date may have encouraged Thomson and his contemporaries seriously to contemplate the possibility of working in more remote and exotic locations, and there were already a number of photographers working in India prior to Thomson's brief visit there, en route for Singapore, in 1861. By the early 1860s, thanks to the efforts of a number of photographic chemists, practising photographers, and other pioneers, the practical aspects of the collodion process had been thoroughly studied and rationalised, making the practical applications of the process in a tropical climate feasible for the first time.

Improvements to wet-collodion after 1860

In 1860, Thomas Sutton reported in the journal *Photographic Notes* that the Photographic Society had 'appointed a Committee to examine samples of photographic collodion, and report upon them, with a view to arriving at a definite formula'.[21] Concern had begun to build up within the photographic community as to the difficulties associated with the 'negative collodion process' and the quality of the resulting negatives.[22] John Thomson would have been well aware of all the theoretical and practical problems relating to the use of the process, particularly when he might already at this point have been contemplating using it in the Far East. Sutton's *Photographic Notes* was probably the most authoritative photographic journal available at this time, and there were a number of outlets in Edinburgh where Thomson might have had access to it. The young Thomson would no doubt have taken note of the concerns and recommendations of the eminent practitioners who reported to the Photographic Society's Committee:

> The reports of Messrs. Delamotte and Fenton are the most valuable on this head, since they have worked on glasses of a large size, viz. 24 inches by 18, and 18 by 15. Their experience is that although the collodion contains too much soluble cotton for these large plates, and occasionally requires thinning down with ether or alcohol in very hot weather, yet that the pyroxyline is nearly of the right kind as regards flowing properties, and may with justice be said to be well calculated to support a smooth and even layer of iodide, without any woolliness[23] or ridges.[24]

In this respect Delamotte and Fenton were referring to samples of collodion supplied to the committee by Hardwich to be used by a group of invited photographers.[25] The committee went on to state that it 'could only pronounce upon that [collodion sample] supplied by Mr Hardwich'.[26] Additional quantities were sent both by Sutton and Mayall, but the committee rather diplomatically deferred by not making any qualitative judgements, stating that 'these gentlemen did not send in collodion in sufficient quantities to admit of it being thoroughly tested'.[27]

Of particular interest to Thomson would have been the comments of Phillip Delamotte concerning the ability of the sensitised plates to record and hold fine shadow detail. 'First with regard to the sensitiveness of the collodion, the opinion of the majority is, that it is unsurpassed.' Francis Frith, in a letter from Cairo dated 1 August 1859, reported to the Committee: 'I find this collodion exceedingly rapid. Three days after iodizing (potassium iodizing solution), it will take a picture with the smallest aperture of the landscape lens (15-ins focus) in five seconds; and I have some hope of getting an interesting series of instantaneous pictures, by using a stop of $1\frac{1}{2}$-in. diameter on the portrait lens ($3\frac{1}{4}$-in. diameter). The lens then covers a $4\frac{1}{2}$-in. plate, with tolerable depth of focus, and I can obtain a sufficiently developed picture with an absolutely instantaneous exposure, sailing boats with ropes sharp, moving figures, &c'.[28]

There is little doubt that Thomson paid serious attention to Frith's observations, taking encouragement from the fact that Frith had been able to operate successfully where temperatures had been above or around 120°F.[29] In a further letter to the Committee, dated 7 August 1859, Frith commented: 'We have just returned after having spent five days in the mud house of an artist at the Pyramids, where we were devoured by thousands of sand-flies; the water very bad, and the heat great. I worked hard and took some fine pictures. Nothing can be more satisfactory than the performances of the collodion. I still get landscapes with the smallest aperture of the view-lens in four seconds, and have taken capital pictures in the heat of the day. I should imagine the temperature in my little tent could not be less than 130°Fht; the developing solution was quite hot'.[30]

It is likely that Thomson would have noted the praise and admiration heaped upon Frith following his return to Britain, and which also heralded his subsequent publication of *Egypt and Palestine Photographed and Described*, a magnificent work which served as a vehicle for displaying his superb photography in the Middle East.[31]

Later in the Report the reactions of Mr Jabez Hughes were sought. He was asked what he considered to be the principal defects in the collodion.[32] He pointed out several shortcomings in the early samples, especially blemishes, and complained of transparent spots with tails, which took the direction of the draining, and showed most distinctly when the collodion was newly iodised.[33] By using simple bromide instead of simple iodide, and developing with (proto)sulphate of iron the spots invariably disappeared. In addition, two or three members of the Committee spoke of narrow black lines like threads in the direction of the dip; these lines sometimes, but not invariably, being remedied by rocking the plate laterally immediately after putting it into the bath.

Many inherent defects are present – to a greater or lesser degree – in almost all wet-collodion negatives, although photographers of the calibre of Frith, Fenton, and Sedgefield, when working the process in the familiar surroundings of their own studio or darkroom spaces, could reliably operate the process and produce virtually flaw-free, perfect negatives. But working in conditions where all is familiar and at hand is a far cry from operating in remote locations, often with chemicals of dubious quality, or which have become contaminated. Black and white spots,[34] 'comets'[35] and flow lines[36] inevitably appeared. Thomson's own negatives bear many of these marks, although the conditions he encountered, and the materials available to him, varied so much that the negatives themselves vary enormously in quality. Other major defects, the result of technical imperfections, can be found in the work of all practitioners of this period. They include irregular clear marks, due to inserting the plate into the silver bath before the collodion has 'set'; a sharp tide-mark across the plate (a bath mark due to the operator failing to dip the plate smoothly into the sensitising solution); and oyster shell markings created by a dirty darkslide or by allowing insufficient time for the silver solution to drain away.

It is interesting to compare Roger Fenton's experiences of working in the hot summer of 1859 with Thomson's. In the opening paragraph of Thomson's article 'Practical Photography in Tropical Regions' he states that 'we have often heard it said "It is almost impossible to obtain fine results in photography where the climate is so hot, the atmosphere so humid and the light so intense"'.[37] During the months of August and September (1859) Fenton revealed that he utilised both the 'iodide and bromide of ammonium and cadmium dissolved in the usual proportions'. He found it to be extremely sensitive and took the dark parts of the picture well. Without doubt this special formulation was found to be particularly useful when working in remote locations. It improved through keeping, even for many weeks, but Fenton found it difficult to use for landscape work in hot weather, because the least overexposure destroyed the intensity, and made the picture thin and flat. A solution of sulphate of iron was used to develop, with mixed pyrogallic acid and nitrate of silver employed as an intensifier. Thomson's use of ammonium bromide, ammonium iodide, cadmium bromide and cadmium iodide shows that he maintained and kept a well-stocked chemical chest which enabled him to adapt and vary his chemical mixes to suit a wide variety of circumstances encountered in the field. His plates were, as a rule, sensitised with bromide and iodide silver halide combinations. It was necessary to utilise bromine compounds with great care to ensure that the proportion of the former never exceeded 20% of the whole.[38] His findings and response to these circumstances mirror very much those of another Scottish photographer, Dr Thomas Keith. It is possible that Thomson had come into contact with Keith in Edinburgh, as Keith, a medical practitioner, was the protégé of the surgeon Sir James Young Simpson, who was a relative of Thomson's friend John Simpson (the cousin of Thomson's future wife). John Simpson worked for Messrs Duncan and Flockhart of North Bridge Edinburgh, who had the licence to make chloroform for Sir James, but who also sold and manufactured photographic chemicals. In any case, Thomas Keith was one of the most serious amateur photographers in Edinburgh in the 1850s.[39]

Practical Photography in Tropical Regions

Thomson was a seasoned photographic traveller. As early as 1866 he boasted of having travelled 1,200 miles in four months, in conditions which averaged 99°F in the shade.[40] Nevertheless, it was extremely difficult – if not virtually impossible – for him, whilst he was in the Far East, to obtain the basic supplies necessary for the successful operation of photography. This can clearly be seen by examining closely the wide varieties of glass sheet he used for the collodion support, more often than not having to recut and re-use glass which had already been utilised for other purposes, including photography. He reported that not even glass acquired from Britain could be relied upon, as it could deteriorate in the long voyage to the East.

Thomson had specific advice to give his fellow professionals about the type of camera to use in the Far East: 'The camera must be strongly made, and the wood the driest, so as not to warp in the hottest sun. It should be portable and of the "Kinnear" form.[41] The only improvement I can suggest on this form of camera is that the sliding front should be capable of being depressed, so that objects below the line of sight may be photographed without altering the level of the camera'.[42] It is not surprising that Thomson would have made such an observation, given some of the unusual circumstances in which he found himself working: locations where judicious and extreme use of the 'falling front' mechanism of a multi-functional view or field camera might be required.

The practice of photography in the tropics could be very dangerous, and Thomson's recollections and advice on working in dark tents (Fig. 32) in the field show how he coped with some of the serious problems which could be encountered. He considered working in portable dark tents

Fig. 32
*Photography
and Exploration.*

Wood-engraving
(from Gaston
Tissandier, *History
and Handbook of
Photography*
(1876)).
National Library of
Scotland

the most unhealthy part of the photographer's operation in the Far East, recalling that even though the photographer may work with a tent in the shade of a tree, and may take every precaution to ventilate its interior, 'after ten minutes' work the rapid evaporation of the chemicals renders the air noxious, particularly when every operation, from coating the plate with collodion to fixing with cyanide is conducted inside'.[43]

Coating, sensitising and developing plates were actions which had to be performed inside a dark tent, in Thomson's case a simple temporary structure of his own design and construction. Working in such conditions took its toll on the photographer: 'I have felt, after a day's work in a tent so thoroughly saturated with chemicals that I might almost be used for coating a plate or printing upon'.[44] When preparing his glass plate negatives Thomson recommended working with a near equal mixture of alcohol and ether,[45] the former used as a means of slowing down the rate of evaporation of the liquid collodion stratum before reaching the gel point, prior to immersion in the silver bath. This enabled the operator to execute all necessary operations quickly, but without undue haste. Owing to the excessively hot and humid conditions, he proffers the following sound advice to help ameliorate or minimise the worst of the chemical side-effects: 'It is a good rule not to remain in your tent a second longer than is absolutely necessary. Coat your plate with collodion outside, and, having developed with iron[46] and washed your plate, fix with cyanide outside, after which the negative may be dried, and set aside to redevelop at your leisure'.[47]

With both salt paper and albumen printing processes there was little or no means of controlling contrast. This crucial and important factor made it vital for the photographer to exercise a high degree of control over the subsequent development, stabilisation, and redevelopment phases of his wet plate operations. The selection and use – either in combination or singly – of a number of developing or intensification agents was an essential part of a wet-plate photographer's repertoire of skills. Both chemical and physical development processes and working procedures are described in great detail in a series of articles written by Thomson for the *British Journal of Photography* in 1866.[48] In addition, Thomson put together a detailed inventory of chemicals and apparatus which he felt were essential acquisitions for the successful practice of practical photography in the tropics.[49] High temperatures and high humidity were not all he had to contend with. He relates, for example, how on one occasion, after exposing a plate, 'no sooner had [he] withdrawn the plate from the shelter of the dark tent, and poured the water over it, than the liquid froze on its surface and hung in icicles around its edge. Ahong [his assistant] was standing nearly knee-deep in snow, with his face buried in his coat sleeves; and as for the bottle, the water within it had frozen into a solid lump'. In spite of these difficulties, he relates, 'we adjourned to a friendly hut, where we thawed the plate over a charcoal fire and washed it with hot water'.[50] It remains a mystery how he had managed to perform the earlier and subsequent photographic operations in these conditions, especially coating the plate with collodion within the confines of a poorly ventilated tent and in close proximity to an undoubtedly primitive and dangerous stove or fire. Explosions and fires were quite frequent occurrences at that time, and it is for this reason that the contents of many important studios and darkrooms were destroyed.[51]

The wet-collodion process undoubtedly had both advantages and disadvantages, and Thomson was well aware of them. He wrote that: 'the wet collodion process, appropriately so named, could not shed its ponderosity and was hedged round with difficulties, as I had reason to know and appreciate, and [was] ill adapted for long journeys. It was the most chemically and mechanically exacting companion to be carried on any expedition, and its shortcomings were accentuated when my wonderings happened to be through forests and tropical jungle' (Fig. 33).[52] In its favour, however, he averred that: 'One special virtue must be noted, and that is that the plates had to be exposed, developed and finished on the spot, so that one was able to judge the success or failure before striking camp.' The main characteristic which ensured the process's survival was that 'the detail in wet collodion negatives was of microscopic minuteness whilst presenting the finest gradation and printing quality which had never indeed been surpassed by any known method'.[53] An observation that few of us today would be willing to dispute.

Fig.33
Portable Photographic Apparatus.

Wood-engraving (from Gaston Tissandier, *History and Handbook of Photography* (1876)). National Library of Scotland

Into Print: Thomson and the Photographic Book*

The appreciation of Thomson's photography in the nineteenth century was not confined to the photographic prints which he produced himself from his own negatives. He sought the use of the publishing industry to mass-produce his photographs in forms convenient for inclusion in printed books which also contained his own writing, and this aspect of his work was as important in forming contemporary opinion of his *oeuvre* as the photographic process itself. The publication of photographs in printed books changed dramatically over the course of Thomson's life, and the rest of this chapter will discuss how Thomson embraced these developments.

From the discovery and exploitation of the earliest reproductive processes, up to the present day, publication has been the ultimate goal for the photographer – a means of achieving both fame and fortune. More importantly, publication also confers on the photographer recognition and respectability, just as it does for artists working in other media. William Henry Fox Talbot himself regarded photography, to some extent, as a means of multiplying images in a way entirely analogous to the traditional processes of printing: indeed the nomenclature that has stuck to many areas of photography, such as the 'print', and 'printing a photograph' could hardly be more bookish.[54]

A major reason for Thomson turning to publication as the best means of disseminating a sizeable body of work to as large and wide an audience as possible, was the inadequacy of alternative means of communication. Exhibitions, for example, did not, in the nineteenth century, offer the same possibilities as they do today. Photographers did exhibit their work to the public framed and hung on the

*The final section of this chapter is by Richard Ovenden.

wall, but such formal displays tended to be large-scale group exhibitions, where the qualification to exhibit was membership of a photographic club, society, or association: the concept of the 'one man show' that we are used to in the late twentieth century was virtually unheard of. Similarly, the glossy photographic periodicals and colour supplements with which we are familar today were not available for Thomson to take advantage of, and although the projection of photographic images by the 'magic lantern' (or oxyhydrogen projector) permitted large-scale projections to potentially very large audiences,[55] this permitted only a fleeting appreciation of each image, without any permanent record of the event. Permanent forms of dissemination, therefore, remained the ultimate goal. For Thomson, these problems were particularly acute as his work required extensive explanation, in the form of accompanying text, to inform an audience which was largely ignorant of the subjects being shown and the context in which they existed.

The technology available to photographers and publishers wishing to reproduce a combination of images and text in printed publications developed rapidly over the course of photography's history, and John Thomson's own publications often stood at the forefront of each stage in this development. He took an active interest in the methods of mass reproduction used by these publications, and, consequently, in the ways in which his work was communicated to Victorian Britain. Perhaps more than any other photographer until Peter Henry Emerson in the 1880s, John Thomson engaged directly with the world of publishing and book production.[56]

During the nineteenth century the use of photography in printed books underwent radical changes. At first, skilled wood-engravers would simply copy photographs onto woodblocks in the same way as they had traditionally copied artists' drawings, and these blocks could then be used to print the image into the page, via printers' ink, at the same time as the text was printed. This basic method remained popular for high-circulation periodicals for the remainder of the century, although a number of technological improvements were made. The most important of these involved the transfer of images directly onto woodblocks by photographic means, the block then being cut or engraved by hand, by a skilled engraver. The block was then electrotyped (i.e. a duplicate printing plate would be made in copper) in order to permit large print-runs to be obtained from it.[57] By the middle of the nineteenth century, there had been established in Britain a growing number of journals which provided news, comment and reviews aimed at the literate and educated upper working and middle classes. These journals, like *The Illustrated London News* (established in 1842) and *The Graphic* (established in 1869), used the medium of the wood-engraved illustration to bring a new, visual dimension to the periodical press, and created, as a by-product, a demand for original art work from artists and photographers. They were certainly immensely popular. Selling for sixpence, *The Illustrated London News*, for example, had a circulation of 123,000 in 1854–55, and *The Graphic* topped 250,000 in 1874. The illustrations proved the key to the mass market.[58] These journals and others embraced photography as a means of illustration.

But shortly after the discovery of photography, books also began to be issued with actual photographic prints pasted onto blank pages by hand. This technique remained in use, to some degree, well into the twentieth century, although it was attended by a number of very serious problems. These problems were of two kinds.

First, the tendency to fade which was inherent in most early photographic prints, particularly the silver-based positive process prints such as salted-paper and albumen. This was the most pressing problem: a phenomenon which John Szarkowski has called the 'specter of impermanence'.[59] Second, there was the problem of reproducing the photographic image in sufficient quantities and at a low enough price to rival the dominant trades of lithography and wood-engraving. Moreover, the pasting-in of positive photographic prints was a cumbersome, expensive, labour-intensive and time-consuming process, which restricted its use to publications which were either paid for by subscription, or underwritten by the author or some other patron. Inevitably these publications had a restricted circulation.

Trying to solve these problems entailed a massive amount of effort. The obvious way to reproduce photographic images in large quantities, at low prices, was to reproduce them in printer's ink, which would also solve the problem of image permanence. To enable this, the photograph had to be transferred to a printing block, but, initially, the quality of reproduction attained could not rival the results achieved by merely pasting a positive photographic print into the book. Eventually, however, solutions began to emerge, but they themselves presented further problems in that the ability to reproduce the glories of continuous tone found in high-definition albumen prints (produced from wet-collodion negatives) on the printed page was beyond the traditional printing technologies as they stood in 1870.

Technological changes, however, drove both photographers and printers to seek other ways to mechanise the reproduction of photographs, and to enable the images to be printed using ink, and then replicated cheaply and in large numbers without sacrificing quality. The methods which were found to solve this problem – known as photomechanical processes – took a large number of forms, and at their best could be almost indistinguishable from high-quality original (or 'real') photographs.

It should come as little surprise, therefore, to learn that the first of Thomson's images to be widely disseminated in printed form were the wood-engraved reproductions of Bangkok which appeared in *The Illustrated London News* in 1867.[60] These were evidently sent to the journal from Singapore, and were probably a piece of hopeful speculation on his part. To the photographer, exposure in a journal of this kind not only meant that his work and name came into the middle-class public consciousness, but also brought in an income, and, once a successful photograph had been made, relatively easily at that. Although it is probable that photographs received a lower fee than commissioned art work, many of these magazines, *The Graphic* in particular, spent large sums per week on illustrations, as the publication depended on the quality of its illustrative material.[61] Thomson returned to these journals as a source of income and exposure on several occasions in the following ten years, and the support of *The Graphic* played an important role in establishing his reputation as the principal visual commentator on China, despite the artistic sacrifices that having his work reproduced in such a way forced on him.

Once the photographer had handed over his originals to a journal, artistic control was relinquished to the wood-engraver whose responsibility it was to translate the image into a final form for the pages of the publication itself. Thomson may well have found this loss of control frustrating. When he finally managed to secure personal control over the design of the printed formats in which his work appeared, his approach gave a greater emphasis to the photographs than had been the case with the magazines which had used his work.

By the middle of the 1860s some senior figures in British photography had begun to campaign for photographers to take greater pains when producing photographically-illustrated books. Stephen Thompson noted in 1862 that 'the application of photography to book-illustration is not by any means a new or novel idea; but its value has hitherto been scarce sufficiently appreciated'.[62] With *The Antiquities of Cambodia*, Thomson's first direct effort at publishing, he was particularly aware of the unique qualities which his photography could bring to an appreciation of subjects like architecture and archaeology. *The Antiquities of Cambodia* was not a large book by any standards, and there were only sixteen images, of which six formed three-part panoramas spread over two conjugate pages. The images were interspersed throughout Thomson's own text, although as pasted-in albumen prints they naturally appeared on otherwise blank pages. But they formed the first photographic record of a site which was beginning to grip not only the academic, but also the popular imagination in Europe. Books with pasted-in prints were naturally expensive to produce, and it was a considerable achievement for Thomson to have persuaded the publishers, Edmonston and Douglas, to take on such a financial risk. Although he had not published before, Thomson had a number of factors on his side. His images had recently appeared in *The Illustrated London News*, and the publishers may have been pursuaded that Thomson was not, therefore, an unknown quantity. Second, Edmonston and Douglas were already active in the field of photographically-illustrated books, and were the publishers of the astronomer and photographer Charles Piazzi Smyth, with whom Thomson may well have had contact of some kind.[63] Finally, the involvement of James Fergusson, although unstated in the book itself, must have assured the publishers of the quality of the information itself. Getting into print for the first time had therefore entailed a great deal of preliminary work on Thomson's behalf, particularly in the field of self-promotion, but luck had also played its part. With this first book issued, it would prove easier to publish the next.

Thomson's next publication, *Views on the North River*, was his first book to be conceived primarily as a medium for the presentation of his photographs: as the title suggests, it is primarily a book of views, whereas *The Antiquities of Cambodia* had been very much a combination of text and images, the two mutually dependent, and the *Visit of the ... Duke of Edinburgh* had essentially been a volume of text with a few photographs inserted almost as an afterthought, and this had not been Thomson's own project. *Views on the North River*, on the other hand, can be seen as the first attempt to present Thomson's experience of China as a visual document (Fig. 34). The book form is being used to recreate the experience of seeing his images in a sequence predetermined by the photographer, and to that extent he was able to retain control over the order and arrangement in which his own photographs were presented, control which he had lost during his association with *The China Magazine*, and when working on *Visit of the ... Duke of Edinburgh*.

Yet despite the success of *Views on the North River* as a photographically-illustrated book, its circulation among the western, English-speaking communities

Fig 34
The Fi-Lai-Sz
Monastery.
c. 1868-69.

170 x 237 mm.
Albumen print from
wet-collodion
negative.
National Library of
Scotland

of Hong Kong and the Treaty ports was somewhat limited, and its impact in Britain, if it had any at all, has left no trace in the contemporary reviewing journals. It remains one of his scarcer books to this day. There was also an additional, nagging problem with this volume, and with his previous efforts at using photography as a tool for illustrating books: the question of image permanence. The tendency of albumen prints (and salted-paper prints before them) to fade, often quite soon after they had been made, drove the development of photographic chemistry during the first forty years of photography's history, and this problem had an equally profound affect on the use of photography in book illustration. The practice of pasting in albumen prints was not only costly, time consuming, cumbersome, and restricting: it also inserted a potential time-bomb into the printed volume which contemporaries were only too well aware of. 'The silver process of photography, too, is of doubtful permanence, and the sun-pictures, it is to be regretted, will not remain for many years, however washed; so that, unless another mode is adopted, the ruins of Thebes will disappear from these ornamental books more rapidly than they do at Thebes itself', wrote one reviewer after handling a volume of photographs of Egypt.[64] Thomson himself was also aware of the problem, and his own efforts at book production for the next thirty years would follow very closely the technical innovations in photomechanical methods of reproducing images in books.

Contemporary views on the albumen process, and his own experiences of publishing books illustrated by it, no doubt influenced his decision to turn to more permanent methods of illustration for his next book. *Foochow and the River Min* therefore contains eighty carbon prints, magnificently printed by Britain's leading firm operating in that field, and as the whole project was conceived and carried through to completion by Thomson himself, we get our closest view of Thomson's own aesthetic stance on the presentation of his images in this book. The page size – double crown – is generous enough to allow the prints to be framed by a large expanse of white paper, and the tones of the carbon prints, pasted onto one side of the page only (in common with all photographically-illustrated books of this date) are dramatically heightened by being set in contrast against the white. The text and images have been separated, so that the reader is allowed to view the images, for their own sake, rather than as explications for the text, or vice-versa. Even more so than *Views on the North River*, this is a book intended as a vehicle for Thomson's images, each of which is intended to be appreciated on its own (with the exception of ten groups of four small images which are printed together on a single leaf). The *Foochow* book was Thomson's most self-consciously aesthetic document, an attempt to convey knowledge purely about his aesthetic response to the Fukien landscape, and the chosen images, and the way in which they are reproduced, reflect this.

Foochow was followed by *Illustrations of China and its People*, which attempts to provide more of a visual encyclopaedia of China, capable of being used and appreciated on several different levels. Indeed, in a review of Thomson's Canton images (later to be used in the book), the *British Journal of Photography* praised 'his efforts to produce, by means of his camera, a sort of pictorial encyclopaedia of scenes illustrative of Chinese manners and customs'.[65] In *Illustrations of China*, the text and images are very closely linked, although the technicalities of production still made it necessary for the images to be printed separately from the text (Fig. 35). The letterpress pages really function as extended captions, positioned next to each relevant image so that each portion of the book aids the reader in the understanding of the other. This sophisticated approach was not a new departure in book-publishing, but in several respects *Illustrations of China* was innovative in its design. It differs from Thomson's earlier books – and *Foochow* in particular – in that the choice of the collotype process as the method of photomechanical reproduction filled the book with soft images, printed on a coated paper, which looked very different from the hard, glossy sharpness of the carbon prints of *Foochow* (which emulated the exhibition-quality albumen print), heightening the difference between the purely artistic purpose of the earlier books, and the multi-purpose intentions which Thomson and his publishers had in mind for *Illustrations of China*. The choice of the collotype process provided other advantages. In the preface to the book Thomson stated them: 'It is a novel experiment to attempt to illustrate a book of travels with photographs, a few years back so perishable, and so difficult to reproduce. But the art is now so far advanced, that we can multiply the copies with the same facility, and print them with the same materials as in the case of woodcuts or engravings'.[66]

The enormous success, both critical and commercial, that greeted *Illustrations of China* prompted Thomson to take a new approach to the marketing of his images and text: one that involved aiming his material once again at the readers of the illustrated weekly magazines, but this time in a full-scale book format, with over five hundred pages of text printed together with over sixty wood-engravings based on his photographs and translated by the skilled wood engraver James Davis Cooper (1823–1904). The resultant book *The Straits of Malacca* brought a much wider audience into contact with the Far East, in particular that section of the reading public that was unable to afford the heavy price tag for the larger *Illustrations of China*. But in order to be able to reach a wider audience, at a much

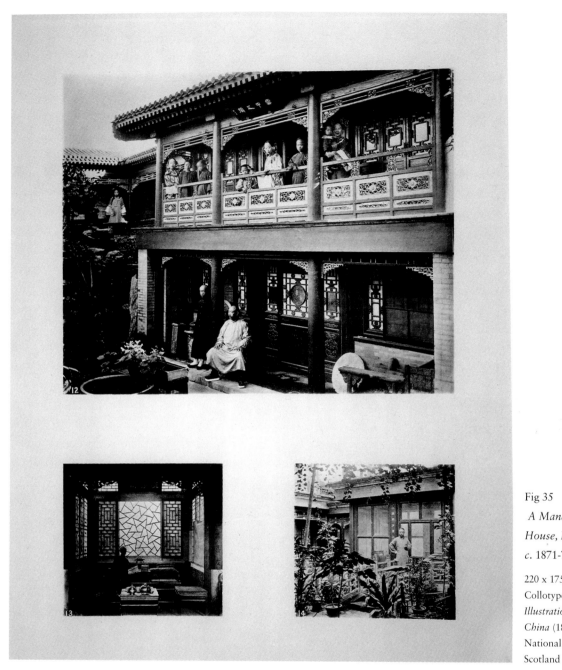

Fig 35
*A Mandarin's
House, Peking.*
c. 1871-72.

220 x 175 mm.
Collotype (from
*Illustrations of
China* (1873–74)).
National Library of
Scotland

lower cost than *Illustrations of China*, Thomson and his publishers had to make some compromises in terms of design and production for *The Straits of Malacca*. Some of the illustrations in this later book are treated as integral vignetted images, in the body of the text, while forty-three were also chosen to be printed as separate plates, and thus inserted (together with a tissue guard) on a higher-quality paper than the letterpress pages. This gives a somewhat uneven feel to the whole, as the choice of images to be treated in each way is not always obvious. Despite the element of compromise, *The Straits of Malacca* was an effective vehicle for disseminating Thomson's visual documentation of China to a wider public, and the success which its publication brought no doubt encouraged him to go further down this road. The result was *The Land and People of China*, published for a mass-market by the Society for the Promotion of Christian Knowledge, which took Thomson's photographs, again transformed them into wood-engravings by a skilled hand (that of Eugene Ronjat (b. 1822), the French illustrator and painter), and also printed them as separate plates, thus according them a special status. But ultimately, such compromises took liberties with Thomson's photography. It also removed the element of control which he had enjoyed with his earlier publications.

By embarking on the project known as *Street Life in London*, Thomson was not only making an innovatory step in the development of photography, he was also reasserting his desire to remain in control of the way in which his photographs were used. To some extent the Woodburytypes used in the publication utilised an 'old' technology. It still required the prints to be pasted onto a page (or mount) by hand. The collotypes in *Illustrations of China* had shown him that this expensive, and labour-intensive, step could be avoided, but Thomson saw that the advantages of the Woodburytype weighed heavily against the use of collotypes for this project. The heightened contrast, the deep blacks, and the brilliant sharpness of the image produced a verity which, as we have seen, suited perfectly Thomson's subject matter, and the way he wished it to be shown (Fig. 36). Despite its drawbacks, the process not only guaranteed permanence, it also provided consistency, and relatively large edition sizes could be provided at low cost.

The decision again to use the Woodburytype process to reproduce his images for

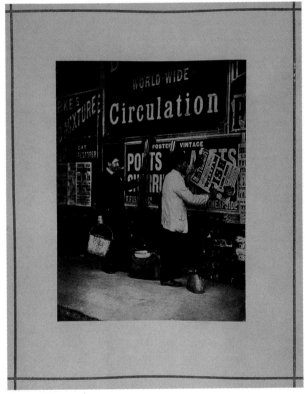

Fig 36
Street Advertising.
c. 1876-77.

Woodburytype (from *Street Life in London* (1876–77)). National Library of Scotland

Through Cyprus with the Camera was a natural one, as the qualities of the process would equally suit a more obviously up-market publication, such as the Cyprus book, albeit one which treated its subject matter very differently from *Street Life*. Whereas in *Street Life in London* the images are mounted on paper which is plain, save for a simple red-ink frame and a caption (also in red), for the Cyprus book, the page-mounts were given a central panel with a dark staining, in which the Woodburytype prints were placed. The overall effect is consciously more aesthetic, like an artist's portfolio interspersed with extended captions, whereas text and image were more consciously integrated in both *Illustrations of China* and *Street Life in London*. In his preface to *Through Cyprus with the Camera* Thomson highlights the two reasons for choosing the Woodburytype process: the faithfulness of the reproductions, and the permanence of the prints. 'The photographs have been printed in permanent pigments', he wrote, 'and therefore, while they supply incontestable evidence of the present condition of Cyprus, they will also afford a source of comparison in after years, when, under the influence of British rule the place has risen from its ruins'.[67]

Thomson's last book, *Through China with a Camera*, embraced yet another technological advance in reproducing photography in book form: the half-tone process. This finally permitted conventional printing presses to reproduce photographic illustrations, unlike the processes that Thomson had used for his earlier books and which required specialised machinery, and printers with special skills. The use of this 'new' technology therefore enabled large numbers of illustrations to be included in *Through China with a Camera* (100 for the first edition of 1898, 114 for the second of 1899). Here again, however, Thomson and his publishers chose not to break with tradition completely by integrating the photographs fully with the text, so some of the photographs have been printed on a coated paper, as separate plates, whereas others have been printed in the body of the text. Quality had to be sacrificed for the benefits of cost reduction with the half-tone process, and therefore, unlike *Illustrations of China* or *Through Cyprus with a Camera*, these two editions are presented more as illustrated travel accounts than as either photographic essays or portfolios of images (although Thomson, in his preface, still expressed the view that nothing in the originals had been lost).[68]

By the time of his death in 1921, John Thomson's life had coincided with almost the entire history of photography up to that point, and his own engagement with photography had seen him embrace many of its crucial developments, both in terms of the making of photographs, and in the way they were reproduced. Although we do not know exactly when Thomson took his first photograph, we do know that he became a master of the wet-collodion process, adapting its operation to suit the very demanding conditions in which he took his finest photographs. In the mid-1870s he began to use the collodion dry-plate, an important technological development which enabled him to travel without the encumbrances of tents, baths, and chemicals associated with the wet-collodion process. This in turn enabled him to develop his street photography in London, adapting to the conditions he found there. Throughout the last two decades of the nineteenth century he experimented with new photographic printing technologies such as the platinum print and the gelatin-silver print.[69] The dissemination of his work through printed publications had also been revolutionised during his working life. From the crude wood-engravings based on his photographs in *The Illustrated London News* of the 1860s, through the sumptuous luxury of the carbon prints in *Foochow and the River Min*, to the striking clarity of the Woodburytypes in *Street Life in London*, and finally to the inexpensive half-tones of *Through China with a Camera*, Thomson's published photographs reached an ever wider public, one that was becoming increasingly hungry for photographic images to enhance their appreciation and understanding of the world.

Travel stands at the centre of John Thomson's achievement as a photographer, and it must be remembered that the experience of travelling was one of the prime motivating forces throughout his career. But Thomson also lived through one of the greatest periods of travel and exploration witnessed by Europeans, and he grew up at a time when the exploits of David Livingstone in Africa held the British reading public in a grip of excitement and anticipation.[70] Thomson later became part of this phenomenon, assisting in the 'opening up' of parts of the world (to his western audience) through the medium of photography. To Thomson, therefore, photography had distinct purposes and functions. One of the most important of these was as a tool for education and information, and many of his own books embrace this role wholeheartedly. When reflecting on Thomson's legacy as a photographer and as an educator, it is worth remembering that to Thomson, this aspect of his work was of crucial importance. It had always been his ambition, he wrote shortly before his death in 1921, 'to see photography take its proper place as a means of illustrating exploration', and as a pioneer both in forming the critical genres of photography for the next century, and in establishing photography as an essential aspect of book illustration, he was brilliantly successful.[71]

NOTES

Abbreviations

AC	John Thomson, *The Antiquities of Cambodia*
BJP	*British Journal of Photography*
Corr.	Unpublished correspondence from Isabel Thomson to John Thomson, 1870–72. Private collection.
Foochow	John Thomson, *Foochow and the River Min*
GRO(S)	General Register Office, Edinburgh
History	Gaston Tissandier, *History and Handbook of Photography*, ed. John Thomson, 2nd edn
HWUA	Heriot-Watt University Archives
IC	John Thomson, *Illustrations of China and its People*, 4 vols
ILN	*The Illustrated London News*
LAC	Lacock Abbey Collection, Fox Talbot Museum
Lee, *Vision*	C. S. Lee, John Thomson: A Photographic Vision of the Far East (1860–72) (Unpublished M.Litt thesis, University of Oxford, 1985.)
NLS	National Library of Scotland
NPG	National Portrait Gallery, London
PC	*The Publisher's Circular*
PRGS	*Proceedings of the Royal Geographical Society*
RGS	Royal Geographical Society
SL	John Thomson, *Street Life in London*
SM	John Thomson, *The Straits of Malacca, Indo-China, and China*
TC	John Thomson, *Through China With a Camera*
TCWTC	John Thomson, *Through Cyprus with the Camera*
VONR	John Thomson, *Views on the North River*
White, *Thomson*	Stephen White, *John Thomson: Life and Photographs*

Introduction

1. See Felix Driver, 'Geography's Empire: Histories of Geographical Knowledge', *Society and Space*, 10 (1992), pp. 23–40.

2. See below pp. 78–88.

3. For the best treatment of Victorian ideas about Empire in Conrad's *Heart of Darkness* see Edward W. Said, *Culture and Imperialism* (London, 1993), pp. 20–35.

4. Louis de Carné, *Travels in Indo-China and the Chinese Empire* (London, 1872), p. 212.

5. Nigel Cameron, *Barbarians and Mandarins: Thirteen Centuries of Western Travellers in China* (Hong Kong, 1989), pp. 149–262. Colin Mackerras, *Western Images of China* (Hong Kong, 1989), pp. 28–42.

6. Herbert Franke, 'In Search of China: Some General Remarks on the History of European Sinology', in *Europe Studies China*, ed. by Ming Wilson and John Cayley (London, 1995), p. 15.

7. Mackerras, *Western Images of China*, pp. 43–65.

8. John Thomson, 'Three Pictures in Wong-nei-chung', *The China Magazine* (1868), pp. 52–56. The quotations are from *The Elements of Drawing in Three Letters to Beginners* (London, 1857) in *The Works of John Ruskin*, ed. by E. T. Cook and Alexander Wedderburn, 39 vols (London, 1904), XV, pp. 161–62, 164.

9. *VONR*, text accompanying 'Looking North from Pau-Lo-Hang Temple'; John Thomson, 'Three Pictures in Wong-nei-chung', p. 56. The verse that is quoted is 'A Hymn on The Seasons', from James Thomson, *The Seasons,* first published 1728.

10. John Hannavy, *Roger Fenton of Crimble Hall* (London, 1975), p. 94. For the Dutch still-life tradition see Ingvar Bergström, *Dutch Still-Life Painting in the Seventeenth Century* (London, 1947).

11. See below pp. 167–75.

12. See Tod Papageorge, 'Before the Gold Rush: Photography and Photographers at the Time of the Miracle', *Times Literary Supplement,* (3 March 1995), pp. 10–11.

13. John Thomson, 'Photography and Exploration', *PRGS*, ns 13 (1891) pp. 669–75.
   The phrase 'sun pictures' was used to describe early photographs. Although it is not known who coined the term, it was used by Talbot to describe the prints used in his book *Sun Pictures in Scotland* (1846).

Chapter 1—Creation

1. GRO(S), Register of Births and Baptisms (Edinburgh, St Cuthbert's) 685^2/35, 1833–42, p. 275.

2. George Heriot's Hospital, Archives, MS 'Record of Heriot's Hospital', XXXI, p. 387.

3. Robert Q. Gray, *The Labour Aristocracy in Victorian Edinburgh* (Oxford, 1976), p. 10.

4. An obituary notice in *The Scotsman*, 6 October 1921, p. 6 ('Death of a Scottish Traveller'), provides a tantalising suggestion that he was educated at the Newlands Institute, Bathgate (now the Bathgate Academy), which had been founded with the aid of a financial benefaction by John Newlands, who was probably a member of Thomson's mother's family. The school was founded in 1833, but records now only survive as far back as the 1870s, and without firmer evidence this suggestion will have to remain just that. See Thomas Davidson, *Bathgate Academy 1833–1933* (Bathgate, 1933). I am grateful to David Williamson and Dr Norman Reid for their assistance in this matter. John's brothers William and Thomas Newlands Thomson were admitted to George Heriot's Hospital in 1845 and 1851 respectively. The School was close to their home in Brighton Street. See George Heriot's Hospital, Archives, MS 'Record of Heriot's Hospital', XXXI, p. 387; XXXIV, p. 282. I am most grateful to Fraser Simm for granting me access to these records.

5. Corr., passim, but especially 4 February 1871.

6. GRO(S), Census of 1851 (St Cuthbert's, Edinburgh) 685^2/719, Enumeration Book 85, p. 4.

7. This implies that his parents came from an upper working-class background, but it was still possible to secure an apprenticeship for a modest premium, or without making any payment at all.

8. I am grateful to Richard Hunter for assistance with this problem.

9. See T. N. Clarke, A. D. Morrison-Low, and A. D. C. Simpson, *Brass and Glass: Scientific Instrument Making Workshops in Scotland as Illustrated by Instruments from the Arthur Frank Collection at the Royal Museum of Scotland* (Edinburgh, 1989), pp. 112–22.

10. NLS, MS Dep 230/6, p. 407; he is also listed as an optician in the 1861 Census. GRO(S) Census of 1861 (Edinburgh, Buccleuch) 685^4/72, pp. 7–8.

11. *Brass and Glass*, p. 112.

12. *Brass and Glass*, pp. 112–13.

13. Ian Inkster, 'The Context of Steam Intellect in Britain (to 1851)', in *The Steam Intellect Societies: Essays on Culture, Education and Industry circa 1820–1914*, ed. by Ian Inkster (Nottingham, 1985), pp. 3–4.

14. HWUA, SA1/1/16.

15. HWUA, SA1/1/15; JW2/1/1.

16. *Brass and Glass*, p. 112. This would also account for the reference to Thomson attending Chemistry Classes at the University that was made in an obituary in the *Geographical Journal*, 58 (1921), p. 470.

17. See Leslie A. Wallace, *1821–1992: A History of Physics at Heriot-Watt University* (Edinburgh, 1993), pp. 15–19.

18. J. W. Hudson, *A History of Adult Education* (London, 1851), pp. 77–78. See also R. D. Anderson, *Education and the Scottish People 1750–1918* (Oxford, 1995), pp. 157–64.

19. See *Catalogue of the Library of the Edinburgh School of Arts* (Edinburgh, 1852), p. 22.

20. *AC*, p. 1.

21. See below, pp. 6–7.

22. *History*, pp. 257–59.

23. They compare with the experiments undertaken by John Benjamin Dancer in 1839–40. See Brian Bracegirdle and James B. McCormick, *The Microscopic Photographs of J. B. Dancer* (Chicago, 1993), p. 5.

24. NLS, MS Dep 230/35. He was recorded as being in arrears of Annual Contributions for the session 1863–64, and was finally struck off the membership roll. NLS, MS Dep 230/38 pp. 69, 96.

25. For more on the foundation and early years of the Society see A. D. C. Simpson, 'An Edinburgh Intrigue: Brewster's Society of Arts and the Pantograph Dispute', *The Book of the Old Edinburgh Club*, ns 1 (1991), pp. 47–73.

26. Scottish Record Office, GD. 356/1, p. 34.

27. See Alison Morrison-Low, 'Photography in Edinburgh in 1839: the Royal Scottish Society of Arts, Andrew Fyfe and Mungo Ponton', *Scottish Photography Bulletin*, 2 (1990), pp. 26–35; Graham Smith, *Sun Pictures in Scotland* (Ann Arbor, 1989), pp. 9–13; Graham Smith, *Disciples of Light: Photographs in the Brewster Album* (Malibu, 1990) pp. 27–39; Larry J. Schaaf, *Out of the Shadows: Herschel, Talbot, and the Invention of Photography* (New Haven, 1992) esp. pp. 30, 34, 35.

28. Alison Morrison-Low, 'Dr John Adamson and Robert Adamson: An Early Partnership in Scottish Photography', *Photographic Collector*, 4 (1983), pp. 198–214.

29. Piazzi Smyth used scientific instruments made at James Mackay Bryson's workshop. See H. A. Brück and M. T. Brück, *The Peripatetic Astronomer: The Life of Charles Piazzi Smyth* (Bristol, 1988), p. 155. Thomson also knew in detail about the camera used by Piazzi Smyth on his expedition to Egypt, and he took one like it to the Far East, but it was stolen before he reached China. John Thomson, 'A Pocket Camera', *British Journal Photographic Almanac 1874* (1874), pp. 156–58.

30. [Josiah Livingston], *Some Edinburgh Shops* (Edinburgh, 1894), pp. 13–15; *William Melrose in China 1845–1855: The Letters of a Scottish Tea Merchant,* ed. by Hoh-Cheung Mui and Lorna H. Mui, Scottish Historical Society, 4th ser., 10 (Edinburgh, 1973), p. xxxi.

31. Like that given by Mr Charles Bird of the Chinese Evangelical Society on the history, resources, and manners of the Chinese Empire. *The Scotsman*, 18 May 1857, p. 1.

32. *Catalogue of the Library of the Edinburgh School of Arts* (Edinburgh, 1852), p. 29.

33. The entry for William in the Thomson family Bible, now in a private collection, provides this date for his leaving Scotland, and also states that he married one Annie Beck in Singapore, on 25 June 1862.

34. For the movement of Scots to India and the Far East see Alex M. Cain, *The Cornchest for Scotland: Scots in India* (Edinburgh, 1986), pp. 16–17.

35. The dates in the family Bible are, however, sometimes confused, and the details may have been entered retrospectively. The comment in Lee, *Vision*, p. 20, that Thomson was back in Britain in 1864 has arisen due to a confusion with the Edinburgh commercial and architectural photographer John Thomson (d. 1881), a partner in the firm of Ross and Thomson, for whom see John Nicol, 'Notes from the North', *BJP*, 28 (1881), p. 148. This confusion was also shared by Weston J. Naef in *Behind the Great Wall of China: Photographs from 1870 to the Present,* ed. by Cornell Capa (New York, 1972), p. [28], and Janet Lehr, 'John Thomson (1837–1921)', *History of Photography*, 4 (1980), pp. 70–71.

36. This has been made in John Falconer, *A Vision of the Past: A History of Early Photographs in Singapore and Malaya* (Singapore, 1987), p. 20.

37. C. M. Turnbull, *A History of Singapore 1819–1988*, 2nd ed. (Singapore, 1989), p. 36.

38. See John Falconer, 'G. R. Lambert & Co., and some Notes on Early Photographers in Singapore', *Photographic Collector*, 5 (1985), pp. 212–19.

39. Turnbull, *Singapore*, p. 43.

40. *SM*, pp. 3–53.

41. 'J. Thomson, Singapore' was proposed for membership of the Bengal Photographic Society at the meeting of 25 October 1864, and elected the following meeting of 22 November 1864. *Journal of the Bengal Photographic Society*, ns 3 (1864), pp. 18, 20. The image of the aftermath of the cyclone is reproduced in White, *Thomson*, plate 7. The cyclone took place on 4 October 1864. I am grateful to John Falconer for his advice on this point.

42. Some of the very rare images from this period are reproduced in Lehr, 'John Thomson 1837–1921', pp. 67–71.

43. N. B. Dennys, *A Descriptive Dictionary of British Malaya* (London, 1894), pp. 364–65.

44. The book was, of course, Mouhout's *Travels*, published in 1864, for which see below, pp. 47–8.

45. *SM*, pp. 79–80.

46. *The Chronicle and Directory for China, Japan, and the Philippines for 1868* (Hong Kong, 1868), p. 88.

47. *SM*, p. 87.

48. See especially Abbot Low Moffat, *Mongkut, the King of Siam* (Ithaca, NY, 1961) passim. See below, pp. 111–13.

49. There is a useful account of her life in Anna Leonowens, *The Romance of the Harem*, ed. by Susan Morgan (Charlottesville, 1991), pp. ix–xxxvii.

50. See *SM*, pp. 129–30. H. G. Kennedy, 'Remarks on the Antiquities of Siam and Camboja, with Some Notice of the Condition of those Countries at the Present Day', *The Journal of the Society of Arts*, 22 (1874), p. 582, additionally accuses her of misunderstanding Siamese court customs.

51. Anna Leonowens, *The English Governess at the Siamese Court* (London, 1870), p. vii.

52. See the introduction by William L. Bradley to the reprint of Frank Vincent's *Land of the White Elephant* (Singapore, 1988), pp. [xi–xii].

53. *The Waking Dream: Photography's First Century: Selections from the Gilman Paper Company Collection*, ed. by Maria Morris Hambourg, et al. (New York, 1993), p. 306.

54. John Thomson, 'The Cambodian Ruins', *China Magazine* (August 1868), p. 17. Kennedy wrote up his account of the journey as 'Report of an Expedition Made Into Southern Laos and Cambodia in the Early Part of the Year 1866', *Journal of the Royal Geographical Society*, 37 (1867), pp. 298–328.

55. Thomson, 'Cambodian Ruins', p. 17.

56. Thomson, 'Cambodian Ruins', p. 18.

57. *The Geographical Journal*, 2 (1893), p. 211. *SM*, pp. 118–63. He later wrote that the trip to Cambodia was 'productive of nothing beyond a series of photographs of its antiquities; a ground plan of Nakon Wat; and a malignant attack of jungle fever brought about by exposure to the excessive heat and miasma of the forests'. John Thomson, 'The Antiquities of Cambodia', *Journal of the North-China Branch of the Royal Asiatic Society*, ns 8 (1873), p. 200.

58. The work of Henri Gsell, official photographer to Labarre's delegation, is little known outside the album now in the collection of the Gillman Paper Company in New York. See Hambourg, et al., *Waking Dream*, p. 306. It bears comparison with much of Thomson's work, although a thorough evaluation of Gsell's images is still awaited.

59. G. Thomson, 'Notes on Cambodia and its Races', *Transactions of the Ethnological Society of London*, ns 6 (1867), p. 246.

60. Thomson, 'Notes on Cambodia', p. 247.

61. *ILN*, no. 1366–1367 (21 April 1866), p. 385.

62. He gave his address as 'Care of John Simpson Esq., Messrs. Duncan and Flockhart, North Bridge, Edinburgh'. *Transactions of the Ethnological Society of London*, ns 6 (1867), p. 8.

63. He gave his address at this stage as 4 Montague Street, Edinburgh. The manuscript of this unpublished paper survives in RGS, Archives, Journal MSS, S.E. Asia 1866, Thomson, J.

64. John Thomson, 'A Visit to the Ruined Temples of Cambodia', *Report of the Thirty-Sixth Meeting of the British Association for the Advancement of Science* (London, 1867), pp. 116–17.

65. *PRGS*, 11 (1867), p. 15.

66. *BJP* (30 November 1866), p. 576.

67. *BJP* (14 December 1866), p. 598–9.

68. *BJP* (1 March 1867), p. 103.

69. 'Ruined Temples of Cambodia', *The Builder*, 25 (27 April 1867), p. 291. *The Builder* had published a review of Fergusson's *History of Architecture* (see below) which had focussed on the section on Cambodia, and gave due credit to Thomson: 'His authority is the photographical collection of Mr. J. Thomson, to whom the revelation of these details is due.' *The Builder*, 25 (30 March 1867), p. 219. Woodcuts based on Thomson's photographs were reproduced in *The Builder*, 25 (30 March 1867), p. 224.

70. Where he is described as 'a photographic artist residing in Bangkok'.

71. The copy in Glasgow University Library has the accession date 1.4.67 on the front pastedown, indicating that it was before that date, but as it had not appeared at the time of his paper to the Glasgow Photographic Association on 21 February. *BJP* (1 March 1867), p. 103. It must have been published sometime in March, although it was first announced on 1 July 1867 in *The Publishers' Circular*.

72. For accounts of Fergusson's contribution to architectural history in the nineteenth century see Maurice Craig, 'James Fergusson', in *Concerning Architecture: Essays on Architectural Writers and Writing Presented to Nikolaus Pevsner*, ed. by John Summerson (London, 1968), pp. 140–52; Nikolaus Pevsner, *Some Architectural Writers of the Nineteenth Century* (Oxford, 1972), pp. 238–51,

73. James Fergusson, *Tree and Serpent Worship*, 2nd ed. rev. (London, 1873), p. 50.

74. James Fergusson, *A History of Architecture in All Countries, From the Earliest Times to the Present Day*, 3 vols (London, 1862–67), II, pp. 713–32.

75. Thomson, 'Notes on Cambodia', pp. 246–52.

76. They may have met at the Bathgate Academy, as the Simpson family came from that town. J. Duns, *Memoir of Sir James Y. Simpson, Bart.* (Edinburgh, 1873), pp. 1–19.

77. Corr., 6 August 1871.

78. E. J. Eitel, *Europe in China: The History of Hong Kong from the Beginning to the Year 1882* (London, 1895), p. 463.

79. *The China Punch* (9 December 1867) p. 106.

80. Lee, *Vision*, p. 42.

81. Clark Worswick and Jonathan Spence, *Imperial China: Photographs 1850–1912* (London, 1979), p. 141.

82. See Worswick, *Imperial China*, pp. 150–51.

83. Lee, *Vision*, pp. 42–44.

84. *The China Punch* (3 April 1868), pp. 162–63.

85. White, *Thomson*, p. 18.

86. White, *Thomson*, p. 18.

87. *The Far East*, published in Japan, being an exception. See Stephen White, '*The Far East*: A Magazine on the Orient for European Eyes', *Image*, 34 (1991), pp. 39–47.

88. NLS, MS 4227, fol. 142v.

89. NLS, MS 30860, p. 471.

90. See below, Bibliography A17.

91. Rev. William R. Beach, *Visit of ... the Duke of Edinburgh to Hong Kong* (Hong Kong, 1869), p. iv.

92. Corr., 9 July 1871.

93. John Newlands Thomson was duly born in March 1871.

94. Corr., 30 June 1870.

95. NLS, MS 4707, fols 81r–82v; 83r–84v.

96. He may well have been in Shanghai in May 1871, for instance, as his name appears on the passenger list of the Steamer *Kwangtung*. See Elliott S. Parker, 'John Thomson, 1837–1921: RGS Instructor in Photography', *Geographical Journal*, 144 (1978), pp. 463–71.

97. *SM*, p. 358.

98. Such as those photographed by Afong Lai in an album of his work in the Riddell Collection of the National Collection of Photography in the National Galleries of Scotland, R38.

99. *SM*, p. 358.

100. Robert Fortune, *A Journey to the Tea Countries of China* (London, 1852), pp. 135–36.

101. Fortune, *Journey*, p. 142.

102. See Alexander Wylie, *Memorials of Protestant Missionaries to the Chinese* (Shanghai, 1867), pp. 201–3.

103. *SM*, p. 307.

104. *SM*, pp. 311–12.

105. Wylie, *Memorials*, p. 269; Corr., 17 February 1872; *Quarterly Journal of the Edinburgh Medical Missionary Society* (1903), p. 391. He was the joint author (with W. Hamilton Jefferys) of *The Diseases of China: Including Formosa and Korea* (London, 1910), and *Leprosy: A Practical Textbook for Use in China* (Shanghai, 1937).

106. Corr., 6 September 1871.

107. *SM*, p. 498.

108. 'Sketches in China', *ILN*, no. 1750 (15 March 1873), p. 254.

109. E. H. Parker, *John Chinaman and a Few Others* (London, 1901), p. 165. The image was eventually published in 'Li Hung Chang', *The Strand Magazine*, 12 (July–December 1896), p. 317.

110. Corr., 10 December 1871.

111. *SM*, pp. 515–16. See Wylie, *Memorials*, pp. 268–69.

112. He is referred to in *SM*, pp. 515–16. The collection is now at the Oriental Museum, Durham University. I am grateful to Nick Pearce for sharing his knowledge of this material with me.

113. Wylie, *Memorials*, pp. 173–75. Thomson thought Wylie 'one of the most distinguished and modest travellers it has been my good fortune to meet'. *SM*, p. 532.

114. Anon, 'Mr Thomson's Photographs of China', *North China Herald and Supreme Court and Consular Gazette*, 11 January 1872, pp. 27–28.

115. *SM*, p. 404.

116. *SM*, p. 433–34.

117. The text of the Convention is reprinted in C. W. J. Orr, *Cyprus under British Rule* (London, 1918), pp. 35–41.

118. 'Photographing in Cyprus', *BJP* (29 November 1878), p. 571.

119. 'I must not omit to pay a just tribute to the hospitality of these simple people, who place at one's disposal the best of everything their houses can provide.' John Thomson, 'A Journey Through Cyprus in the Autumn of 1878', *PRGS*, ns 1 (1879), p. 99.

120. Who evidently turned out to be almost useless. 'Photographing in Cyprus', *BJP* (29 November 1878), p. 571.

121. 'Where the archimandrite and the monks showed us great attention.' Thomson, 'Journey Through Cyprus', p. 100.

122. On 13 January 1879. See Thomson, 'Journey Through Cyprus', p. 97.

123. *TCWTC*, vol. 1, p. vi.

124. Remarks by Captain F. J. Evans, Hydrographer to the Admiralty, in Thomson, 'Journey Through Cyprus', p. 105.

125. Volume one also contains a Woodburytype portrait of Wolseley, by Lock and Whitfield.

126. Thomson, 'Photographing in Cyprus', p. 571.

127. *PC* (1 February 1879), p. 105.

Chapter 2—Publication

1. BL, Add. MS 41945, fol. 23v.

2. Anon, 'Mr Thomson's Photographs of China', *North China Herald and Supreme Court and Consular Gazette*, 11 January 1872, pp. 27–28.

3. Corr., 17 February 1872.

4. John Thomson, 'Life in China I', *The Graphic* (30 November 1872), p. 510. W. L. Thomas, 'The Making of *The Graphic*', *The Universal Review* (September–December 1888), pp. 80–93.

5. *Foochow*, p. 5.

6. *Foochow*, p. 9.

7. BL, Add. MS 41907, fol. 47v.

8. BL, Add. MS 41916, fol. 71v.

9. This extra-illustrated copy was sold at Sotheby's Belgravia, 17 June, 1981, lot 195. It is now in the Tokyo Fuji Art Museum. It contained 114 carbon prints, as opposed to the 80 listed in the normal edition. The extra material dealt with the Formosa trip.

10. See Arthur Warren, *The Charles Whittinghams Printers* (New York, 1896), passim; Janet Ing, 'Foreword', in *Charles Whittingham Printer 1795–1876: An Exhibit of his Works at Bailey/Howe Library at the University of Vermont* ([s.l.], 1983), pp. 9–10.

11. Anne Kelsey Hammond, 'Aesthetic Aspects of the Photomechanical Print', in *British Photography in the Nineteenth Century: The Fine Art Tradition*, ed. by Mike Weaver (Cambridge, 1989), pp. 170–73.

12. *History*, pp. 184–85. For more details about Thomson's use of and views on the process see below pp. 179–80.

13. For the Autotype Company see H. Baden Pritchard, *The Photographic Studios of Europe*, 2nd ed. (London, 1883), pp. 29–36; K. J. M. Mitchell, *The Rising Sun: The First 100 Years of the Autotype Company* ([s.l.], 1976), passim. Unfortunately the Records of the firm at the Science Museum do not cover the period when Thomson's books were being produced. Science Museum Library, MSS Autyp. 1–6.

14. E. Marston, *After Work: Fragments from the Workshop of an Old Publisher* (London, 1904), pp. 275–76.

15. BL, Add MS 41897, fol. 143v.

16. BL, Add. MS 41907, fols 81r, 100r, 121r, 133v, 140v.

17. The term autotype has its origins in a comment by the art critic Tom Taylor, and was adopted by the Autotype Company, and its subsidiary, The Autotype Fine Art Company, to give the firm its name. They used the term simultaneously to refer to both the carbon and collotype processes. Hammond, 'Photomechanical', pp. 172–3.

18. *IC*, vol. 1, Introduction, p. [1].

19. See Tom Reardon and Kent Kirby, 'Collotype: Prince of the Printing Processes', *Printing History*, 14 (1991), pp. 3–18.

20. Hammond, 'Photomechanical', pp. 174.

21. *The Chinese Recorder and Missionary Journal* (March–April 1874), pp. 109–10.

22. *The Graphic* (24 May 1873), p. 491.

23. *The Graphic* (24 May 1873), p. 491; *IC*, vol. I, plates I, XVII, XX, XXIV.

24. *The Athenaeum*, no. 2378 (24 May 1873), p. 659; no. 2397 (4 October 1873), p. 427; no. 2415 (7 February 1874), pp. 190–191; no. 2425 (18 April 1874), p. 520.

25. N. Prejevalsky, *Mongolia, the Tangut Country, and the Solitudes of Northern Tibet: being a Narrative of Three Years' Travel in Eastern High Asia*, 2 vols (London, 1876), I, p. vi.

26. See for example the advert in *The Athenaeum*, no. 2612 (17 November 1877), p. 613.

27. BL, Add. MS 41907, fol. 133v.

28. It was not, however, the most expensive book on Sampson Low's list at this time. That honour went to William Bradford's massive and magisterial *The Arctic Regions* at twenty-one guineas, another important photographically illustrated book. See *PC* (16 November 1874), p. 887.

29. *PC* (16 October 1874), p. 760.

30. Although the Copyright Library copies were deposited at Stationers' Hall on 30 November 1874, the adverts for the book did not appear until 1875, the date on the titlepage. London, Stationers' Hall, Copyright Libraries Receipt Books, vol. 8.

31. Sampson Low's list included books ranging in price from a shilling up to twenty-one guineas.

32. Marston, *After Work* , pp. 195–96.

33. *ILN*, no. 1849 (16 January 1875), p. 66.

34. *Nature*, 11 (1875), pp. 207–8.

35. *The Athenaeum*, no. 2459 (12 December 1874), p. 787.

36. Originally published in French as *Les Merveilles de la photographie* (Paris, 1874).

37. Announced in *The Publishers' Circular* as 'ready' on 16 November 1875.

38. *History*, pp. 142, 173–75, 184–85.

39. *BJP* (10 December 1875), p. 597.

40. For the best account of Woodbury see Steven Wachlin, *Woodbury & Page: Photographers Java* (Leiden, 1994), pp. 9–34.

41. See the review in *BJP* (26 March 1875), p. 155.

42. For which see below xx.

43. This style is described by Ruari McLean, *Victorian Publishers' Book-Bindings in Cloth and Leather* (London, 1974), pp. 11–12.

44. See the advert in *PC* (16 August 1877), p. 594.

45. *The Athenaeum*, no. 2569 (20 January 1877), p. 80.

46. *The Scotsman*, 30 January 1877, p. 3.

47. Beaumont Newhall, *The History of Photography from 1839 to the Present* (New York and London, 1982), p. 103; Helmut and Alison Gernsheim, *The History of Photography: From the Earliest Use of the Camera Obscura in the Eleventh Century up to 1914* (London, 1955), p. 340; Ian Jeffrey, *Photography: A Concise History* (London, 1981), pp. 65–67.

48. *PC* (18 January 1877), p. 5.

49. *PC* (1 February 1877), p. 5.

50. *PC* (1 February 1877), p. 5.

51. The subsequent parts were announced as ready in *The Publishers' Circular* on the first of each month following. For the phenomenon of serial publication, see Laurel Brake, '"The Trepidation of the Spheres": The Serial and the Book in the 19th Century', in *Serials and Their Readers*, ed. by Robin Myers and Michael Harris (Winchester, 1993), pp. 83–101.

52. *PC* (2 October 1877), pp. 679, 715, 787.

53. *PC* (2 November 1877), p. 829.

54. *PC* (1 June 1877), p. 375.

55. LAC, Letter, John Thomson to Sampson Low, Marston, Searle and Rivington, 6 May 1877.

56. LAC, Letter, Sampson Low to William Henry Fox Talbot, 30 May 1877.

57. LAC, Letter, Sampson Low to Talbot , 5 June 1877.

58. LAC, Letter, Sampson Low to Talbot, 14 June 1877.

59. LAC, Letter, Sampson Low to Talbot, 10 July 1877.

60. LAC, Letter, Sampson Low to Talbot, 10 August 1877.

61. *PC* (1 February 1878), p. 103.

62. *BJP* (21 December 1877), p. 609.

63. *The Exhibition of the Royal Scottish Academy of Painting, Sculpture, and Architecture ... The Fifty First* (Edinburgh, [1877]), pp. 26, 44.

64. Anon, 'Death of a Scottish Traveller', *The Scotsman*, 6 October 1921, p. 6; John Gifford, Colin McWilliam, and David Walker, *The Buildings of Scotland: Edinburgh* (Harmondsworth, 1984), p. 193.

65. It was founded in 1894; Thomson was elected in 1896. See *Royal Societies Club: Foundation & Objects, Rules & By-Laws, List of Members* (London, 1897), p. 143. For the Club, see also *Survey of London*, Vol. 30: *The Parish of St James Westminster*, Part One: *South of Piccadilly* (London, 1960), p. 472.

66. It would only move to its present location in Lowther Lodge in 1911. See Ian Cameron, *To the Farthest Ends of the Earth: The History of the Royal Geographical Society 1830–1980* (London, 1980), p. 198; Hugh Robert Mill, *The Record of the Royal Geographical Society 1830–1930* (London, 1930), pp. 181–82.

67. Frances Dimond and Roger Taylor, *Crown & Camera: The Royal Family and Photography 1842–1910* (Harmondsworth, 1987), p. 213.

68. Dimond and Taylor, *Crown and Camera*, pp. 211–12.

69. Windsor Castle, Royal Photographic Collection, 11.113, pp. 11, 12.

70. NPG: x3807.

71. Windsor Castle, Royal Photographic Collection, 11.114, p. 5.

72. Windsor Castle, Royal Photographic Collection, 11.114, p. 22.

73. NPG: x15500.

74. NPG: x4101.

75. NPG: x16927.

76. RGS: x252/022125.

77. RGS: PR/026691.

78. RGS: PR/026876–7.

79. RGS: PR/026561.

80. RGS: PR/026474.

81. RGS: PR/026698.

82. See Sotheby's London, 19/7/1994 lot 325.

83. NPG: x13142–3 (Phillipa Strachey), x13158–9 (Ralph Strachey), x38528 (Lady Strachey), x13105 (Elinor Rendel). For more on the family see Malcolm Rogers, *Camera Portraits: Photographs from the National Portrait Gallery 1839–1989* (London, 1989), pp. 138–39.

84. *Report of the Sixth International Geographical Congress, held in London, 1895* (London, 1896), Appendix A, p. 79; *Sixth International Geographical Congress, London, 1895: Catalogue of Exhibition* (London, 1896), p. 14.

85. RGS Archives, Letter, Thomson to H. W. Bates, 28 December 1886.

86. RGS Archives, Letter, Thomson to H. W. Bates, 25 January 1886.

87. RGS Archives, Letter, Thomson to A. R. Hicks, 7 November 1917.

88. RGS Archives, Letter, Thomson to A. R. Hicks, 10 February 1921.

89. They may well have been reproduced by The Platinotype Company, who operated their business on the Bromley Road. See H. Baden Pritchard, *Photographic Studios*, pp. 76–80.

90. The British Library and National Library of Scotland copies were bound by the great bookbinder, Roger de Coverly. See below, Bibliography no. A85. For De Coverly see *The British Bookmaker*, 5 (February, 1892), pp. 179–80.

91. Although there were some which were bound in a more elaborate and luxurious style, such as those for the Duchess of Devonshire and the Princess of Wales. See Marianne Tidcombe, *The Doves Bindery* (London, 1991). Nos 416, 418.

92. Edwin Hodder, *Cities of the World: Their Origin, Progress, and Present Aspect* 3 vols (London, [1882]), II, pp. 251–74.

93. Robert Brown, *The Countries of the World: Being A Popular Description of the Various Continents, Islands, Rivers, Seas, and Peoples of the Globe* 6 vols (London, [1882]), V, pp. 23–65, 127–47.

94. Brown, *Countries of the World*, V, p. 65.

95. *The Leeds Mercury*, 8 February 1898.

96. H. J. Mackinder, 'A Journey to the Summit of Mount Kenya, British East Africa', *Geographical Journal*, 15 (1900), pp. 453–86; Rev. J. W. Arthur, 'Mount Kenya', *Geographical Journal*, 58 (1921), p. 23.

97. RGS Archives, Letter, A. R. Hinks to Thomson, 14 November 1917.

98. *The British Journal Photographic Almanac 1922* (1922), p. 306.

99. Anon, 'Death of a Scottish Traveller', *The Scotsman*, 6 October 1921, p. 6.

100. J. S[cott] K[eltie], 'John Thomson', *The Geographical Journal*, 57 (1921), p. 470.

Chapter 3—Ruins and Structures: The Romantic Vision and the Melancholy Past

1. For overviews of travel photography as a genre see Robert Hershkowitz, *The British Photographer Abroad: The First Thirty Years* (London, 1980); Rainer Fabian and Hans-Christian Adam, *Masters of Early Travel Photography* (London, 1983); 'Extending the Grand Tour', in *The Waking Dream: Photography's First Century: Selections from the Gilman Paper Company Collection*, ed. by Maria Morris Hambourg, et al. (New York, 1993), pp. 84–117.

2. See Janet Dewan and Maia-Mari Sutnik, *Linnaeus Tripe: Photographer of British India* (Toronto, 1986), pp. 13–22.

3. Arthur Ollman, *Samuel Bourne: Images of India*, The Friends of Photography, Untitled 33 (Carmel, Calif., 1983), pp. 6–7.

4. John Falconer, 'Photography in Nineteenth-Century India', in *The Raj: India and the British 1600–1947*, ed. by C. A. Bayley (London, 1990), pp. 264–65; Isobel Crombie, 'China, 1860: A Photographic Album by Felice Beato', *History of Photography*, 11 (1987), pp. 25–37.

5. I am grateful to John Sanday of the World Monuments Fund for his comments and advice on Angkor.

6. Bruno Dagens, *Angkor: Heart of an Asian Empire* (London, 1995), pp. 13–43.

7. The first presentation of Mouhot's 'discoveries' was in a paper read after his death to the Royal Geographical Society on 10 March 1862. *PRGS*, 6 (1861–62), pp. 80–82. It was printed as 'Notes on Cambodia, the Lao Country, &c.', *The Journal of the Royal Geographical Society*, 32 (1862), pp. 142–63. His obituary appeared in the *ILN*, no. 1158 (9 August 1862), p. 166.

8. M. Henri Mouhot, *Travels in the Central Parts of Indo-China (Siam), Cambodia, and Laos, During the Years 1858, 1859, and 1860*, 2 vols (London, 1864), I, pp. 279–80.

9. *SM*, pp. 126–30.

10. *SM*, p. 136.

11. *AC*, p. 33.

12. Louis de Carné, *Travels in Indo-China and the Chinese Empire* (London, 1872), p. 40.

13. Falconer, 'Photography in Nineteenth-Century India', p. 264.

14. Reproduced in *Masterpieces of Photography from the Riddell Collection*, ed. by Sara Stevenson and Julie Lawson (Edinburgh, 1986), plate 30.

15. Thomson, as a member of the Bengal Photographic Society may have been familiar with Tripe's work.

16. *AC*, p. 45.

17. *IC*, vol. IV, text accompanying plate XIX.

18. *IC*, vol. IV, text accompanying plate XIX.

19. A. Wylie, 'On an Ancient Buddhist Inscription at Keu-yung Kwan, in North China', *Journal of the Royal Asiatic Society*, ns 5 (1871), pp. 14–44.

20. *IC*, vol. II, plate VIII.

21. *IC*, vol. II, text accompanying plate VIII.

22. *John Thomson: China and its People*, ed. by Ruth Charity and William Schupbach (London, 1991), p. 25.

23. *TC*, p. 147.
24. *Foochow*, p. 8.
25. 'A Visit to Yuan-Foo Monastery', *The Chinese Recorder and Missionary Journal* (March 1871), 296.
26. 'A Visit to Yuan-Foo Monastery', p. 298.
27. See Ann Paludan, *The Imperial Ming Tombs* (New Haven, 1981); and the same author's *The Chinese Spirit Road: The Classical Tradition of Stone Tomb Statuary* (New Haven, 1991).
28. *IC*, vol. III, plate XII.
29. *IC*, vol. IV, plate XX.
30. *TCWTC*, II, p. 50.
31. *TCWTC*, I, p. 15.

Chapter 4—Hearts of Darkness: The Street and its Types

1. The concept of 'type' derives originally from the scientific classification of the natural world, and ultimately from the work of Carl Linnaeus. See David Knight, *Ordering the World: A History of Classifying Man* (London, 1981), pp. 58–81.
2. Mary Cowling, *The Artist as Anthropologist: The Representation of Type and Character in Victorian Art* (Cambridge, 1989), p. xix.
3. See White, *Thomson*, plates 1, 6.
4. *SM*, p. 9.
5. See Syed Hussein Alatas, *The Myth of the Lazy Native* (London, 1977), pp. 72–80.
6. Eitel, *Europe in China*, p. 468.
7. *SM*, p. 200.
8. NLS, MS 503, fol. 26r. For Dickson see John Clark, *Japanese-British Exchanges in Art 1850s–1930s: Papers and Research Materials* (Canberra, 1989), pp. 130–31.
9. *SM*, p. 268.
10. Reproduced in *SM*, plate 13, as a wood-engraving from Thomson's original. The original negative is now lost, but an albumen print can be found in the Tokyo Fuji Art Museum. It is illustrated in White, *Thomson*, plate 73.
11. See for example the lithograph, *Hussain, a Malay of Malacca*, from J. T. Thomson's, *Sequel to Some Glimpses into Life in the Far East* (London, 1865), frontispiece.
12. Joseph Conrad, *Youth: A Narrative and Two Other Stories* (Edinburgh, 1902), p. 54.
13. *SM*, p. 297.
14. *IC*, vol. II, plate IV, no. 9.
15. For a discussion of the use of photography for this purpose, see *Anthropology and Photography 1860–1920*, ed. by Elizabeth Edwards (New Haven and London, 1992), passim.
16. M. Le Baron de Hübner, *A Ramble Round the World, 1871*, 2 vols (London, 1874), II, pp. 232–33.
17. Hübner, *A Ramble Round the World* , p. 233.
18. Hübner, *A Ramble Round the World*, p. 235.
19. *IC*, vol. IV, plate IX; *SM*, pp. 496–502.
20. *SM*, p. 497.
21. *SM*, p. 498.
22. See below under 'The Crawlers', p. 87.
23. See Alex Potts, 'Picturing the Modern Metropolis: Images of London in the Nineteenth Century', *History Workshop*, 26 (1988) esp. pp. 28–29, citing Carl Gustav Von Carus in 1844.
24. See Ialeen Gibson-Cowan, 'Thomson's *Street Life* in Context', *Creative Camera*, 251 (1985), pp. 10–15.

25. Adolphe Smith, *Report of the International Trade Union Congress held at Paris from August 23rd to 28th 1886* ([London, 1886]), and *A Critical Essay on the International Trade Union Congress held in London, November 1888* (London, 1889). After his involvement with Thomson, Smith became a leading figure in the Social Democratic Foundation, the precursor of the modern Labour Party, and wrote for its newspaper, *Justice*. See for example, A. Smith, 'France and the International Congress', *Justice* (27 December 1884), p. 3.

26. See for example his defence of Russian Nihilists in 'A Russian Secret State Trial', *Contemporary Review*, 58 (July–December 1890), 863–75.

27. See Eric de Maré, *The London Doré Saw: A Victorian Evocation* (London, 1973); Ira Bruce Nadel, '"London in the Quick": Blanchard Jerrold and the Text of *London: A Pilgrimage*', *The London Journal*, 2 (1976), pp. 51–66. Jerrold later wrote one of the classic biographies of Doré. Blanchard Jerrold, *Life of Gustave Doré*, (London, 1891). Thomson translated Baron D'Avillier's *Spain*, which Doré illustrated in its first appearance in print in French (1874).

28. See for example *The Pall Mall Gazette*, 5 February 1877, p. 5.

29. Anthony S. Wohl, *The Eternal Slum: Housing and Social Policy in Victorian London* (London, 1977), pp. 73–108. James Winter, *London's Teeming Streets 1830–1914* (London, 1993), pp. 45–47, 107–109.

30. Thomson and Smith probably took the phrase, 'the Silent Highway' from Mayhew. *London Labour and the London Poor*, 4 vols (London, 1851–62), I, p. 53.

31. See Gareth Stedman Jones, 'Working-Class Culture and Working-Class Politics in London, 1870–1900: Notes on the Remaking of a Working Class', *Journal of Social History*, 7 (1974), pp. 484–86.

32. Winter, *London's Teeming Streets*, p. 103. See also Richard Maxwell, 'Henry Mayhew and the Life of the Streets', *Journal of British Studies*, 17 (1978), pp. 99–100.

33. See Helmut Gernsheim, *The Origins of Photography* (London, 1982), pp. 134–41; Bernard V. and Pauline F. Heathcote, 'Richard Beard: An Ingenious and Enterprising Patentee', *History of Photography*, 3 (1979), pp. 313–29.

34. See Peter Keating, 'Words and Pictures: Changing Images of the Poor in Victorian Britain', in Julian Treuherz, *Hard Times: Social Realism in Victorian Art* (London, 1987), pp. 126–30.

35. Steadman Jones, 'Working Class Culture and Working Class Politics', pp. 465–71.

36. *SL*, preface.

37. See '*The Graphic*', in Julian Treuherz, *Hard Times: Social Realism in Victorian Art* (London, 1987), pp. 53–64.

38. '*The Graphic*', in Treuherz, *Hard Times*, p. 61.

39. '*The Graphic*', in Treuherz, *Hard Times*, p. 61.

40. See Sara Stevenson, *Hill and Adamson's The Fishermen and Women of the Firth of Forth* (Edinburgh, 1991), passim.

41. Taken between 1868 and 1871, and formally published in 1878–79. See Thomas Annan, *Photographs of the Old Closes and Streets of Glasgow 1868/1877 With a Supplement of 15 Related Views*, ed. by Anita Ventura Mozley (New York, 1977), pp. v–xv; Sara Stevenson, *Thomas Annan 1829–1887* (Edinburgh, 1990), pp. 13–18.

42. See Julie Lawson, 'The Problem of Poverty and the Picturesque: Thomas Annan's *Old Closes and Streets of Glasgow 1868–1871*', *Scottish Photography Bulletin*, 2 (1990) pp. 40–46.

43. See Julie Lawson's comments in *Masterpieces of Photography from the Riddell Collection*, ed. by Sara Stevenson and Julie Lawson (Edinburgh, 1986), pp. 116–18.

44. See Gertrude Mae Prescott, 'Architectural Views of Old London', *The Library Chronicle of the University of Texas at Austin*, ns 15 (1981), passim.

45. See Hammond, 'Aesthetic Aspects of the Photomechanical Print', esp. pp. 173–75; Beaumont Newhall, *Photography and the Book* (Boston, 1983), pp. 33–35; for a detailed account of the elements of the process see the entry on the Woodburytype factory in Baden-Pritchard, *Photographic Studios*, pp. 96–101.

46. *PC* (18 December 1875), p. 1211.

47. *History*, p. 221.

48. As favoured by other photographers more interested in portraying the picturesque qualities of such a scene as a 'safe' tourist memento, like those which appear in William Notman's *Sports and Pastimes of Canada*. See Miles Orvell, *The Real Thing: Imitation and Authenticity in American Culture 1880–1940* (Chapel Hill, 1989), p. 81.

49. See especially the criticisms of Jeff Rosen, 'Posed as Rogues: The Crisis of Photographic Realism in John Thomson's *Street Life in London*', *Image*, 36 (1993), pp. 9–39.

50. A similar appreciation of this aspect of Thomson's work has recently been made by Colin Westerbeck and Joel Meyerowitz, *Bystander: A History of Street Photography* (London, 1994) pp. 73–80. Jacob Riis was similarly constrained by the (very different) conditions he was confronted with: see Greenough, 'The Curious Contagion of the Camera', p. 138. *The British Journal of Photography* praised Thomson's photography for overcoming these difficulties: *BJP* (14 December 1877), p. 595.

51. See Rosen, 'Posed as Rogues', pp. 17–21; Anne McCauley, 'An Image of Society', in *A History of Photography: Social and Cultural Perspectives*, ed. by Jean-Claude Lemagny and André Rouillé (Cambridge, 1987), pp. 62–63.

52. See Sean Shesgreen, 'The First London Cries', *Print Quarterly*, 10 (1993), pp. 364–73.

53. See Felicity Ashbee and Julie Lawson, *William Carrick 1827–1878* (Edinburgh, 1987), pp. 11–17.

54. Greenough, 'Curious Contagion', pp. 139–40.

55. Sotheby's, Belgravia, *Photographic Images and Related Material* (27 June 1980), lot 231. They were published as *Street Types of Great American Cities* (Chicago, 1896).

56. See Mick Gidley, 'Hoppé's Impure Portraits: Contextualising the American Types', in *The Portrait in Photography*, ed. by Graham Clarke (London, 1992), pp. 132–54.

57. Greenough, 'Curious Contagion', p. 140.

58. Published as August Sander, *Antlitz der Zeit* 'Face of Our Time' (Munich, 1929). See Robert Kramer, *August Sander: Photographs of an Epoch 1904–1959* (New York, 1980), p.11.

59. *SL*, p. 2.

60. *SL*, p. 3.

61. *SL*, pp. 88–90.

62. Gustave Doré and Blanchard Jerrold, *London: A Pilgrimage* (London, 1872), p. 127.

63. *SL*, pp. 43–44.

64. See for example Roger Whitehouse, *A London Album: Early Photographs Recording the History of the City and its People from 1840 to 1915* (London, 1980) no. 172, where this image is captioned as 'A Mother and Child in a London Doorway'. He obviously failed to read the accompanying text.

65. *SL*, p. 81.

66. Rosen, 'Posed as Rogues', pp. 34–35.

67. *The Athenaeum*, no. 2616 (15 December 1877), p. 778. Rosen, 'Posed as Rogues' p. 34.

68. *The Graphic* (1 December 1877), p. 523.

69. *The Lancet* (10 February 1877), p. 213.

70. Anon, 'Politics, Sociology, Voyages, and Travels', *The Westminster Review*, ns 52 (July–October 1877), p. 241.

Chapter 5—Formal Portraits

1. [Lady Elizabeth Eastlake], 'Physiognomy', *The Quarterly Review*, 90 (1851–52), p. 62.

2. Moffat, *Mongkut*, 52.

3. *Siam and Laos as Seen by our American Missionaries*, ed. by Mary Backus (Philadelphia, 1884), p. 326.

4. John Bowring, *The Kingdom and People of Siam*, 2 vols (London, 1859), I, p. 441.

5. *SM*, p. 93.

6. Moffat, *Mongkut*, p. 12.

7. David K. Wyatt, *Thailand: A Short History* (New Haven and London, 1984), pp. 183–85.

8. Moffat, *Mongkut*, p. 194.

9. *SM*, p. 89.

10. Wyatt, *Thailand*, p. 182.

11. Moffat, *Mongkut*, p. 25.

12. *SM*, p. 93.

13. *SM*, p. 94.

14. *SM*, pp. 94–95.

15. de Hübner, *Ramble Around the World*, II, pp. 293–94.

16. *IC*, vol. I, text accompanying plate I.

17. The Baron records that he received the photograph a little while after he spoke with the Prince. Hübner, *Ramble Around the World*, II, pp. 293–94.

18. *SM*, p. 512.

19. See Ting-yee Kuo and Kwang-Ching Liu, 'Self-strengthening: The Pursuit of Western Technology', in *The Cambridge History of China Volume 10: Late Ch'ing, 1800–1911, Part I*, ed. by John K. Fairbank (Cambridge, 1978), pp. 504–7.

20. John Thomson, 'Life in China, XVI – The Foreign Office, Peking', *The Graphic* (18 October 1873), p. 362.

21. *TC*, p. 252.

22. *BJP* (29 November 1872), p. 569.

23. W. H. Medhurst, *The Foreigner in Far Cathay* (London, 1872), pp. 80–81.

24. *IC*, vol. I, plate XI.

25. *IC*, vol. I, text accompanying plate XI.

26. *IC*, vol. I, text accompanying plate XIV.

27. See especially Roger Taylor, 'Photographers to Her Majesty', in Frances Dimond and Roger Taylor, *Crown & Camera: The Royal Family and Photography 1842–1910* (Harmondsworth, 1987), pp. 211–12.

28. Lady Violet Greville, 'The Devonshire House Ball', *The Graphic* (10 July 1897), p. 78.

29. Greville, 'The Devonshire House Ball', pp. 78–79.

30. 'Ball at Devonshire House', *The Times*, 3 July 1897, p. 12.

31. 'The Devonshire House Ball', *St. James's Gazette*, 3 July 1897, p. 8.

32. Martin Mayer, *The Met: One Hundred Years of Grand Opera* (London, 1983), p. 13. See also the Foreword to *The Library of the Late Ogden Goelet of New York* (American Art Association, Anderson Galleries, 3–4 January 1935).

33. 'The Devonshire House Ball', *Pall Mall Gazette*, 3 July 1897, p. 7.

34. For Ingres Odalisques, see Julie Lawson, 'The Painter's Vision', in *Visions of the Ottoman Empire* (Edinburgh, 1994), pp. 20–22. For Fenton's *Seated Odalisque*, see Weston J. Naef, *Handbook of the Photographs Collection J. Paul Getty Museum* (Malibu, 1995), p. 68.

35. Lady Sarah Wilson was the daughter of the 7th Duke of Marlborough.

36. Lady Elizabeth Montagu, Duchess of Buccleuch, died in 1827. Thomson's photograph is based on the painting by Thomas Gainsborough now (as then) in the collection of the Duke of Buccleuch, at Boughton.

37. Still at Belvoir Castle in the possession of the Duke of Rutland. For a description see Frederick B. Daniell, *Catalogue Raisoneé of the Engraved Works of Richard Cosway, R.A.* (London, 1890), p. 31. See also Stephen Lloyd, *Richard & Maria Cosway: Regency Artists of Taste and Fashion* (Edinburgh, 1995). I am particularly grateful to Stephen Lloyd for his advice on this portrait.

Chapter 6—Man and Nature: The Sublime and Picturesque Landscape

1. [John Thomson], 'Three Pictures in Wong-Nei-Chung', *China Magazine* (August 1868), p. 53.
2. *BJP* (30 November 1866), p. 576.
3. John Thomson, 'Practical Photography in Tropical Regions', *BJP* (10 August 1866), p. 380.
4. See Peter Bicknell, *Beauty, Horror, and Immensity: The Picturesque Landscape in Britain, 1750–1850* (Cambridge, 1981), pp. xii–xiii.
5. John Beasley Greene (1832–56). See Bruno Jammes, 'John B. Greene, an American Calotypist', *History of Photography*, 4 (1981), pp. 305–24.
6. Especially *The Lone Lagoon* (1893). See Nancy Newhall, *P. H. Emerson: The Fight for Photography as a Fine Art* (New York, 1978).
7. See Roger Taylor, *Samuel Bourne 1834–1912: Photographic Views in India* (Sheffield, 1980); Arthur Ollman, *Samuel Bourne: Images of India,* The Friends of Photography, Untitled 33 (Carmel, Calif., 1983).
8. Captain Charles Wilson, *Ordnance Survey of Jerusalem* (London, 1865); Captain Charles Wilson and H. S. Palmer, *Ordnance Survey of the Peninsula of Sinai* (London, 1869); Paul Fort, 'Ordnance Survey Work in the Middle East during the 1860s', *Photographic Collector*, 6 (1987), pp. 58–67.
9. For the tradition of Chinese landscape art see Marjorie L. Williams, *Chinese Painting: An Escape from the 'Dusty World'* (Cleveland, 1981), p. 24; Anne Farrer, *'The Brush Dances & The Ink Sings': Chinese Paintings and Calligraphy from the British Museum* (London, 1990), pp. 33–35; Sherman E. Lee, *Chinese Landscape Painting* (Cleveland, 1954), pp. 5–10. Thomson collected some early Chinese scroll-paintings: see *SM*, p. 283.
10. See Patrick Conner, *George Chinnery 1774–1852: Artist of India and the China Coast* (Woodbridge, 1993).
11. *VONR*, p. [5].
12. *SM*, p. 219.
13. *VONR*, text accompanying 'Looking North from the Pau-Lo-Hang Temple'.
14. *VONR*, text accompanying 'Road to the Village of Wong Tong'.
15. Thomson's studio was at no. 29, Afong's at no. 54.
16. See *Van Bombay tot Shanghai=From Bombay to Shanghai: Historical Photography in South and South-East Asia,* ed. by John Falconer, Steven Wachlin and Anneke Groeneveld (Amsterdam, 1995), p. 49.
17. *BJP* (29 November 1872), p. 569.
18. *TC*, p. 8.
19. NGS, R38.
20. See Simon Schama, *Landscape and Memory* (London, 1995), p. 408.
21. See the image reproduced in Sotheby's London, 4/5/95 lot 35.
22. NLS, MS 9843, fol. 2v.
23. *Foochow*, p. 10.
24. Reproduced in *Ansel Adams: Letters and Images 1916–1984,* ed. by Mary Street Alinder and Andrea Gray Stillman (Boston, 1988), p. 388.
25. See Barbara M. Stafford, 'Towards Romantic Landscape Perception: Illustrated Travels and the Rise of "Singularity" as an Aesthetic Category', *Art Quarterly*, ns 1 (1977), pp. 108–9.
26. Thomson, 'Photographing in Cyprus', p. 571.
27. *TCWTC*, II, p. 35.
28. *TCWTC*, II, p. 35.
29. See Schama, *Landscape and Memory*, especially pp. 207–14.
30. The journey is summarised in Alexander Hosie, 'A Journey in South-western China, from Ssŭ-ch'uan to Western Yünnan', *PRGS*, ns 8 (1886), pp. 383–84.
31. *SM*, p. 446.
32. *SM*, p. 447.
33. *IC*, vol. III, text accompanying plate XXIV.
34. [John Thomson], 'Three Pictures in Wong-Nei-Chung', *China Magazine* (August 1868), p. 53.

Chapter 7—'A Congenial, Profitable, and Instructive Occupation': John Thomson and Photography

1. H. J. P. Arnold, *William Henry Fox Talbot: Pioneer of Photography and Man of Science* (London, 1977); Gail Buckland, *Fox Talbot and the Invention of Photography* (London, 1980); Larry J. Schaaf, *Out of the Shadows: Herschel, Talbot & the Invention of Photography* (New Haven, 1992); Sara Stevenson and John Ward, *Printed Light: The Scientific Art of William Henry Fox Talbot and David Octavius Hill with Robert Adamson* (Edinburgh, 1986); Hubertus von Amelunxen and M. W. Gray, *Die Aufgehobene Zeit* (Berlin, 1988).

2. The calotype negative could be exposed whilst either wet or dry.

3. Gallic acid and protosulphate of iron.

4. Victor Regnault discovered shortly afterwards that collodion plates were more quickly developed with pyrogallol (pyrogallic acid) and fixed with potassium cyanide. Both are, however, capable of being developed and fixed with the same chemical compounds.

5. John Thomson, 'Geographical Photography', *Scottish Geographical Magazine*, 25 (1904), pp. 14–19.

6. Thomson recommends that when the iodised collodion has been evenly spread over the plate the operator should run off the excess liquid from the two opposing corners, thus reducing the tendency of the collodion layer to thicken at one end when poured off from one point only.

7. Success or failure of the whole process was decided at this point, and depended entirely upon the operator's chemical and manipulative skills. If the iodised collodion stratum was correctly laid down, thinly and evenly distributed on the glass plate, without flaws, dust, or contamination, excellent results could be obtained. No form of after-treatment could compensate for, or rectify any errors or incorporated blemishes resulting from a poorly collodionised plate.

8. Double decomposition occurs when, for example, as in the salt paper process, solutions of silver nitrate and sodium chloride are mixed together; silver, having a greater affinity for chlorine, forms silver chloride whilst sodium couples with the nitrate to form sodium nitrate. This process only takes place in the presence of moisture ($AgNo_3 + NaC_1 = AgC_1 + NaNo_3$). It is slightly more complex than this however, as the chlorine ions (C_1) have first to enter into combination with water, to form hydrochloric and hypochlorous acid before being taken up by the silver; sodium nitrate is hygroscopic and helps retain moisture within the fibres of paper and assists in a passive manner the reduction of the silver salts to its metallic form as a redox agent. By the mid-1850s most practitioners were using ammonium as opposed to sodium chloride as the primary salt. Being more hygroscopic and less likely to form insoluble sulphur compounds in the subsequent stages of processing, it was generally the preferred option of albumen printers.

9. For portraiture using the albumen process, a density range of 1.2 – 1.5 was favoured.

10. Until the advent of modern emulsion-based photographic papers it was not possible to produce chemically developed-out printing papers which could vary contrast grade. Printing out papers offer only limited contrast control.

11. Wrapped in a black-lined, light-coloured cloth which protected the plate in the short term from light and heat.

12. The prospects for failure were legion at almost every stage of the process. If there were any residual iron compounds remaining on the insufficiently washed plate, the addition of potassium cyanide would lead to the formation of potassium ferricyanide, a highly active and efficient bleaching agent.

13. *History*, p. 125.

14. Joseph Maria Eder, *A History of Photography*, 4th ed. (New York, 1972), p. 342.

15. $C_6H_4(OH)_2$, 1:2:3 Pyrogallol, Trihydroxybenzene, Phentriol – 1:2:3 (erroneously called pyrogallic acid). See Henri Braconnot, 'Observations sur la préparation et la purification de l'acide gallique, et sur l'existence d'un acide nouveau dans la noix de galle', *Annales de chimie et de physique*, 2ᵉ série, 9 (1818), pp. 181–89.

16. Eder, *History*, p. 178.

17. Eder, *History,* p. 342.

18. Eder, *History,* p. 342.

19. Such as paper, linen fibres, straw, wood, and cactus skins.

20. Simon Peers, *The Working of Miracles: Photography in Madagascar 1853–1865* (London, 1995).

21. 'Report of the Collodion Committee', *Photographic Notes,* 5 (1860), pp. 52–55.

22. 'Report of the Collodion Committee', p. 52.

23. If the collodionised plate had been dipped, drained, and inserted into the camera before it had 'set' with the solution having been mixed too thinly, then the silver salts held in suspension would have been flowing slowly down the plate. The resultant (negative) image would appear out of focus in localised areas.

24. Caused by the collodion being incorrectly 'flowed'. Under these conditions it forms ridges and 'pools' parallel to the direction in which it is drained.

25. Amongst whom were Phillip Delamotte, Roger Fenton, Francis Bedford, Jabez Hughes, and Russell Sedgefield.

26. 'Report of the Collodion Committee', p. 52.

27. 'Report of the Collodion Committee', p. 52.

28. 'Report of the Collodion Committee', p. 53.

29. Reported by Thomas Sutton, who had received two letters from Cairo sent by Frith. See 'Report of the Collodion Committee', pp. 52–55.

30. For Thomson working in the Far East however, high levels of temperature and humidity would have entailed variations in the ether–alcohol mix to account for the evaporation of the collodion stratum to take place at the required rate.

31. Helmut Gernsheim, *Incunabula of British Photographic Literature* (London, 1984), p. 88.

32. 'Report of the Collodion Committee', p. 53.

33. 'Report of the Collodion Committee', p. 54.

34. Due to dust or small airborne crystal particles of potassium cyanide.

35. Due to small particles or fragments of dried collodion which have contaminated the solution.

36. Contemporaries also referred to this as 'diagonal ribbing'. It was attributed to the plate being insufficiently or improperly rocked when coating with collodion; or the collodion being too thick. To solve the problem, photographers were recommended to thin the collodion with alcohol. See H. Snowden Ward, *Photographic Annual incorporating the Figures, Facts, & Formulae of Photography* (London, 1908).

37. Thomson, 'Practical Photography', p. 380.

38. Neville Story Maskelyne had discovered in 1846 that silver bromide extended the spectral response from the blue partially into the green.

39. Thomas Keith, 'Dr Thomas Keith's Paper on the Waxed Paper Process', *Photographic Notes* 1 (17 July 1856), pp. 100–4.

40. Thomson, 'Practical Photography', p. 436.

41. C. G. H. Kinnear is generally acknowledged as being the designer of the first 'field' camera: i.e. one that allowed the position of the lens in relation to the focal plane to be manipulated in order to correct perspective.

42. Thomson, 'Practical Photography', p. 404.

43. He regarded the most suitable shape of a tent for long journeys to be conical. It should be made from three thicknesses of black cotton cloth, and one of yellow. There should be a window of yellow cloth sewn into the left side of the tent. The tripod on which the tent is fixed should be made of three lengths of bamboo, cut locally each time the tent is erected, and then discarded. The tent is therefore much more transportable without the frame, and was used by Thomson to wrap his box of chemicals when travelling. Thomson, 'Practical Photography', p. 404.

44. Thomson, 'Practical Photography', p. 404.

45. Four parts, ether to five parts, alcohol.

46. Ammonia sulphate of iron.

47. The chemical development is the process by which the latent negative photographic image is brought out by a chemical reagent. Initially, photographers using the wet-collodion process used gallic acid, but then moved on to pyrogallol (erroneously, but extensively, referred to as pyrogallic acid), which was a more powerful reducing agent. Both gallic acid and pyrogallol were difficult and inconvenient to use in practice, and especially in the field, due to the ease and speed with which both compounds oxidised. Physical development was more akin to the process of intensification as we still recognise it today. The developing solution contains additional silver nitrate, which, during the subsequent treatment and processing of the wet-collodion negative, deposits additional metallic silver onto the partially formed image. The image is blacker in appearance than that formed through the action of the proto-sulphate of iron developer, and produces a distinct relief when examined in raking light. This variation enables the photographer to obtain negatives of extremely high contrast when working in conditions which do not produce high-contrast negatives.

48. Thomson, 'Practical Photography', p. 404.

49. See 'Photographic Chemicals and Apparatus', in Justus Doolittle, *Vocabulary and Hand-Book of the Chinese Language* 2 vols (Foochow, 1872), II, pp. 319–20.

50. *SM*, pp. 474–75.

51. Bill Jay, 'Death in the Darkroom', *BJP*, 127 (1980), pp. 976–99.

52. Thomson, 'Geographical Photography', p. 16.

53. Thomson, 'Geographical Photography', p. 16.

54. Thomson even referred to Talbot as the 'Caxton' of photography. LAC, Letter, John Thomson to Sampson Low & Co., 6 May 1877.

55. John Thomson was a particularly successful magic lantern lecturer, and developed his own technology to enable his presentations to be as effective as possible. See John Thomson, 'The Magic Lantern', in *Science for All*, ed. by Robert Brown, 2 vols (London, [1882]), II, pp. 208–14. He was the first to urge the Royal Geographical Society to use the magic lantern to illustrate lectures. RGS Archives, letter dated 7 November 1917.

56. See especially Nancy Newhall, *P. H. Emerson: the Fight for Photography as a Fine Art* (New York, 1978).

57. See Estelle Jussim, *Visual Communication and the Graphic Arts: Photographic Technologies in the Nineteenth Century* (New York, 1983), pp. 58–66.

58. Richard D. Altick, *The English Common Reader: A Social History of the Mass Reading Public 1800–1900* (Chicago, 1957), pp. 343–44, 394–95.

59. John Szarkowski, *Photography Until Now* (New York, 1989), p. 177.

60. 'Bangkok, Capital of Siam', *ILN*, no. 1428 (25 May, 1867), pp. 512, 514.

61. W. L. Thomas, 'The Making of *The Graphic*', *The Universal Review* (September–December 1888), p. 88.

62. S. Thompson, 'Photography in its Application to Book Illustration', *BJP* (1 March 1862), p. 88.

63. For Thomson's possible connection with Piazzi Smyth see above, pp. xx–xx. Piazzi Smyth was also interested in the application of photography to book illustration. See C. Piazzi Smyth, 'On Photographic Illustrations for Books', *Transactions of the Royal Scottish Society of Arts*, 5 (1858), pp. 87–92.

64. Review of W. Abney's *Thebes and its Great Temples* in *The Athenaeum*, no. 2573 (17 February 1877), p. 220.

65. 'Our Editors Table: Views in Canton by John Thomson', *BJP* (24 September 1869), p. 463.

66. *IC*, Vol. 1, Preface.

67. *TCWTC*, Vol. 1, Preface.

68. *TC*, Preface.

69. Platinum prints by Thomson survive in the Royal Geographical Society, and were given to that institution in the period 1904–17. Other platinum prints survive in the Museum voor Volkenkunde in Rotterdam, being prints made by Thomson from photographs taken by J. C. Photz whilst in Persia. They were given to the Museum in 1885. I owe my knowledge of this collection to Anneka Groeneveld. They were not taken by Thomson, as suggested by Nissan N. Perez in *Focus East: Early Photography in the Near East (1839–1885)* (New York, 1988), pp. 226–72.

70. See especially Felix Driver, 'David Livingstone and the Culture of Exploration in Mid-Victorian Britain', in *David Livingstone and the Victorian Encounter with Africa*, ed. by Peter Funnell (London, 1996), pp. 109–38.

71. RGS Archives, Letter, Thomson to Mr Hinks, 10 February 1921.

BIBLIOGRAPHY

A. Writings of John Thomson Published in his Lifetime

1. 'Practical Photography in Tropical Regions', *BJP* (10 August 1866), p. 380; (17 August 1866), p. 393; (24 August 1866), p. 404; (4 September 1866), pp. 436–37; (5 October 1866), pp. 472–73; (12 October 1866), p. 487.

2. *The Antiquities of Cambodia: A Series of Photographs Taken on the Spot With Letterpress Description by John Thomson F.R.G.S., F.E.S.L.* (Edinburgh: Edmonston & Douglas, 1867).
   71, [2] pp. ; 16 albumen prints, 1 photo-lithographic plate.
   On verso of titlepage: Shirley, Printer, Edinburgh.
   Trade binding: Green quarter cloth, lettered in gilt on front board: Antiquities of Cambodia Illustrated by Photographs Taken on the Spot
   Plates 1–3, 10–12 are each composite of 3 images forming panorama.
   Gernsheim, *Incunabula*, no. 368; Goldschmidt & Naef, *Truthful Lens*, no. 166.

3. 'Enlargements from Small Negatives', *BJP* (4 January 1867), p. 3; (11 January 1867), pp. 13–14.

4. 'The King of Siam's State Barge' and 'Bangkok, The Capital of Siam', *ILN*, no. 1428 (25 May 1867), pp. 512, 514.

5. 'A Visit to the Ruined Temples of Cambodia', *Report of the Thirty-Sixth Meeting of the British Association for the Advancement of Science* (London, 1867), pp. 116–17.

6. 'Notes on Cambodia and its Races', *Transactions of the Ethnological Society of London*, ns, 6 (1868), pp. 246–52. With four lithographs after Thomson photographs. Attributed to 'G. Thomson, Esq.'

7. 'The Ruined Temples of Cambodia', *ILN*, no. 1467 (1 February 1868), pp. 104, 118.

8. *Photographic Album Accompanying 'The Ever Victorious Army'* (Hong Kong: [s.n.]; Glasgow: [s.n.], 1868).
   [16] pp. ; 22 mounted albumen prints.
   'This album is issued as an accompaniment to Mr Andrew Wilson's work, published by Messrs. Blackwood, entitled "The Ever Victorious Army": A History of the Chinese Campaign under Lieut.-Col. C. G. Gordon ... and of the Suppression of the Tai-Ping Rebellion'. Preface signed J. T., July 1868.
   Gernsheim, *Incunabula*, no. 411.

9. 'The Cambodian Ruins (Part One)', *The China Magazine* (August 1868), pp. 17–19.

10. 'Three Pictures in Wong-nei-chung', *The China Magazine* (August 1868), pp. 52–56.

11. 'Morning Walk in Cochin China', *The China Magazine* (September 1868), pp. 60–62.

12. 'The Cambodian Ruins (Part Two)', *The China Magazine* (September 1868), pp. 80–82.

13. 'An Anamese Village', *The China Magazine* (September, 1868), pp. 123–24.

14. 'Hak-Kas', *The China Magazine* (September 1868), pp. 134–36.

15. 'An Anamese Chief', *The China Magazine* (September, 1868), pp. 150–51.

16. 'Chinese House at Cholon', *The China Magazine* (September, 1868), pp. 166–67.

17. 'An Anamese Scholar', *The China Magazine* (September 1868), pp. 180–81.

18. Rev. William R. Beach, *The Visit of His Royal Highness the Duke of Edinburgh, K.G., K.T., G.C.M.G. to Hong Kong, Compiled from Local Journals and Other Sources ...* (Hong Kong: Noronha & Sons. Government Printers. London: Smith, Elder and Co., 1869).
iv, [2], 59, [1] pp. ; Seven albumen prints by Thomson, two of which form a fold-out panorama.
Bound in half-paper boards, sides of red cloth, lettered in gilt: 'Visit to Hong Kong of His Royal Highness the Duke of Edinburgh in 1869'.
Gernsheim, *Incunabula*, no. 477.

19. 'Prince Alfred at Hong Kong', *ILN*, no. 1578 (29 January 1870), pp. 111–12.

20. 'A Visit to the Interior of South Formosa', *The Cycle*, 27 (August 1870)

21. *Views on the North River. By J. Thomson, F.R.G.S., &c.* (Hong Kong: Noronha & Sons, Printers. 1870).
[38] pp. ; Fourteen albumen prints.
Quarter-cloth, paper covered boards, decorated and lettered on front and rear boards 'Views on the North River'.
Gernsheim, *Incunabula*, no. 497; Goldschmidt & Naef, *Truthful Lens*, no. 167.

22. 'A Visit to Yuen-foo Monastery', *The Chinese Recorder and Missionary Journal* (March, 1871), p. 296.

23. 'Photographical Chemicals and Apparatus. By John Thomson Esq.', in Justus Doolittle, *Vocabulary and Hand-Book of the Chinese Language. In two volumes Romanized in the Mandarin Dialect. By the Rev. Justus Doolittle. Author of Social Life of the Chinese.* 2 vols (Foochow: China, Rozario, Marcal and Company London: 60 Paternoster Row: Trubner and Company, New York: Anson, D. E. Randolf and Company. San Francisco, A. L. Bancroft and Company, 1872.), II, pp. 319–20.

24. 'Hong-Kong Photographers', *BJP* (29 November 1872), p. 569; (13 December 1872), pp. 591–92.

25. 'Life in China I', *The Graphic* (30 November 1872), pp. 504, 508, 510.

26. 'Life in China II', *The Graphic* (7 December 1872), pp. 534, 578.

27. 'Life in China III', *The Graphic* (14 December 1872), pp. 556, 559.

28. 'Life in China IV', *The Graphic* (21 December 1872), pp. 587, 592.

29. 'Life in China V', *The Graphic* (28 December 1872), p. 607.

30. 'Life in China VI', *The Graphic* (4 January 1873), pp. 3, 12.

31. 'Life in China VII', *The Graphic* (11 January 1873), pp. 21, 35.

32. 'Life in China VIII', *The Graphic* (18 January 1873), pp. 58, 64.

33. 'Life in China IX', *The Graphic* (25 January 1873), pp. 71, 74, 85.

34. 'Life in China X', *The Graphic* (8 February 1873), pp. 124, 130.

35. 'Life in China XI', *The Graphic* (15 February 1873), pp. 160, 161.

36. 'Life in China XII', *The Graphic* (1 March 1873), pp. 194, 209.

37. 'Life in China XIII', *The Graphic* (22 March 1873), pp. 274, 280.

38. 'Sketches of Life in China XIV', *The Graphic* (17 May 1873), pp. 459, 473.

39. 'Life in China XV', *The Graphic* (24 May 1873), pp. 482, 484.

40. 'Life in China XVI', *The Graphic* (18 October 1873), pp. 362, 377.

41. 'Notice of a Journey in Southern Formosa', *PRGS*, 18 (1873), pp. 144–48

42. 'The Antiquities of Cambodia', *Journal of the North China Branch of the Royal Asiatic Society*, ns 7 (1873), pp. 197–204.

43. *Foochow and the River Min* (London: Printed by the Autotype Fine Art Company, 1873).
[12] pp ; 80 carbon prints.
Verso of titlepage: Chiswick Press: Printed by Whittingham and Wilkins, Tooks Court, Chancery Lane.
Printed in an edition of 46 copies.
Not in Goldschmidt and Naef, *Truthful Lens*. Not in Betram Dobell, *Catalogue of Books Printed for Private Circulation* (London, 1906).

44. *Illustrations of China and its people: a series of two hundred photographs with letterpress description of the places and people represented. By J. Thomson, F.R.G.S.*
(London: Sampson Low, Marston, Low, and Searle, Crown Buildings, 188, Fleet Street, 1873–1874).
4 vols ; 200 Autotypes (i.e. collotypes).
On verso of titlepage: Chiswick Press: Printed by Whittingham and Wilkins, Tooks Court, Chancery Lane. Bound in black cloth, elaborately gilt-tooled and blocked with illustration taken from Thomson's image of the Confucian Temple, Peking. Gilt edges.
Goldschmidt & Naef, *Truthful Lens*, no. 168.

45. *Illustrations of China and its people: a series of two hundred photographs with letterpress description of the places and people represented. By J. Thomson, F.R.G.S.* Second edition
(London: Sampson Low, Marston, Low, and Searle, Crown Buildings, 188, Fleet Street, 1874).
4 vols ; 200 Autotypes (i.e. collotypes).
On verso of titlepage: Chiswick Press: Printed by Whittingham and Wilkins, Tooks Court, Chancery Lane.
On p. [6]: Note: The Photographs are produced by the Autotype Mechanical Printing Process of Messrs. Spencer, Sawyer, Bird and Co., London.
Bound in black cloth, elaborately gilt-tooled and blocked with illustration taken from Thomson's image of the Confucian Temple, Peking. Gilt edges.

46. 'A Pocket Camera', *British Journal Photographic Almanac 1874* (1874), pp. 156–58.

47. *Treasure Spots of the World: A Selection of the Chief Beauties and Wonders of Nature and Art* ed. Walter B. Woodbury (London: Ward, Lock, and Tyler, Paternoster Row, 1875).
Unpaginated.
Bound in blue cloth elaborately embossed in gilt and black. Gilt edges.
Contributions: 'Bangkok, Capital of Siam'; 'Amoy Harbour, China'; 'On the Merced, Yosemite Valley'.

48. 'Sketches of Travel in China: Hong Kong to Peking', in *Illustrated Travels: A Record of Discovery, Geography, and Adventure* ed. H. W. Bates, 6 vols (London: Cassell, Petter, & Galpin, [1875]), V, pp. 119–22, 243–47.

49. *The Straits of Malacca, Indo-China, and China, or Ten Years' Adventures and Residence Abroad* (London: Sampson Low, Marston, Low, and Searle, 1875).
xvi, 546 p. ; 68 wood-engravings (by J. D. Cooper) taken from the author's sketches and photographs.
Preface signed: J. T. Brixton, November 1874.
Red cloth, blocked in black and gilt.

50. *The Straits of Malacca, Indo-China, and China, or Ten Years' Adventures and Residence Abroad* (New York: Harper and Brothers, 1875).
xv, 546 pp., 68 wood-engravings (by J. D. Cooper) taken from the author's sketches and photographs.
Issued in both red and blue cloth. Spine lettered: 'W. Thomson' on some copies.
American reprint of A49.

51. 'Proverbial Photographic Philosophy', *British Journal Photographic Almanac 1875* (1875), pp. 128–29.

52. 'Across Siam to Cambodia-I', in *Illustrated Travels: A Record of Discovery, Geography, and Adventure,* ed. H. W. Bates, 6 vols (London: Cassell, Petter, & Galpin, [1875]), V, pp. 307–30.

53. 'Across Siam to Cambodia [II]', in *Illustrated Travels: A Record of Discovery, Geography, and Adventure,* ed. By H. W. Bates, 6 vols (London: Cassell, Petter, & Galpin, [1876]), VI, pp. 43–44.

54. *The Land and People of China: a Short Account of the Geography, Religion, Social Life, Arts, Industries, and Government of China and it's People* (London: Society for the Promotion of Christian Knowledge ... ; New York: Pott, Young & Co., 1876).
iv, 28, [4] pp., fold-out map ; 12 wood-engravings after original photographs.
Final two leaves contain catalogue of SPCK publications.
Bound in green cloth, embossed in gilt and black.

55. Baron Charles D'Avillier, *Spain*. Translated by John Thomson, illustrated by Gustave Doré. (London: Sampson Low, Marston, Low, and Searle, Crown Buildings, 188, Fleet Street 1876).
xii, [1], 512 pp.; 112 full-page wood-engravings.
Verso of titlepage: London: Printed by William Clowes and Sons, Stamford Street and Charing Cross.
Bound in red cloth, blocked in black and gilt. Gilt edges.

56. Baron Charles D'Avillier, *Spain*. Translated by John Thomson, illustrated by Gustave Doré (New York: Scribner, Welfont and Armstrong, 1876).
xii, [1], 512 pp.; 112 full-page wood-engravings.
Bound in red cloth, blocked in black and gilt.
American reprint of A55.

57. 'Thomson's Reise auf Formosa', *Globus*, 29 (1876).

58. Gaston Tissandier, *A History and Handbook of Photography Translated from the French of Gaston Tissandier*. (London: Sampson Low, Marston, Low & Searle, 1876).
[2], xvi, 326, 14, 40 pp.; 15 full-page wood-engravings, photo-tint frontispiece.
A translation by Thomson of Tissandier's *Les Merveilles de la photographie*.
Final two sections consist of adverts for photographic equipment, and a catalogue of books published by Sampson Low. Endpapers and flyleaves also contain adverts.
Bound in green cloth, embossed in gilt.

59. Gaston Tissandier, *A History and Handbook of Photography Translated from the French of Gaston Tissandier* (New York: Scovill Manufacturing Co., 1877).
[2], xvi, 326 pp., 15 full-page wood-engravings, photo-tint frontispiece.
American reprint edition of A58.

60. Adolphe Smith and John Thomson, *Street Life in London: With Permanent Photographic Illustrations*. (London: Sampson Low, Marston, Searle, and Rivington, 1877–78).
12 monthly parts ([2], 100 pp.); 36 Woodburytypes.
Variant: the parts were issued as a complete work after publication of the final part, with a collective titlepage, list of 'Illustrated Contents of Vol. 1' and a trade binding. Binding: Green and black gilt-embossed cloth. Gilt edges.

61. *Dix ans de voyages dans la Chine et l'Indo-Chine ouvrage traduit de l'anglais avec l'autorisation de l'auteur par MM. A. Talandier et H. Vattemare et illustré de 128 gravures sur bois* (Paris: Librarie Hachette et Cie, 1877).
[4], 492 p.; 128 wood-engravings, not all by Thomson.
A French translation of A49.

62. 'Taking a Photograph', and 'The Magic Lantern', in *Science for All*, ed. by Robert Brown (London: Cassell, Petter, Galpin & Co., [1877–82]). 2 vols
'Taking a Photograph', Vol. 1: 258–62. 'The Magic Lantern', Vol. 2: 208–14.
Illustrated with wood-engravings.

63. Pierre Jules Hetzel, *Public and Private Life of Animals. Adapted from the French of Balzac, Droz, Jules Janin, E. Lemoine, A. de Musset, Georges Sand &c. by J. Thomson* (London: Sampson Low, Marston, Searle, & Rivington, 1877).
x, [2], 387, [1], 24 pp.
A translation of: *Scènes de la vie privée et publique des animaux*.
Final 24 pages contain 'List of Books Publishing [sic] by Sampson Low, Marston, Searle, & Rivington. April 1876.'
Bound in brown cloth, blocked in gilt and black, by Burn & Co. Gilt edges.
Illustrated by Jean Ignace Isidore Gérard, called: Grandville.

64. Pierre Jules Hetzel, *Public and Private Life of Animals. Adapted from the French of Balzac, Droz, Jules Janin, E. Lemoine, A. de Musset, Georges Sand &c. by J. Thomson* (London: Sampson Low, Marston, Searle, & Rivington. Philadelphia: J.B. Lipincott, 1877).
x, [2], 387, [1], 24 pp.
A translation of: *Scènes de la privée et publique des animaux*.
Final 24 pages contain 'List of Books Publishing [sic] by Sampson Low, Marston, Searle, & Rivington. April 1876.'
Bound in brown cloth, blocked in gilt and black, by Burn & Co.
Illustrated by Jean Ignace Isidore Gérard, called: Grandville.
American edition of A63.

65. Gaston Tissandier, *A History and Handbook of Photography Translated from the French of Gaston Tissandier. Edited by J. Thomson … with upwards of 70 illustrations and some specimens of permanent processes.* 2nd. rev. ed. (London: Sampson Low, Marston, Searle & Rivington, 1878).
xx, 400 pp.; 70 wood-engraved illustrations and five photomechanical plates.
The final 18 pages contain adverts.
With an appendix by William Henry Fox Talbot.

66. 'Mountain Views in Cyprus', *ILN*, no. 2054 (8 November 1878), pp. 432, 434.

67. *Through Cyprus with the Camera in the Autumn of 1878. By John Thomson, F.R.G.S. … In Two Volumes. With Sixty Permanent Photographs* (London: Sampson Low, Marston, Searle and Rivington, Crown Buildings, 188, Fleet Street. 1879).
2 vols., 59 Woodburytypes.
Dedicated, with a portrait, to Sir Garnet Wolseley, K.C.B., G.C.M.G., Lord High Commissioner of Cyprus. The images were printed either by the Woodbury Company, or the Autotype Company. Bound in elaborately gilt-blocked red cloth. Gilt edges.

68. 'A Journey Through Cyprus in the Autumn of 1878', *Proceedings of the Royal Geographical Society*, ns 1 (1879), pp. 97–105.

69. *L'Indo-Chine et la Chine. Récits de voyages abrégés par H. Vattemare* (Paris: Librarie Hachette et Cie, 1879).
190, [2] pp. ; 43 wood-engravings.
Part of the series: Bibliothèque des Ecoles et des Familles.
Decorated paper wrappers.
A French translation of A49.

70. 'A Panoramic Lantern', *Photographic News* (17 December 1880), pp. 608–9.

71. 'Gelatino-Bromide Plates', *British Journal Photographic Almanac 1880* (1880), p. 54.

72. Adolphe Smith and John Thomson, *Street Incidents. A Series of Twenty-One Permanent Photographs with Descriptive Letter-press* (London: Sampson Low, Marston, Searle, and Rivington, Crown Buildings, 188, Fleet Street, 1881).
iii, 100 pp., 21 Woodburytypes.
Re-issue of sheets I-P⁴, (pages 45–100) from A60.
Red cloth, embossed in gilt and black, with designs derived from two Thomson images. Gilt edges.

73. Baron Charles D'Avillier, *Spain*. Translated by John Thomson, illustrated by Gustave Doré. (London: Bickers & Son, 1 Leicester Square, 1881).
xiii, [1], 520 pp.; 112 full-page wood-engravings.
Verso of half-title: [Printed in Edinburgh by] The Ballantyne Press, Ballantyne & Hanson Edinburgh & London.
Bound in green cloth, blocked in black and gilt.
Re-issue of A55.

74. Alfred de Rothschild, *A Description of the Works of Art Forming the Collection of Alfred de Rothschild. The photographs by J. Thomson,* [sic] *FRGS*, ed. Charles Davis. ([London: [s.n], 1884])
2 v. ; 205 platinum prints by Thomson.
Verso of title page: Chiswick Press: C. Whittingham and Co., Tooks Court, Chancery Lane, London.

75. 'Pictures Received: Portrait of R. L. Maddox, M.D.', *Photographic Times* 14 (1884), p. 431.

76. 'Exploration with the Camera', *BJP* (12 June 1885), pp. 372–73.

77. *L'Indo-Chine et la Chine. Récits de voyages.* 2ᶜ éd. (Paris: Librairie Hachette, 1885).
192 pp. ; 43 wood-engravings.
Part of the series: Bibliothèque des écoles et des familles.
Decorated paper wrappers.
A French translation of A49.

78. *L'Indo-Chine et la Chine. Récits de voyages.* 3ᶜ éd. (Paris: Librairie Hachette, 1888).
192 pp. ; [43] wood-engravings.
Part of the series: Bibliothèque des écoles et des familles.
Decorated paper wrappers.
A French translation of A49.

79. 'Photography and Exploration', *PRGS*, ns 13 (1891), pp. 669–75.

80. 'Rainfall in Formosa and some of the Effects on the Island and Mainland of China', *British Association for the Advancement of Science*, 62 (1892), pp. 811–12.

81. *La China: Viaggi di J Thompson* [sic] *e T. Choutzé* (Milano: Fratelli Treves, editori, 1895).
   [3], 419 pp. ; 167 wood-engravings largely from Thomson photographs.
   [Part I]: 'Viaggio in Cina, di. J. Thompson', pp. 1–179.
   Italian translation of A49.

82. *Through China with a Camera* (Westminster: A. Constable & Co., 1898).
   xiv, 284 pp., 100 half-tone plates.
   Bound in green cloth, gilt blocked device on front board.

83. *Through China with a Camera* (London and New York: Harper & Brothers, 45 Albemarle Street, 1899).
   xvi, 269, [1] pp., 114 half-tones.
   A second edition, with a new introduction.
   Bound in blue cloth, gilt blocked device on front board.

84. *Bunyan Home Scenes. Illustrated. By John Thomson and Sidney Robjohns.* (Bedford: J. Thomson, Photographer to the Queen, 72, High Street, Bedford).

85. *The Devonshire House Fancy Dress Ball July 2nd 1897: A Collection of Portraits in Costume of Some of the Guests* (Hammersmith: Privately printed [by the Chiswick Press] for the Committee, 1899).
   16 pp. ; [287 photogravure plates].
   Photogravures by a number of photographers including Thomson.
   The photogravures were printed by Walker and Boutall.
   50 copies were bound in 1899 in quarter pigskin with vellum sides at the Doves Bindery.
   See Marianne Tidcombe, *The Doves Bindery* (London, 1991), nos. 416, 418.

86. 'Photography', in *Hints to Travellers: Scientific and General edited for the Council of the Royal Geographical Society* by E. A. Reeves ... 9th ed. rev. and enlarged 2 vols (London, 1906), II, pp. 51–62.

87. 'Geographical Photography', *Scottish Geographical Magazine*, 23 (1907), pp. 14–19.
   (Read before Section G (Geography) at the York Meeting of the British Association.)

B: Modern Reprints of Thomson's Writings and Principal Modern Scholarly Studies

1. Robert Doty, 'Street Life in London: A Review of an Early Use of Photography in Social Documentation', *Image*, 6 (1957), pp. 240–45.

2. 'The First PhotoJournalist: John Thomson', *Creative Camera*, 43 (1968), pp. 22–25.

3. Robert Doty, 'John Thomson: *Street Life in London*', *Album*, 9 (October 1970), pp. 18–23.
   Reprint of B1.

4. 'Illustrations of China and its People', *Album*, 9 (October 1970), pp. 24–32.

5. 'Proverbial Photographic Philosophy', *Image*, 14 (1971), pp. 12–13.
   Reprint of A51.

6. Weston J. Naef, 'John Thomson's *Illustrations of China and its People*', *Metropolitan Museum of Art Bulletin*, (February–March 1972), pp. 194–95.

7. J. Thomson and Adolphe Smith, *Street Life in London* (Wakefield, 1973).
   Facsimile of A60.

8. John Warner, 'John Thomson: Compassionate Photographer', *Arts of Asia*, 6 (1976), 42–53.

9. *China, The Land and its People: Early Photographs by John Thomson* [Edited by John Warner]. (Hong Kong, 1977).
   Reprints much of A44.

10. *Public and Private Life of Animals. Illustrated by J.J. Grandville. With a New Introduction by Edward Lucie-Smith.* (London: Paddington Press, 1977).
    Facsimile reprint of A63.

11. Colin Westerbeck Jr., 'John Thomson: Victorian Adventurer and Inventor of Candid Street Photography', *American Photographer*, 1 (1978), pp. 66–72.

12. Elliott S. Parker, 'John Thomson, 1837–1921: RGS Instructor in Photography', *Geographical Journal*, 144 (1978), pp. 463–71.

13. Janet Lehr, 'John Thomson (1837–1921)', *History of Photography*, 4 (1980), pp. 67–71.

14. Helmut Gernsheim and Janet Lehr, 'Correspondence', *History of Photography*, 4 (1980), p. 343.

15. *Street-Life in London: Eine Foto-reportage aus dem Jahre 1876* (Dortmund, 1981). Die bibliophilen Taschenbücher, 217. Reprint of A60.

16. John Thomson, *China and its People in Early Photographs: An Unabridged Reprint of the Classic 1873/4 Work. With a New Foreword by Janet Lehr* (New York, 1982). Reprint of A44.

17. Ialeen Gibson-Cowan, 'John Thomson on Cyprus', *Photographic Collector* 3 (1985), 309–19.

18. *Through Cyprus with the Camera in the Autumn of 1878. A Note on John Thomson* [by] *Ialeen Gibson Cowan* (London, 1985). Reprints all of the photographs and text of A67. Not a facsimile.

19. Stephen White, *John Thomson: Life and Photographs* (London, 1985). Preface by Robert A. Sobieszek. Reissued in America as *John Thomson: A Window to the Orient* (Albuquerque, NM, 1989).

20. C. S. Lee, 'John Thomson: A Photographic Vision of the Far East, 1860–1872'. (Unpublished M.Litt thesis University of Oxford, 1985.)

21. Ialeen Gibson-Cowan, 'Thomson's *Street Life* in Context', *Creative Camera*, 251 (1985), 10–15.

22. 'From the Archives: *The Antiquities of Cambodia* by John Thomson', *The Archive: Center for Creative Photography*, 25 (1988), pp. 40–47. Reprints parts of A2.

23. *John Thomson: China and its People*, ed. by Ruth Charity and William Schupbach (London, 1991).

24. *Straits of Malacca, Siam, and Indo-China: Travels and Adventures of a Nineteenth-Century Photographer. Introduction by Judith Balmer* (Singapore, 1993). Photographically reprints the first half of A49.

25. *Thomson's China: Travels and Adventures of a Nineteenth-Century Photographer. With an Introduction and New Illustration Selection by Judith Balmer* (Hong Kong, 1993). A photographic reprint of the China section of A49.

26. Jeff Rosen, 'Posed as Rogues: The Crisis of Photographic Realism in John Thomson's *Street Life in London*', *Image*, 36 (1993), pp. 9–39.

27. *Victorian Street Life in Historic Photographs by John Thomson. Text by John Thomson and Adolphe Smith* (New York, 1994). Reprint of A60.

28. 'King Mongkut Faces the Camera', in *Adventures and Encounters: Europeans in South-East Asia*, ed. by J. M. Gullick (Kuala Lumpur, 1995), pp. 81–91.

Glossary of Photographic Terms

The following list is intended as an aid to understanding the often confusing and difficult terminology associated with the early history of photography. Only those terms which appear in the text have been included.

Further Reading

Gordon Baldwin, *Looking at Photographs: A Guide to Technical Terms* (Malibu and London, 1991).
Brian Coe and Mark Haworth-Booth, *A Guide to Early Photographic Processes* (London, 1983).
Luis Nadeau, *Encyclopedia of Printing, Photographic and Photomechanical Processes* (Fredericton, NB, 1989).

Albumen Print

Invented in 1850, the albumen print was the most commonly used positive print on paper until the last decade of the nineteenth century. Prints were made by coating a sheet of paper with a solution containing egg white (albumen) and salt. After this coat had been applied, the paper was dried and then coated again with a solution of silver nitrate (the light-sensitive element). Prints were normally toned after exposure and development, almost always with gold chloride, deepening their tonal range, often enhancing their colour, and improving their longevity. The main advantage of the albumen process over the Salted-Paper Process was that the prints were sharper and had a glossier surface.

Further Reading

Helen Ronan, '"Minions of the Sun": An Introduction to the Albumen Print', *Visual Resources*, 7 (1990), pp. 23-31.

Autotype Process

See Collotype

Calotype

Discovered by William Henry Fox Talbot in September 1840, the calotype process was the first photographic process from which an infinite number of identical prints could be made from a single negative master. In September 1840 Talbot was able to complete the work first begun in 1835 to the point where he was able to develop a latent negative image and so establish in principle and practice the process which forms the basis of photography in use today. In the calotype process a sheet of good quality paper is floated on two separate baths of potassium iodide and silver nitrate, forming silver iodide. This was rendered light sensitive with a further application of silver nitrate, gallic and acetic acids. Following a short (1-5 minute) exposure in the camera, the latent negative was brought out by using a further application of gallic acid, fixed, washed, and then waxed with a hot iron. The process was widely used until the late 1850s, when it was gradually superseded by the Wet-Collodon Process.

CARBON PROCESS

The Carbon Process was used to produce positive prints mainly on paper, but occasionally on other surfaces (especially glass). These were virtually permanent, and produced pronounced dark tones. The process used carbon black for pigmentation, although other colours could be produced by varying the colourants. Prints were first patented in 1855, but did not become commercially viable until Swan's variation was patented in 1864. A sheet of tissue was coated with gelatin containing potassium bichromate and a pigment (usually carbon black). When this tissue was then contact-printed, the parts of the gelatin that were exposed to light through the negative hardened. The tissue was developed in water and brought into contact with another sheet of paper, onto which adhered the hardened gelatin. The sandwich thus formed was then immersed in water and the unexposed gelatin was washed away. The image was then attached to the second sheet.

Further Reading

Michael Gray, 'Carbon Printing: Black as Colour', in *Photography 1900: The Edinburgh Symposium*, ed. by Julie Lawson *et al* (Edinburgh, 1994), pp. 89-97.

COLLODION

See WET-COLLODION

COLLOTYPE

The collotype was a photomechanical process based on photolithography, and developed by several innovators during the 1850s. A glass plate was coated with a base layer of gelatin hardened with sodium silicate, and with another gelatin layer to make it light sensitive (by the addition of potassium or ammonium bichromate). The plate, once dried, was contact printed under a negative. The second gelatin layer hardened in proportion to the amount of light received. After washing, the excess bichromate ran off and the gelatin swelled, producing a finely veined pattern of wrinkles called reticulation. The plate was treated with glycerine to aid water retention, and then dampened, and rolled with ink. As in lithography, the greasy ink was repulsed by the water-swollen bumps produced by the reticulation: the ink plate was then used to print paper, producing a finely detailed image with a subtle tonal range. There were many variations of the process, the most common in Britain being known as the Autotype.

Further Reading

Tom Reardon and Kent Kirby, 'Collotype: Prince of the Printing Processes', *Printing History*, 14 (1991), pp. 3-18.

GELATIN-SILVER PRINT

From the early 1870s the gelatin-silver process became the most commonly used process for printing from negatives. Paper was coated with gelatin impregnated with either silver bromide or silver chloride. Silver-bromide papers were the more common of the two, being the principal paper used for enlarging. Advantages over albumen papers were that gelatin-silver papers were more stable, less prone to yellowing, and were simpler and quicker to produce. Silver-bromide prints are generally warm black in tone, silver-chloride prints being cooler, blue-black in tone. Gelatin-silver prints normally have a surface gloss.

HALF-TONE (LETTERPRESS) PROCESS

The half-tone process is another process used for reproducing photographic images in print-runs. It was the photomechanical printing process most commonly used from the 1880s until the end of the 1970s. The key element of the process involved re-photographing an original image through a screen, which breaks the image up into dots, the sizes of which vary according to the levels of light and dark areas of the original. Simultaneously introduced into Britain and the United States by Mersenbach and Ives respectively, the process made it possible to print text and images at the same time using a flat-bed letterpress machine. The main breakthrough came as a result of the invention of an accurate and reliable glass cross-line screen, and Levy's acid etch bath to prevent loss of detail in the shadow areas.

PHOTOGRAVURE

Photogravure is another process used for reproducing photographic images in print-runs. The process was invented by the Austrian Karel Klíč, although his work was prefigured by some of Talbot's discoveries in the 1850s. A tissue coated on one side with gelatin sensitised by potassium bichromate was exposed under a transparent positive (created by contact printing from the original negative). When wet, this tissue was pressed onto a sheet of copper, prepared by an application of a resin powder. In water the gelatin which had not been exposed to light dissolved. The copper plate, still unevenly covered with gelatin, was placed in an acid bath, in which the remaining gelatin acted as a resist, the acid biting deepest where the gelatin was thin or absent. This action corresponded to the relative tonal density of the original image. When inked, the plate retained ink in proportion to the tonal range of the image.

Further Reading

> Johan de Zoete, *A Manual of Photogravure: A Comprehensive Working-Guide to the Fox Talbot Klíč Dustgrain Method* (Haarlem, 1988).

PLATINUM PRINT

Platinum printing is a positive printing technique, invented in the early 1870s, and made commercially viable from about 1878. A sheet of paper sensitised with a solution of potassium chloro-platinate and ferric oxalate (an iron salt) was contact printed under a negative until a faint image was produced by the reaction of the light with the iron salt. The paper was developed by immersion in a bath of potassium oxalate that dissolved out the iron salts and reduced the chloro-platinate salt to platinum in those areas where the exposed iron salts had been. The print was then washed in baths of weak hydrochloric or citric acid, and finally in water. The process was favoured because of its permanence, and because of the soft tones which it rendered possible.

Further Reading

> Mike Ware, 'The Eighth Metal: The Rise of the Platintotype Process', in *Photography 1900: The Edinburgh Symposium*, ed. by Julie Lawson *et al.* (Edinburgh, 1994), pp. 99-111.

SALTED-PAPER PROCESS

Salted-paper prints were the earliest positive prints on paper. They were usually made by contact printing from a CALOTYPE (or paper negative), but glass negatives were also used. A sheet of paper was sensitised with sodium chloride, and then coated on one side with silver nitrate. After drying, the paper was contact printed under a negative. After exposure to the sun, the image appeared, and the print was fixed with hyposulfite of soda (which halted any further chemical reaction). The prints were usually toned with gold chloride for greater permanence and for enhancing the tones. The process was discovered by William Henry Fox Talbot in 1835, and was the most commonly used positive printing process (with variations) until its gradual replacement by the albumen process.

Further reading

> James M. Reilly, *The Albumen & Salted Paper Book: The History and Practice of Photographic Printing 1840–1895* (Rochester, NY, 1980).

STEREOGRAPH

Stereographs consist of a pair of photographic images, which have been made by using a dual-lens camera, of which the centres of the lenses have been set the same distance apart as the centres of human eyes. Each photograph is intended to replicate what one eye sees. The images have to be viewed through a device known as a stereoscope in order to convey human binocular vision, and to convey the illusion of depth. The stereograph was immensely popular in the late-nineteenth century.

Wet-Collodion

The wet-collodion process used to create a negative image on a glass base was invented by F. Scott Archer in 1848, and published in 1851. The collodion was made from gun cotton (cotton soaked in nitric and sulfuric acid and then dried). Gun cotton was dissolved by the photographer in a mixture of ether, alcohol, and potassium iodide. The collodion was then poured onto a clean glass plate, and after a few seconds the plate was dipped in a bath of nitrate, which reacted with the potassium iodide to form silver-iodide which was light sensitive. The plate was then exposed in the camera while wet (hence 'wet-plate process'). The plate had to be developed immediately after exposure in a solution of pyrogallic and acetic acids. The process provided shorter exposure times than its rival processes, and produced very high resolution of detail.

Woodburytype

The Woodburytype was a photomechanical process. It was patented by Walter Woodbury in 1864. A relief image was made in bichromated gelatin, and then placed in a hydraulic press together with a block of lead which produced a mould in shallow relief. The block could then be used to print with ink (in fact, pigmented gelatin – the pigment was usually carbon black, but colours could vary) in an adapted press. Woodburytype prints have no grain or internal structure, but retain the tones of a 'real' photograph.

INDEX

The Stationery Office

Published by The Stationery Office and available from:

The Stationery Office Bookshops
71 Lothian Road, Edinburgh EH3 9AZ
(counter service only)
South Gyle Crescent, Edinburgh EH12 9EB
(mail, fax and telephone orders only)
0131-479 3141 Fax 0131-479 3142
49 High Holborn, London WC1V 6HB
(counter service and fax orders only)
Fax 0171-831 1326
68-69 Bull Street, Birmingham B4 6AD
0121-236 9696 Fax 0121-236 9699
33 Wine Street, Bristol BS1 2BQ
0117-926 4306 Fax 0117-929 4515
9-21 Princess Street, Manchester M60 8AS
0161-834 7201 Fax 0161-833 0634
16 Arthur Street, Belfast BT1 4GD
01232 238451 Fax 01232 235401
The Stationery Office Oriel Bookshop
The Friary, Cardiff CF1 4AA
01222 395548 Fax 01222 384347

The Stationery Office publications are also available from:
The Publications Centre
(mail, telephone and fax orders only)
PO Box 276, London SW8 5DT
General enquiries 0171-873 0011
Telephone orders 0171-873 9090
Fax orders 0171-873 8200

Accredited Agents
(see Yellow Pages)
and through good booksellers

Printed in Scotland for The Stationery Office Limited by CC No. 70343 30c 6/97